# THE
# CHINESE ASTROLOGY BIBLE

# THE
# CHINESE ASTROLOGY BIBLE

## Derek Walters

## THE DEFINITIVE GUIDE TO
## USING THE CHINESE ZODIAC

 A GODSFIELD BOOK

An Hachette Livre UK Company
www.hachettelivre.co.uk

First published in Great Britain in 2008
by Godsfield Press, a division of
Octopus Publishing Group Ltd
2–4 Heron Quays, London E14 4JP
www.octopusbooks.co.uk

ISBN: 978-1-84181-338-7

A CIP catalogue record for this book is available
from the British Library.

Printed and bound in China

10 9 8 7 6 5 4 3 2 1

# Contents

# What is Chinese astrology?

The familiar names of the 12 Animals of the Chinese zodiac are just one facet of the fascinating world of Chinese astrology. In Chinese astrology, a person's fate is not dictated by the influence of good or bad planets, but by the rise and fall of natural rhythms which follow as regularly as night and day, the changing seasons, the tides and the phases of the moon.

# How is Chinese astrology different?

In the Western world, when people refer to astrology they might be thinking of the daily 'horoscopes' found in popular newspapers, based on the signs of the zodiac or a person's birth date. Some may be familiar with the deeper aspects of Western astrology, which concerns itself with the positions of the planets at the moment of birth. But what has generally come to be known as 'Chinese Astrology' includes many different techniques and philosophies that would certainly not match the Western definition of the word.

The Chinese principle is based on the idea that three kinds of fate rule our lives: Heaven's Fate, or time over which we have no control; Earth's Fate, or place, which we can change to a certain extent; and Human Fate, our actions, which are entirely dependent upon ourselves. The purpose of Chinese astrology is to understand Heaven's Fate, which is given to us by the Lord of Time at the moment of birth.

Unlike Western astrology, Chinese astrology is not based on what is happening in the Heavens at the moment of an individual's birth, but relies instead on more natural Earthly rhythms – the hours, the seasons, the tides and the waxing and waning of the Moon. How we choose to work with these patterns determines the successes or failures we may experience in our life. By following beneficial trends we can harness our resources to the greatest advantage.

*The Moon is the symbol of the yin or receptive force. When the yin force is strong, it benefits all things of a feminine nature.*

## PRIMEVAL FORCES

'From the earliest human existence through succeeding generations, was there ever a time when the rulers failed to observe the Sun, Moon and Planets, record their motions and expound their meanings?

Raise your head and contemplate the vastness of the Heavens; look around you and marvel at the manifestations on Earth. For such are the primeval forces described by the sages of long ago.'

*Sima Qian, the first historian of China, writing in the 2nd century BCE*

# The Chinese zodiac

The most recognizable feature of Chinese astrology is the Chinese zodiac, a charming procession of 12 animals – Rat, Ox, Tiger, Rabbit, Dragon, Snake, Horse, Sheep, Monkey, Rooster, Dog and Pig. One of the animals (the Ox) matches one of the signs of the Western zodiac (Taurus the Bull) but there all similarity ends.

The Western zodiac is a belt of stars across the sky through which the Moon and planets appear to travel, whereas the Chinese zodiac is a kind of calendar. Yet it has more right to be called a 'zodiac' (the word derives from Latin and Greek meaning 'circle of animals') since all the Chinese zodiac signs are animals, whereas four of the Western zodiac signs are human – Gemini the Twins, Virgo the Virgin, Sagittarius the Archer and Aquarius the Water Carrier – while Libra the Scales, isn't even a living being.

## Buddhist origins

Strangely enough, this most familiar aspect of Chinese astrology is, in Chinese historical terms, a relatively recent invention, to replace the technical term known as 'Branches' (see page 15) which we shall meet later. No mention of the animals of the zodiac is found in the great classical writings compiled 2,000 years ago. Furthermore, they are unlikely to be Chinese, having been brought to China by Buddhist monks from Siberia about 1,500 years ago. Although nearly all Chinese men, women and children know the animal signs of the years they were born, the signs were never regarded as 'official'; until the middle of the last century Chinese calendars and almanacs would only grudgingly, and in small print at the bottom of the page, condescend to add the animal name of the current year.

It is important to remember that the qualities associated with the 12 signs of the Chinese zodiac are not drawn from each animal's natural characteristics. The animal names were chosen because those particular animals best

*The spread of Buddhism had a lasting influence on Chinese astrology.*

symbolized the qualities that had already been observed by Chinese astrologers over thousands of years. Thus, when describing a Rat person as likely to be lively and creative at night, for example, this is not because rats have those qualities, but because the qualities associated with that particular sign can be likened to those of the rodent.

## Origin of the animal names

There are many children's stories regarding the origin of the names of the 12 animals. The most popular says that the Buddha called all the animals to a meeting, and as they arrived, so their names were given to the cycles of 12 years which are named after them. It is true that the names arrived in China at about the same time as Buddhism, so perhaps there is some reasoning behind the tale. After all, there are no equivalent legends about Confucius or the Yellow Emperor or any other figure in the Taoist paradise naming the years after the animals, which is what might have been expected if the animal names existed in China before Buddhism arrived.

## Tribal totem or time symbol?

Some historians suggest that the 12 Animals were originally tribal totems. Perhaps in ancient times a new chief was elected each year to rule over all the tribes, being chosen from whichever tribe was next in the cycle of 12. Familiarity with the animal names stretches well beyond the boundaries of China, through Mongolia and Siberia and even further west to Iran and Turkey

Alternatively, the names of the animals may have been chosen according to how well they represented the months of the year and the time of day. To begin with, in ancient China the sign for midnight was a baby, since it represented the dawn of a new day.

## Hours, seasons and constellations

As rats are particularly active at midnight, the Rat would have seemed an appropriate symbol for night-time. The second sign, the Ox, corresponds with the month when oxen would be yoked to the plough. Then came the official start to the year, and the animal with the authority to officiate at the New Year could be no other than the royal Tiger. Rabbits hop across the grass in the early morning as the Sun rises, thus the dawn hour and springtime are both symbolized by the Rabbit. The next two signs, Dragon and Snake, are simply taken from the Chinese names of constellations which could be seen in the sky at that time of the year.

*According to the Chinese calendar, Winter comprises the Pig, Rat and Ox months, corresponding to November, December and January.*

When the Sun, known in China as the Great Yang is at its highest point at noon and on the longest day, the animal which most symbolizes the yang or male principle is the Horse. Its companion sign, the yin principle, is symbolized by the Sheep, since flocks of sheep are all female. The long day draws to a close, but there is still work to be done, so the active Monkey best represents the energy needed to complete the day's tasks. Then as the Sun sets, birds come home to roost and so the Rooster symbolizes the end of the day. Now it is time to lock up for the night and put the Dog on guard; and when everyone has gone to bed, all that can be heard is the gentle Pig-like grunting of the sleeping family.

# Principles of Chinese astrology

If the animal names are a relatively new import, what did Chinese astrologers use before the names were invented? Two thousand years ago, the great historian and imperial astronomer Sima Qian had a staff of 28 observers to study the skies day and night, not only watching the Moon, stars and planets, but the Sun, the clouds and every kind of manifestation in the sky.

They observed the motions of the planets, recorded comets and meteor showers, and noted that some stars varied in brightness. They watched for spots in the Sun, observed clouds, haloes and the aurora borealis, and noted the occurrence of eclipses so accurately that it is possible to give the precise dates of historical events from their records.

## Heaven's messengers

Such phenomena were regarded as messages from Heaven, and astronomy was the means by which the emperor could ascertain Heaven's approval or displeasure. The messages determined whether the emperor went to war, signed treaties or took a wife, and were state secrets. For anyone outside the Imperial Guild of Astronomers to study the movements of the planets was tantamount to spying on the emperor himself, an offence of treason punishable by death.

Fortunately, two of Heaven's messengers were not confined to the Imperial Court. The Sun's course through the sky, rising and setting at different times throughout the year, is there for anyone to see, as is the Moon, which not only progresses through the stars, but waxes and wanes, its phases reckoning the months in a different year to the Sun's.

## Oracle bones

Since the dawn of writing, shamans recorded the excursions of the Sun and Moon by scratching a pair of signs on fragments of bone. These 'oracle' bones bearing the shaman's

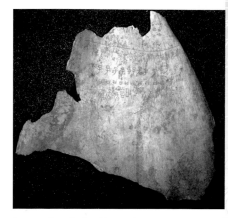

*Scraps of ancient writing on bones are often records of astronomical events.*

predictions, the eventual outcome and sometimes the nature of the gift presented by the client are the oldest known examples of Chinese writing. From pre-historic times, the stems and branches have been all the information that the astrologer needs to construct a horoscope.

## Stems and Branches

In parts of the world the seven-day week is a relatively new invention. The ancient Chinese had a ten-day week which has survived in the Chinese calendar without interruption to the present day. Each day was represented by a sign called a 'Stem'; months and hours were represented by a sequence of 12 signs called the 'Branches', which we now know as the 12 Animal signs. More than 5,000 years ago, the two sequences of ten daily Stems and 12 Branches were combined to form a double sequence of 60 Stem-and-Branch combinations, and these were used to reckon the days more precisely (see Part 7, pages 222– 265).

# How the Universe was created

The ancient Chinese philosophers' view of creation is uncannily similar to the view held by astrophysicists today. To begin with, there was nothing – or rather, there was nothing and not-nothing. Everything was bound together into one, the Tai Yi or Great Unity. From the Great Unity came the two principles of yang and yin.

Yang is what is and yin is what it is not. If there is nothing, there must be something which is not nothing. The great 6th-century-BCE thinker Laozi explained the importance of yang and yin with the image of a cup. The body of the cup is yang while the interior, where there is nothing, is yin. If the cup were solid, it would have no purpose; without the yin component, the yang is useless.

## Yin and yang

In Chinese astrology, the principles of yang and yin are symbolized by the Sun and Moon: even today, the usual Chinese word for the Sun is the Tai

*In traditional China, men were considered to be yang because their work was mainly outside in the open air while women (yin) worked indoors in the shade.*

Yang (the Great Yang), while the Moon is Tai Yin (the Great Yin). Because it was customary for men to work outside in the Sun, yang became associated with males and masculine activities and women and the feminine embodied the yin principle. Following the creation of yang and yin forces, the five active principles – the Five Elements – were formed, which in turn gave rise to every material thing in the Universe. Central to the understanding of the Chinese horoscope is the role played by what is called the Five-Element Doctrine.

# The Five Elements

The names of the Five Elements were originally the names of the five planets known to the ancients of Western philosophy, but there are startling differences in the way that the influences of these planets were interpreted, which implies that Eastern and Western astrology developed independently.

Although both concur that Mars, the red planet, is associated with Fire, and that swift-moving Mercury is related to Water, this is where the similarity ends. Jupiter was known to ancient Chinese astronomers as the Wood planet, ruling over the east, the spring, generation and consequently motherhood. By contrast, Venus, in the west regarded as the symbol of love and all things female, was to the Chinese sky-watcher the Metal Star, with responsibility for items such as scythes and swords, and of course, males. Saturn is called the Earth star in Chinese astrology, perhaps because its colour is the yellow ochre of central China.

The elements were also associated with the seasons of the year – Water, cold and wet, belonged to winter, while Fire belonged to summer; they were also associated with the times of day and the four cardinal points. Every aspect of life could be classified according to one of the Five Elements of Wood, Fire, Earth, Metal and Water.

*Jupiter, the Wood planet, is associated with all things feminine and creative, as well as all forms of plant life.*

## North versus south

Associating the elements with the seasons has led to controversy. Much of the imagery and symbolism associated with Chinese philosophy relates to the progress of the seasons, and for inhabitants of the Southern Hemisphere, it seemed that traditional reasoning did not apply to them. As a result, some teachers of Chinese astrology and feng shui whose work was mainly in the Southern Hemisphere re-invented the philosophical principles to suit the reversed seasons of the south.

# The four seasons

Although the arguments for making significant changes in horoscope interpretations for the Southern Hemisphere are very persuasive, it is important to consider why most traditional Chinese astrologers strongly refute them.

Firstly, the imagery of the seasons and their qualities is just that – visual imagery. Saying that Metal in autumn chops down the Wood of spring presents a picture which the abstract mathematical signs of the stems and branches cannot. But the imagery, which does not suit the reversed seasons of the Southern Hemisphere is at fault, not the actual underlying principle. In any case, the imagery does not always suit the Northern Hemisphere either. It is the imagery that needs to be changed not the principles.

## Where to draw the dividing line?

The second argument against the 'reformed' interpretation is the question of boundaries. Where does one draw the line between the hemispheres? It is too simple to say the Equator, for what happens in Ecuador, Brazil or Malaysia, where the Equator might cross the street or run through one's house? Should the 'Equator' be the Earth's Equator, measured from pole to pole, or the plane of the Earth's orbit around the Sun? Remember that in the tropics, half of the year is spent in the north of the Sun's plane and the other half south of it.

*The Sun rises in the east and sets in the west in both hemispheres.*

## Sunrise and sunset

Another cogent factor is that no matter whether the Sun is in the south at mid-day (as in the Northern hemisphere) or in the north, it still rises in the east and sets in the west. Furthermore, the place of the Sun, as well as the Moon and planets, against the celestial background is the same for both hemispheres (which cannot be seen during the day no matter which hemisphere one observes from). When the Sun passes through the constellation of the Bird in August, it will do so no matter whether August is in summer, autumn, winter, the wet season or the dry one.

## The compass needle

There is still one more arresting argument why the traditional factors of Chinese astrology and feng shui should not be changed. The vital apparatus of the professional feng shui consultant is the *Luopan* or compass. And that points in the same direction whether you live in east London, England, East London, South Africa or east London, Canada.

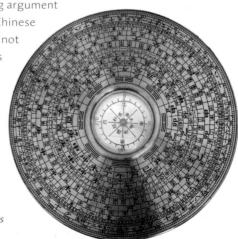

*The Chinese astrological compass has the names of stars round its rim.*

# East and West

'How is Chinese astrology different from Western astrology?', is a frequently asked question and the person posing the question wants to know if the results of the two systems are the same, complement each other or are totally different.

The best way to consider the two types of astrology is to think of two artists making a portrait of someone in their own individual styles. Both will probably produce recognizable likenesses, but each one will have highlighted some aspect of the person's character, personality or appearance that will make the portrait unique.

## Technique, interpretation and emphasis

The differences between Chinese and Western astrology are not just confined to technique, but also to the interpretation of results, and the quite different emphasis on what is regarded as important. The most obvious difference is apparent at the first encounter with Chinese astrology. Western people new to the subject might ask, 'I was born in March, what sign is that?' whereas a Chinese person unfamiliar with the Western zodiac would say 'I'm 32, what zodiac sign is that?'. In popular Western astrology, whether someone is a Capricorn or a Sagittarius depends on the time of the year in which that person was born; in Chinese astrology, whether the person is a Rat or Rooster depends on the year he or she was born – and consequently is revealed by a person's

*Children all born in the same year often display traits which are particular to that group.*

age. This might seem one of the drawbacks to Chinese astrology: does it mean that everyone born in a particular year is doomed to failure or success because they all have the same animal sign?

## The Four Columns of destiny

Of course, there are many other factors to take into consideration, not just the year, but the month, day and time as well – what the Chinese call 'the Four Columns' of a person's destiny.

But this is one way in which astrology is vindicated. Teachers who have yearly intakes of new recruits invariably comment on how one particular cohort would be outstanding, another quiet and yet another boisterous. All the members of the year's intake are individuals, but taken as a group, they share the same animal sign, and take on what might be termed a 'corporate identity'. Any wine merchant would agree that in some years the vine crop was fruitier, sweeter or in some way more capable of producing a remarkable vintage. Perhaps the very factors of weather, climate or air quality affect the developing children of particular years in some subtle, psychological way.

# Two zodiacs

The differences between the Western zodiac and Chinese animal signs do not rest in the nature of the members of the two zodiacs, but what they signify. The Western zodiac signs are names of constellations in the sky that we can see at night, while the Chinese animal names are labels attached to abstract mathematical concepts that would otherwise be very difficult for ordinary people to grasp.

A few hundred years ago, some inventive Chinese astrologers expanded their techniques and introduced a new set of exotic star names into their calculations. They included such exotic phenomena as the Square Creature, Yin-Yang, Twin Maids, Celestial Tree-weevil, Man-Horse and Precious Vase, but it is the White Sheep, Golden Bull and Lion that reveal the new concepts to be none other than Western zodiac signs in oriental dress.

During the latter part of the 19th century, when Chinese fortune-tellers were becoming familiar with Western clients, the differences between the Western and Chinese calendars obviously caused problems. If asked to draw up a horoscope for a Western client's birthday and a prognostication for the year ahead, the confused astrologer would draft two forecasts, one based on the birthday according to the Western calendar and the other worked out according to the Chinese date.

## Horoscope shape

Another odd cross-over during
this period was the actual layout
of a horoscope. When Chinese
astrologers of old laid out a chart
based on the planets and stars,
they used a circular format with a
kind of spider's web arrangement
of 12 segments to represent the
divisions of the sky: a very
convenient way of visualizing the
heavens. Western horoscopes,
however, were traditionally drawn
up in a curious box shape that
might have had some mystical or
aesthetic appeal, but was visually
awkward and mathematically
inconvenient. Then, towards the
end of the 19th century, Chinese
astrologers thought it more
stylish to adopt the Western box-
type horoscope format, but by
that time Western astrologers had
already discarded the awkward
box shape in favour of the circular
chart that the Chinese had been
using for centuries!

*Animal names (such as 'Marten', see page 273) are labels
used for abstract concepts that are difficult to grasp.*

# The stars

Chinese astronomy had developed its own techniques for observing the Heavens long before any contact had been made with Western sky-watchers. The sky is full of bright points of light which the imagination sees joined together as constellations. The seven principal stars of the Great Bear (the Plough), and the shoulders, belt and sword of Orion were as familiar to early observers in both East and West as they are to star-gazers today.

The rest of the starry sky is for the most part a confused scattering of fainter lights, which ancient observers resolved into distinctive constellations of their own devising. The early astronomers of Western Asia and Europe visualized certain patterns of stars to which they gave names often connected with the sea, such as whale, fish, crab and dolphin.

## Chinese constellations

Early Chinese astronomers saw rather different images, which to them represented objects to do with city life: markets, houses, mansions and courtyards. There were other technically significant differences, too. Because the sky is constantly rotating and changing position every night and throughout the night, astronomers needed some kind of reference point to say where the stars will be at a particular date and time. Against the background of the stars, the Moon and planets mark

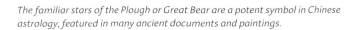

*The familiar stars of the Plough or Great Bear are a potent symbol in Chinese astrology, featured in many ancient documents and paintings.*

a steady journey through the sky along a common path – the ecliptic. (This is the path that the Sun appears to travel through the year as the Earth makes its journey around the Sun). Western astronomers divide this path into 12 divisions (the zodiac) and use the imaginary line as a base line. Chinese astronomers used a quite different system: the sky was divided like the segments of a grapefruit from the Pole Star to the Equator, each of the segments having the name of its most obvious constellation, such as Orion, the Pleiades or the Square of Pegasus, which they knew as the Mansions of the Moon. And it is these Mansions of the Moon that are the very foundations of Chinese astrology.

# How to use this book

Provided that your birthday is not in January or February, go straight to the table on pages 36–37 and find the animal sign for the year in which you were born. You can then read about your general characteristics and personality in the section 'The 12 animals' on pages 30–61.

If your birthday is earlier than 1 March, it is best to find the year animal for a friend until you have grasped the problems of the start of the Chinese year. When you feel confident enough, try finding the animal signs for people born in January and February.

Once you have found the animal sign for a person, you can find the best partnerships for that sign (see 'Relationships') and even what the coming year has in store ('The Year Ahead').

You will want to polish your skill as an astrologer by finding the animal signs for the hour, day and month which is explained in Part 5 (see pages 166–187). Within this section it becomes clear that there are four animal signs significant to each individual – those representing the hour, day, month and year of birth – and referred to as the Four Animals. You can look more deeply into the characteristics and personality shown by the 'Patterns of Harmony' (see pages 181–187).

In fact, once you are familiar with the techniques of Chinese horoscope calculation, in many cases you will be able to work out three of the animal signs in your head, without reference to any tables.

*Every Chinese horoscope begins with the time, day, month and year of birth.*

## Another dimension

To develop the horoscope still further, you will need to look at the Four Stems, partners to the Four Animals. The step-by-step instructions for assembling the complete horoscope chart are given in 'The Broader Horoscope' pages 188– 121.

Once you have compiled a horoscope built on the Four Columns you will find avenues available for demonstrating and perfecting your skills. Part 8, pages 266– 391, of the book suggests practical ways your knowledge can be applied, from finding lucky days for various activities, to the most favourable directions for moving house. You will also find descriptions of cases from history and literature using the methods and techniques that you will have acquired through these pages.

## The 12 Animals

But it is the 12 Animals that reign over Chinese astrology today. Before embarking on our journey into the intricate world of Chinese astrology and its far-reaching influences, let us begin with its most familiar aspect – the Animal of the Year.

# The 12 animals

In Chinese astrology, a person's zodiac sign is determined not by his or her birthday, but the year in which that individual was born. This section explains how to find a your Chinese animal zodiac sign, and the characteristics and qualities for each of the 12 signs.

# finding your Chinese zodiac sign

When someone refers to his or her Chinese zodiac sign, that person is usually referring to the year that he or she was born, since that is how the years are popularly reckoned in China. The year 2000, for example, was the Year of the Dragon.

It should be a simple matter, then, to associate every Western year with one of the Chinese animal signs: if 2000 was the year of the Dragon, then every 12 years after that – 2012, 2024, 2036 and so on – would also be Dragon years. For the most part this holds true, as can be seen from the table on page 36. Indeed, for everyone whose birthday is in March through to December there is absolutely no problem. Unfortunately, one sixth of the world's population was born in January or February, and that is where the problems begin.

## Chinese New Year

When does the Chinese year start? For present purposes, as can be seen from the table on page 36, the Chinese astrological year begins on 4 February, which is called *li chun* or the 'Beginning of Spring'. For someone born on 4 February or later, the animal of the year is shown in the main table. Accordingly, for someone born between 1 January and 3 February their zodiac sign would be the one belonging to the previous year.

*Chinese communities love to celebrate New Year with spectacular lion dances.*

Unfortunately, matters are not that simple. Until about 50 years ago, even in post-Revolutionary China, the Chinese used a lunar calendar in which every month began with the New Moon. The 'New Year' itself began with the second New Moon after the winter solstice, which could be any time between the middle of January and the middle of February. When Chinese people celebrate the New Year, it is the Lunar New Year Festival which they commemorate. The Lunar New Year Festival is everyone's birthday. A baby born a few days before the Lunar New Year Festival would have its first birthday while it was still in the cradle!

## More confusion

But there is an added complication. While some Chinese astrologers draw up horoscopes based on the lunar calendar, it is general practice to use an astronomical calendar in which the year starts at the precise half-way point between the shortest day and the spring equinox. For most of the second half of the 20th century this has been 4 February, although it gradually gets earlier every 70 years or so.

The confusion arises when someone's birthday falls between the Lunar New Year Festival and the astronomical New Year or *li chun*. In 1953, the Lunar New Year fell on 14 February, marking the Year of the Snake. But for someone born, say, on 10 February 1953, according to the astronomical calendar beginning 4 February their zodiac sign would have been Snake, but for the general public, because the birthday was before the Chinese New Year Festival, the zodiac sign was a Dragon!

Or the converse might be true. The Lunar New Year Festival of the Dragon Year, 1952, began on 27 January, so most Chinese people would say that someone born on 1 February 1952 was born in the year of the Dragon; however, a professional Chinese astrologer compiling the horoscope would say that the person was born in the Rabbit year!

## Problem solved

The problem is a common one that Chinese astrologers resolved centuries ago. When calculating a horoscope, the *li chun* or 4 February astronomical New Year is used, but in everyday terms, the animal sign based on the Lunar New Year Festival would be used. A supplementary table of Lunar New Year Festivals is also given here for completeness (see page 37).

## Other versions of the New Year

For the sake of completeness, it should be mentioned that there are schools of thought that prefer to use other starting points for the year. There are still many people (particularly in China) who have no idea of their birthday and only know their age. A Chinese fortune-teller today might just use the Western calendar equivalent and not bother with the niceties of the New Moon or 'Beginning of Spring'.

At the other end of the scale, there are serious academic astrologers who believe that the astronomical year begins with the winter solstice, and construct all their calculations accordingly. For them, the New Year begins on 22 December and anyone born on Christmas Day would be reckoned to have the animal sign of the following year.

So, to emphasize the main point of the arguments considered above, regard the Chinese astrological year as beginning with the *li chun* ('Beginning of Spring'), 4 February, and use that as the starting point of the calendar.

## THE ANIMAL SIGN FOR THE YEAR

According to the Astronomical Year beginning with the *li chun*

| Before February 4th | | Birth Year | | | *After February 4th |
|---|---|---|---|---|---|
| Pig | 1936* | 1960* | 1984 | 2008 | Rat |
| Rat | 1937 | 1961 | 1985 | 2009 | Ox |
| Ox | 1938 | 1962 | 1986 | 2010 | Tiger |
| Tiger | 1939* | 1963 | 1987 | 2011 | Rabbit |
| Rabbit | 1940* | 1964* | 1988 | 2012 | Dragon |
| Dragon | 1941 | 1965 | 1989 | 2013 | Snake |
| Snake | 1942 | 1966 | 1990 | 2014 | Horse |
| Horse | 1943* | 1967 | 1991 | 2015 | Sheep |
| Sheep | 1944* | 1968* | 1992 | 2016 | Monkey |
| Monkey | 1945 | 1969 | 1993 | 2017‡ | Rooster |
| Rooster | 1946 | 1970 | 1994 | 2018 | Dog |
| Dog | 1947 | 1971 | 1995 | 2019 | Pig |
| Pig | 1948* | 1972* | 1996 | 2020‡ | Rat |
| Rat | 1949 | 1973 | 1997 | 2021 | Ox |
| Ox | 1950 | 1974 | 1998 | 2022 | Tiger |
| Tiger | 1951 | 1975 | 1999 | 2023 | Rabbit |
| Rabbit | 1952* | 1976* | 2000 | 2024 | Dragon |
| Dragon | 1953 | 1977 | 2001 | 2025‡ | Snake |
| Snake | 1954 | 1978 | 2002 | 2026 | Horse |
| Horse | 1955 | 1979 | 2003 | 2027 | Sheep |
| Sheep | 1956* | 1980* | 2004 | 2028‡ | Monkey |
| Monkey | 1957 | 1981 | 2005 | 2029 | Rooster |
| Rooster | 1958 | 1982 | 2006 | 2030 | Dog |
| Dog | 1959 | 1983 | 2007 | 2031 | Pig |

**Note:** The start of the Chinese astronomical year gradually creeps forward, a difference of one day every seventy-odd years. For most of the second half of the 20th century, *li chun* was 4th February, but in years marked * the *li chun* was 5th February, and in years marked ‡ the *li chun* will be 3rd February.

# DATES OF THE CHINESE LUNAR NEW YEAR FESTIVAL

The table below shows the dates of the Chinese New Year Festival, which is held on the second New Moon after the winter solstice. A cursory examination of the table will reveal what was known to the ancients; the Moon's phases follow a pattern which repeats every 19 years. Look, for example at the dates of the lunar New Year for 1924, 1943, 1962, 1981, 2000 and 2019.

| | | | | | |
|---|---|---|---|---|---|
| 30 Jan 1911 | 17 Feb 1931 | 6 Feb 1951 | 27 Jan 1971 | 15 Feb 1991 | 3 Feb 2011 |
| 18 Feb 1912 | 6 Feb 1932 | 27 Jan 1952 | 15 Feb 1972 | 4 Feb 1992 | 23 Jan 2012 |
| 6 Feb 1913 | 26 Jan 1933 | 14 Feb 1953 | 3 Feb 1973 | 23 Jan 1993 | 10 Feb 2013 |
| 26 Jan 1914 | 14 Feb 1934 | 3 Feb 1954 | 23 Jan 1974 | 10 Feb 1994 | 31 Jan 2014 |
| 14 Feb 1915 | 4 Feb 193 | 24 Jan 1955 | 11 Feb 1975 | 31 Jan 1995 | 19 Feb 2015 |
| 3 Feb 1916 | 24 Jan 1936 | 12 Feb 1956 | 31 Jan 1976 | 19 Feb 1996 | 8 Feb 2016 |
| 23 Jan 1917 | 11 Feb 1937 | 31 Jan 1957 | 18 Feb 1977 | 7 Feb 1997 | 28 Jan 2017 |
| 11 Feb 1918 | 31 Jan 1938 | 18 Feb 1958 | 7 Feb 1978 | 28 Jan 1998 | 16 Feb 2018 |
| 1 Feb 1919 | 19 Feb 1939 | 8 Feb 1959 | 28 Jan 1979 | 16 Feb 1999 | 5 Feb 2019 |
| 20 Feb 1920 | 8 Feb 1940 | 28 Jan 1960 | 16 Feb 1980 | 5 Feb 2000 | 25 Jan 2020 |
| 8 Feb 1921 | 27 Jan 1941 | 15 Feb 1961 | 5 Feb 1981 | 24 Jan 2001 | 12 Feb 2021 |
| 28 Jan 1922 | 15 Feb 1942 | 5 Feb 1962 | 25 Jan 1982 | 12 Feb 2002 | 1 Feb 2022 |
| 16 Feb 1923 | 5 Feb 1943 | 25 Jan 1963 | 13 Feb 1983 | 1 Feb 2003 | 22 Jan 2023 |
| 5 Feb 1924 | 25 Jan 1944 | 13 Feb 1964 | 2 Feb 1984 | 22 Jan 2004 | 10 Feb 2024 |
| 25 Jan 1925 | 13 Feb 1945 | 2 Feb 1965 | 20 Feb 1985 | 9 Feb 2005 | 29 Jan 2025 |
| 13 Feb 1926 | 2 Feb 1946 | 21 Jan 1966 | 9 Feb 1986 | 29 Jan 2006 | 17 Feb 2026 |
| 2 Feb 1927 | 22 Jan 1947 | 9 Feb 1967 | 29 Jan 1987 | 18 Feb 2007 | 6 Feb 2027 |
| 23 Jan 1928 | 10 Feb 1948 | 30 Jan 1968 | 17 Feb 1988 | 7 Feb 2008 | 26 Jan 2028 |
| 10 Feb 1929 | 29 Jan 1949 | 17 Feb 1969 | 6 Feb 1989 | 26 Jan 2009 | 13 Feb 2029 |
| 30 Jan 1930 | 17 Feb 1950 | 6 Feb 1970 | 27 Jan 1990 | 14 Feb 2010 | 2 Feb 2030 |

# The Rat

## Keyword: Creativity

The Rat is the leader of the Chinese zodiac, perhaps not the most powerful member, but the most innovative. Forget the Western notions of 'rat' being a term of abuse, synonymous with low-life or desertion; our astrological Rat is known for its quick thinking, wariness and nocturnal sprightliness. (Of course, those who are not happy being called a Rat might prefer an alternative translation such as mouse, squirrel, mole, hamster or some other small furry animal of their choice.)

Being the symbol for midnight, it is during these dark hours, when all others are asleeping, that the Rat's imaginative brain suddenly jumps into action. All kind of new ideas spring into mind – but the Rat's failing is that it needs a willing partner to put the ideas into practice. Without the right person at hand when these brilliant stratagems surface, enthusiasm quickly wanes and is unlikely to be followed up. But that does not matter; another idea will be born tomorrow.

## Reluctant participant

Although the Rat is a creative innovator, he or she is often reluctant to put these ideas into practice because the Rat can foresee how much of his or her time and personal commitment will be involved once the project has started. Rats, unfortunately, are easily distracted and will quickly move on to a new project before they have finished the current.

Rats have a strange sense of humour that other people do not always grasp, so that someone unfamiliar with the Rat's ways is apt to take his or her cynical comments too literally. Nothing is more likely to bemuse the poor Rat as when a suggestion made in jest is hailed as a dazzling stroke of genius. The even more astonishing thing is that the idea turns out to be just that – genius.

## Work

Rats work at their best when the mood takes them. They will put far more into their working hours if they are given the freedom to act when they are driven from inside.

The Rat is very good at communication, both in the spoken word and correspondence, and his or her flair for inspiring others often makes the Rat a memorable teacher. The Rat loves to travel and enjoys seeking out new places and experiences. Most satisfying of all is the ability to sleep on long journeys, since for the economically minded Rat this is a constructive way of resting. Even after a few minutes' nap a Rat will be alert again.

*The Rat hour is midnight, when Rat people are at their most alert.*

# The Ox

## Keyword: Stability

Steadfast and reliable are the words most commonly used to describe the Ox. Every Chinese almanac begins with a picture of an ox being led by a farmer; usually called the 'Spring Ox', it actually represents the last month of the Chinese winter, when oxen are taken out to plough the fields. Thus the Ox symbolizes all the hard work that has to be done in order to prepare for a prosperous future.

Ox people are those who lay the foundations for success; they are steady, reassuring and reliable. Every family and every business concern needs the strength and sense of permanence which the Ox provides. The downside to this sign is its obstinacy. Because of the Ox's demand for perfection, others are likely to be irritated by his or her refusal to accept new but untried ideas and methods, preferring instead to follow established practice. But time usually shows that the Ox was right all along.

The Ox makes a good friend and a formidable enemy. In dealing with the Ox, it is always important to be straightforward with the facts. Friends know this, but those who try to disguise bad news as favourable do so at their peril. The Ox can see through flattery and spin, and knows instinctively when important information is being held back. Power and position do not impress the Ox, who judges people on their merits and achievements rather than the trappings of authority.

## Work

Because of his or her love of permanence and stability, the Ox is drawn to matters to do with land and buildings. Brown fields or green fields are all the same to the industrious Ox; whether for farming or for

development, the Ox will see that the maximum benefits are drawn from the potential that land has to offer. Perhaps because of this connection to the Earth element, it is best for the Ox to avoid areas where water dominates; for the Ox character, a desert is seen as preferable to the seaside!

People should not assume that they know every facet of the Ox person's character, since there is a deeper quality that does not often surface. Though the outer garment may be that of a rough countryman, there is an artist within. Although the Ox does not avoid a social life, in reality this is a very private person with a romantic streak which the Ox prefers to keep hidden. Perhaps it is the solid reliability of the Ox which is its most obvious trait.

*Almanacs usually open with an Ox led by a farmer –foretelling the year's weather.*

# The Tiger

## Keyword: Authority

Everyone wants to be a Tiger, the animal that best symbolizes luxury, authority and royalty. Why, even on the Tiger's forehead Nature has marked the Chinese character for 'king'. Although the Rat heads the procession of the 12 Animals, it is the Tiger who is in charge, for it is the royal Tiger, not the Rat, who rules over the first month of the Chinese year.

Presiding over the first month of spring, the Tiger symbolizes the revitalizing energies as the ground takes on its bloom of green, animals come out of hibernation, and fight for supremacy over their territories. So it is that the Tiger personality has all the qualities of resolution and competitiveness and a determination to succeed.

In family matters the Tiger can be stern and a touch disciplinarian, but always loving and understanding.

The Tiger has wonderful charisma and attracts many admirers, but this may cause some resentment among those who are less successful. The Tiger provides stimulating company whether with friends or among strangers. Always ready with interesting anecdotes, the Tiger is never short of invitations to dinner, providing that it does not matter if fellow guests are somewhat overshadowed. Because of this, in social circles the Tiger should be careful not to cause offence by taking on a leading role when it is not expected.

# Work

Tigers are drawn to professions where there is tradition and formality, particularly where uniforms or recognizable dress are worn. The Tiger can be astute in business affairs, but makes the greatest gains when helping others on the road to fortune. They quickly ascend the career ladder and will hold high positions, though they are generally more adept at chairing meetings, rather than speaking at them. The difficulty that Tigers face occurs when they are promoted to take charge of an already existing situation; they will see much that needs to be altered and are likely to meet resistance to their proposed changes. This is when the Tiger needs a little-used touch of diplomacy.

*The mark on a tiger's head looks similar to the Chinese character for 'king'.*

Because the Tiger is such a strong masculine sign, Tiger ladies may find that they have no difficulty in competing both socially and in business with their male rivals. In earlier times, Chinese families were very wary of women born in the year of the Tiger, lest they usurp the man's rightful place at the head of the family!

Tiger people dress carefully and neatly, paying great attention to every detail of their outfit, avoiding flamboyance, yet making a statement which says 'expensive!'.

# The Rabbit

## Keyword: Compassion

The gentle Rabbit was chosen to represent the month of the year when burgeoning spring brings the promise of new life and opportunities. Thus more than anything else, the Rabbit symbolizes all matters to do with children and those in need of care.

When Chinese people look at the Moon, they see, not the Man in the Moon, but a Rabbit stirring a vat of herbs to make the elixir of immortality, and it is this aspect of the Rabbit personality that draws many people born under this sign to the healing and caring professions.

Plants and flowers are gathered at early dawn for many different purposes, not just medicine. The artistic Rabbit may pick them in order to create artistic displays, particularly as gifts; or the industrious Rabbit may gather them for making dyes and pigments to colour fabrics or they may indeed be used for medicines.

## Family-minded

In the Rabbit's family, it is the children that take priority over all other considerations. Rabbit parents are prepared to make great sacrifices to ensure the well-being of their children, while in later life the care of elderly parents becomes their major concern. The Rabbit person without children is likely to be surrounded by pet animals, since there is so much love to be shared.

*The Rabbit is a symbol of the Wood element, which rules over herbs and plants, whether they are used for medicines, or for dyeing clothes.*

## Work

The ideal working situation for the Rabbit is one that is 'early to bed, early to rise'. The Rabbit's constitution does not favour late hours, which can lead to stress and physical debilitation. Astrologically, the placid Rabbit is the partner of the ferocious Tiger; both achieve their ambitions but in different ways, and in business the Rabbit succeeds by being the quiet diplomat who by persuasion is able to win over the most obstinate of adversaries. Despite this, if the Rabbit senses danger to those in its care, it will become a furious champion for its charges.

The Rabbit enjoys natural fibres and hand-woven fabrics, and is likely to have a taste for ethnic designs.

# The Dragon

## Keyword: Magic

Ancient astronomers associated this sign, the only mythical animal
among the 12, with stars and planets long before it was named the
Dragon. One of the sacred books of China, the *I Ching* or *Book of
Changes*, begins with a description of the Dragon constellation
rising above the horizon and sailing through the sky during the
course of a night.

Dragons, the symbol of imperial might, were embroidered on the
robes of the emperor. Unlike in the West, where dragons were monsters
to be slain by knights and saints, in China the Dragon was a powerful,
all-knowing being who could bestow rich rewards on those who
deserved its favours. In Chinese art, the Dragon is usually shown with
pearls issuing from its mouth and gold coins from its other end.

## Otherworldly

The Dragon character always has a touch of the exotic, a kind of other-
worldliness which sets it apart from the commonplace. Dragons are
attracted to magic and spectacle, and especially the theatre, which is
all about transformation and illusion.

Chinese people refer to exceptionally gifted youngsters as 'Dragon
children' even though they may be born in other years. A 'Dragon lady' is
a formidable business woman who will no doubt become a millionairess!

*The Dragon is associated with pearls and they are often shown close to its mouth.*

## Work

When the Dragon is not appearing on the stage, a career in any field that needs flamboyance, flair and knowledge of current trends will suit the Dragon's special personality. Although Dragons are associated with wealth and good fortune, there is also a downside: the Dragon's fortune may disappear as swiftly as it comes. The bright lights of the theatre are not the only ones that tempt the Dragon: the flashing neon lights of Las Vegas casinos have a magnetic attraction, too. People born under the Dragon sign should be wary of speculation and gambling; after a few initial successes they could be easily seduced into thinking that they had a magic touch: alas, what comes so easily can disappear just as fast.

The Dragon's family life is likely to be exciting but hectic. Decisions are made hastily without thought for the consequences. Family members will come and go, and the house is likely to be full of friends and acquaintances turning up for breakfast and dinner, always expecting a welcome and always getting one.

The Dragon's dress sense is never conventional. What the Dragon wears today may not be next year's fashions, but astonished observers may be fooled into thinking so.

# The Snake

## Keyword: Spirituality

Elegant and sensuous, the Snake, the Dragon's companion, is another sign of magic and mystery. But where the Dragon is exuberant and vibrant, the Snake is more restrained and discreet. A lover of the finer things in life, one of the Snake's luxuries is the chance to sit in quiet contemplation, enjoying the hidden aura of everyday things. In these moments of detachment, the Snake can tune in to its spiritual inner nature. Many people born under the sign of the Snake will admit to having had some form of contact with beings from other worlds, be they ghosts or aliens.

Because natural snakes live in cracks in the ground, this means they are in close contact with the Earth itself, and when an earthquake is imminent they surface. Similarly, the astrological Snake's highly tuned senses can detect plots and secrets; when a Snake realizes that someone is not being completely honest, instead of challenging the liar to be truthful, the Snake will store the information and use it to good advantage when the time comes. On a practical level, by keeping in the background but always being vigilant and watchful, the Snake is skilled at gathering all kinds of information. There are no scandals or intrigues that pass by the Snake unnoticed. The typical Snake's eye for detail mean that many Snake personalities are good with figures, and can solve complex mathematical problems in their heads.

## Work

In career matters, the Snake can put its talents into research, investigation or anything where meticulous attention to detail is needed. For this reason the Snake is usually very precise when dealing with money and makes a good accountant. In business deals Snakes will haggle well beyond the decimal point. At home, their attention to careful budgeting may cause resentment among family members, who may sometimes wish the wallet was opened a little more often. But the

apparent economies enable the fastidious Snake to afford the occasional luxuries. One such indulgence would be his or her taste in clothes, discreetly understated but nevertheless quietly impressive.

Snake people are intrinsically truthful, but at the same time they are unwilling to share their knowledge. They have their own strict codes of morality and conduct by which they rule their own lives, and expect family members to do the same. Essentially a very private person and suspicious of strangers, the Snake is reluctant to admit outsiders into its home.

*The Snake may appear to be sleeping, but it is ever alert and vigilant.*

# The Horse

## Keyword: Fellowship

In Chinese astrology the ancient sign of the Horse represented mid-day, when the Sun (the Great Yang), is at its highest point. Because of its association with the yang force, the Horse stands for all matters traditionally regarded as male interests, such as physical prowess, sports and fast cars. But not everybody born in the year of the Horse, male or female, wants to be a football player. Rather, the qualities of the Horse are teamwork, social life and being one of the gang.

Because men were considered to be the dominant partners in a relationship, in traditional Chinese society it was considered unfavourable if the woman was born in a Horse year. Parents dreaded having a baby girl born in Horse years as it would be difficult for them to find a suitable marriage partner: the choice was limited to men of the same age who would also be Horses. Worse still was if the girl was born in a Fire Horse year (1966 being the latest Fire Horse year) as such turbulent characters would give the husband no chance of a peaceful life.

Men born in Horse years are likely to have fixed views about the role of men in society, believing that certain domestic tasks are a woman's duties while it is the man's job to be the breadwinner. Horses are happiest when they are able to separate work and social life from home and family. Paradoxically perhaps, women born in Horse years take the

*The Horse symbolizes masculine qualities and interests above all else.*

opposite views and feel that both husband and wife should share the household chores, social activities and family responsibilities. According to the female Horse, the purpose of working is to earn money to support the family.

## Work

The leadership qualities of the Horse personality mean that they make good committee members, are active in the community and may be attracted to political careers. Horse people tend to have firmly entrenched views, and they are not easily swayed by reasoned argument; the most successful way to influence the Horse's opinion is via the printed page.

Horse people will follow the trends of their social group, whatever the current fashion, and will even wear items of clothing or accessories that they are not perfectly happy with, if they feel that this will enable them to blend in with their companions.

Once you have made friends with a Horse, you can be sure that you have a friend for life.

# The Sheep

## Keyword: Family

Just as the Horse is the symbol of the yang force, so it is that the Sheep symbolizes yin. It is the most feminine of all the signs and rules over all the qualities associated with family, motherhood and marriage. It makes no difference if the Sheep person is male or female; stability and companionship are important. Ties with family, siblings and cousins are therefore more likely to be very close, while those who for various reasons have lost contact with their parents will feel a strong need for companionship within a new family of their own.

One of the Sheep's shortcomings is its failure to understand that not everyone has the same tastes and preferences. It may come as a shock, for example, to learn that a planned surprise treat was not welcomed with as much enthusiasm as had been expected.

## Too trusting

Sheep may be too trusting of people they have come to regard as friends and may suffer the consequences of a close colleague unexpectedly dissolving an established partnership in what had always been regarded as a joint enterprise. It is best when this happens early in life, as this helps the Sheep personality to be more careful in his or her judgement of character, and also helps to strengthen that person's defences should there be more serious breaches of trust in the future.

But the Sheep has unexpected reserves of belligerence. Because the Sheep is normally so easy-going and acquiescent, it is easy to overlook any signs of resentment that may build up if the Sheep is constantly treated unfairly or unthinkingly. When this bitterness surfaces, the results can be devastating and lead to major changes.

## Work

Sheep people like to be near crowds, but don't want to get lost in them. All Sheep have their individual personalities, and may prefer to show their independence by remaining on the edge of a group, rather than throwing themselves into the throng. Social activities such as dancing and musical

*Since flocks of sheep are all females, the Sheep symbolizes femininity.*

performance suit the Sheep's personality, because these activities give opportunities not only to work with a group of people, but also to shine as a soloist, and for this reason Sheep personalities may follow a career in the arts.

Sheep personalities always appear confident and self-assured, and are clever at choosing outfits that can be easily adapted to suit the occasion, whatever it may be.

# The Monkey

## Keyword: Skill

The ancient Chinese sign, now known as the Monkey, originally showed a hide of leather being tanned on a frame to suggest an exhausted worker stretching out at the end of the day. The sign represented the completion of the day's tasks and symbolized the satisfaction obtained when an enterprise is eventually brought to a close.

Although the Monkey is usually associated with manual dexterity, it also signifies those who have skill with words, and who can talk themselves out of the most difficult situations. Of course, if they were not Monkey personalities, they would not be in difficulties in the first place. Unfortunately, many of the problems that the Monkey has to face are actually the consequences of his or her own actions, rather than the result of some unavoidable external influence. But in fairness, all turns out well eventually.

## Work

The Monkey is adept in many ways, combining a sharp mind and incisive wit with technical expertise, but whether its talents are put to good use or not depends very much on the whim of the moment. The career choice will reflect the Monkey person's need to express his or her imagination through its technical skills. Some Monkeys' accounting systems seldom catch up with reality; their budgeting experiments can mean that they reel from affluence to shortage in the blink of an eye, but the skilful Monkey always has some clever scheme in reserve.

The old symbol of 'stretching' at the end of a day's work does not signify that after a job is complete the Monkey relaxes and takes life easy. Quite the reverse; no sooner has the Monkey finished one scheme, but he or she begins to plan the next course of action. It is an exciting life, but one with which the family may not be able to keep up. Restless and impatient, the Monkey can soon tire of his or her surroundings and want to move on. This restlessness may be all very well in the workplace, but can put a strain on family life. In personal relationships such an attitude can be disastrous. The partners of Monkey people need to assess their relationship carefully, for it is easy to lose patience with the Monkey's unpredictable ways.

The complex nature of the Monkey is reflected in its love of intricate designs and choice of clothes with detailed patterns.

*Though boisterous and playful, Monkeys can be creatively constructive.*

# The Rooster

## Keyword: Commerce

Some Chinese texts claim that the original sign for the Rooster is an image of a bird settling on its nest, which is why the Rooster was chosen. True, it represents the west and the setting sun, the time when birds do indeed come home to roost, but in fact, the original sign represented a wine jar, which indicated that it was time to leave the tasks of the day, sit back with a bottle of wine, listen to music and watch the sun set.

As the Rooster's original sign of the wine jar also identified the autumn equinox, people born in Rooster years whose birthdays are close to about 21 September (especially if their birth time was about sunset), seem to have too many empty wine bottles in their horoscope. Consequently, they may need to watch their intake of stimulants, whether alcohol or tobacco!

The sign of the Rooster represents all things to do with leisure activities, whether it is enjoying music and the fine arts, or less-cultural evening entertainment.

## Work

But there are other aspects to the Rooster. Because the west is associated with the Metal element, representing coinage, this sign also rules over commerce and trade. Being a yin or feminine sign, it favours

*In many ways, the extrovert Rooster is the yin counterpart of its rival, the Tiger.*

enterprises that are connected with women's interests, such as fashion or women's magazines. The sign is the feminine equivalent of the Tiger, and helps people born under this sign who have hopes of promotion. Men born under the Rooster sign gain by being gifted with the kind of intuition normally regarded as the province of the female, a talent that helps them to understand the wiles of the opposite sex much more astutely than they realize.

Roosters are stimulating people, but are better talkers than listeners. They speak frankly and sometimes fail to realize that criticism, especially when justified, is not always welcome. They like to be active and like their farmyard counterparts are early risers, a merit not always appreciated by the Rooster's partner!

Women blessed with this sign have great fashion sense and attract many admirers who may be overawed by the Rooster's charisma. Man or woman, the Rooster's style will always be at the cutting edge of what is fashionable.

# The Dog

## Keyword: Property

The Dog symbolizes the time when preparations are made to close up the house for the night and put the Dog on guard. Thus, it represents the safety and security of the home, defences against intruders and by extension, supportive people who offer protection when it is needed and friends who can be relied upon in times of difficulty.

The Dog personality is fiercely defensive of friends and family. Wary of meeting people for the first time, the Dog is happy to socialize with a wide number of people, but true friendships are limited to a special few. Within this tightly closed circle, loyalties are deep and the bonds unbreakable.

Within the family, the Dog will share many interests with older and younger generations and is happiest when special occasions call for activities that involve the whole family. The Dog is always happy to receive visitors into the home, but there will be a tacit understanding that they do not overstay their welcome.

## Work

It is not only intruders whom the Dog guards against. The vigilant Dog will keep an eye on the fabric of the house to ensure that it is wind- and waterproof. Dog personalities tend to enjoy fixing things in the house; indeed, those Dog personalities who choose a career connected with building or real estate will have followed their ideal calling. Dog people prefer to own their houses rather than rent, but those who choose the latter course still have the same pride of ownership over their little kingdom. Throughout life, instead of staying in one fixed location, the Dog will always try to move to more spacious and more impressive properties.

Despite the Dog's concern to ensure that the walls of the house are secure, it is surprising that he or she likes to spend so much time outside. Indeed, the cherished house is more a place to return to, rather than the place to stay put – the Dog is a lover of the countryside and open spaces, from where he or she can proudly admire the prized house from a distance, rather than from within. It is to be hoped that the Dog's partner will share this love of the outdoors.

*Whoever has a trusty and loyal Dog for a friend has a friend for life.*

The Dog's preferred style of dress immediately suggests the country lover. When the occasion calls for something more formal, the effect may be slightly intimidating.

# The Pig

## Keyword: Home

The Chinese zodiac leaves its nicest character to the last. While it may not be very flattering to be thought of as a Pig personality, the sign embodies all the favourable qualities associated with family, a comfortable home and warm friendliness. Indeed, it is worth bearing in mind that the Chinese character for 'family' depicts a pig with a roof over it, to signify that no home is complete without its happy pig. It shows contentment and security – the old astrological sign showed two people in bed asleep.

People born under the sign of the Pig always have a welcome in their home. They love luxurious comfort and their furnishings are more likely to be chosen for the feel rather than the look. Some houses are so pristine and polished that the visitor is afraid of sitting down in case something is scratched – this doesn't apply in the Pig's house.

## Work

Those outside the family might be forgiven for thinking that the Pig is awash with money, but the reason that the Pig can afford life's comforts is due to sheer industriousness. The Pig works hard in order to enjoy the benefits that a little extra cash can bring; but having done so, work is left behind. Work is a topic that the Pig does not like to discuss at home; what is the point of working hard if the troubles and anxieties of daily toil are allowed to intrude on a peaceful home life?

Sadly, the Pig's gentle kindness can be a weakness, too. In his or her eagerness to please, the Pig is liable to misjudge people's intentions, and his or her charitable nature is likely to be imposed upon. The Pig should try to be firmer with those who repeatedly come to him or her for help. It may be hard to refuse, but when people come to the Pig as a 'last resort' it is worth considering where that person would go if the naïve Pig wasn't there to help.

Pig people have a great sense of style; while they prefer to relax in comfortable shapeless clothes, they love to dress to meet the occasion, matching the mood of the moment but always with a surprising extra touch that enables them to stand out and be noticed.

Because the Pig is the last sign of the zodiac, it is a symbol of finishing and completion. As a result, once the Pig has achieved its objective, it may have no motivation to start afresh.

*The Pig symbolizes a well-earned rest after a hard day's work.*

# Relationships

Which signs are the ideal partners for each of the animal signs? Few Chinese parents would allow their children to marry without first seeing if their zodiac signs were compatible. The following pages offer traditional wisdom on this critical matter.

# Compatibility

Chinese folklore is full of proverbs concerning the suitability of prospective marriage partners, nearly all of them concerning the animal zodiac signs of the intended couple. Most warn of the unfavourable conflicts ahead when two animal signs clash, such as 'Ox and Horse cannot share the same stable'. Sadly, very few are as positive as the simple statement 'When the Rabbit meets the Snake, there is true happiness.'

In former times (and even now in certain Chinese social circles), when the parents of a young man wished to discover if a young lady's parents were in favour of a match (the young couple themselves would be lucky to have a say in the matter), the man's parents would send a card bearing the young man's name and the eight signs which gave his hour, day, month and year of birth. If the girl's family was happy with the prospect, her parents would return the card with the girl's birth date written on it. Then both sets of parents would consult their astrologers to see what the future held for the couple. On the other hand, if the girl's parents thought their daughter's other suitors had better prospects, they would send the card back to say their astrologer had considered the match unsuitable. That way, an offer of marriage could be rejected politely without any offence being taken.

*Many people believe that compatible astrological signs are a sure guide to their future happiness.*

## Compatibility in business

Of course, compatible animal signs don't merely apply to couples with romance in mind, they can be very useful for prospective employers wanting to engage the right kind of person for the job. That may seem a little far-fetched, but perhaps not as fanciful as some of the CVs submitted by job-hunters. An employer might want a creative person, someone who can take orders easily or someone with experience. All these can be evident through the usual interview channels. But how will the employer know whether the candidate will be trustworthy or loyal? Waiting to find out could be a costly process. Chinese employers, however, would have the answer at their finger tips: just look at the date of birth and see if the animal sign is compatible.

## Birth planning

Another way in which the animal signs are considered is when a family is planning to have a child – particularly now in China where the number of children a family may have is restricted. Much better if the child is born in an astrologically harmonious year!

In the following pages, the most favourable astrological relationships are marked with a ★.

# The Rat's companions

## With another **Rat**

Rats together can forge long-lasting relationships. They have much in common: among friends there are shared interests, while those in closer relationships are able to support each other. They are aware of each other's strong points and shortcomings simply because they have had the same experiences. They make good working companions because in emergencies they are able to take over the other's schedule. Rat children may seem to be distant from their parents, but there is inner love.

## With the **Ox**

Rat and Ox make excellent partners, since one is the creative innovator and the other the perfectionist who completes every project. In romantic relationships, it is the Rat who should take the lead, but the Ox will always be happy to follow the mood of the moment. The somewhat erratic Rat needs the stabilizing influence of a very sensible partner. Children born in Ox years are likely to stay with their parents longer than might have been expected.

## With the **Tiger**

Rat and Tiger personalities may not seem to have much in common but they respect each other's different outlooks on life. There is a fondness

that is expressed in subtle ways both recognize, although outsiders might seem amused at some of the strange things they say to each other. It is sometimes easier if the wife is the older partner in this relationship, as this will help to balance the Tiger's bold charisma.

## With the **Rabbit**

It is not surprising that the Rat was attracted to this beautiful (or handsome) partner, but there are some difficulties in trying to understand what it is that the Rabbit really wants in life. Sometimes the Rat may feel rejected, and this can be very hurtful, but love can conquer all. The Rabbit child of Rat parents may leave home early in life.

## With the **Dragon** ★

The Dragon makes a stimulating and exciting companion. The Rat will always be ready with ideas that the Dragon will develop in his or her own individual way. Friends will envy the lifestyle of these two career people, but they need to remember that they are both equally good at disposing of income as they are of getting it – something to keep in mind in both romantic and business situations. The Dragon child will have a brilliant career.

## With the **Snake**

The Snake will bring a touch of mystery into the Rat's life. The Rat will continue to be fascinated by the Snake's captivating ways as long as there remains the hint of more excitement to come. But as the prospects of a better relationship prove to be nothing but empty promises, the Rat will long for something more physical and tangible.

## With the **Horse**

These two people have such different interests that they must have very deeply held feelings for each other in order to remain together! While the Rat will try to share the Horse's interests, the Horse is unlikely to do the same for the Rat. They can stay together forever provided that each understands the other's separate needs.

## With the **Sheep**

Perhaps the Sheep is not the best partner for the Rat, but he or she will bring calmness into the home. Sometimes the Rat may wish the Sheep was a little more exciting, but then, you can't have everything.

## With the **Monkey**★

The Monkey is stimulating company for the Rat. Not only do they plan exciting schemes together, but the Monkey helps to put these plans into action. As business partners, they will be very successful if they can get someone to monitor their riskier enterprises. Their romantic life may be unconventional but very satisfying.

## With the **Rooster**

This relationship is better as a business partnership, when both can go home at the end of the day. The Rat is likely to find that the Rooster makes sudden demands on time, energy and perhaps pocket, which the

Rat considers unreasonable, and the Rooster feels are justified. In a romantic partnership, the Rat can be easily swayed by the Rooster's charisma, which may not be wholly reciprocated.

## With the **Dog**

Although in nature the Dog and Rat may not be the best of companions, astrologically they are a compatible couple. The Rat may find the Dog partner somewhat taciturn, but nevertheless, the Dog is always there at hand to help whenever necessary. Friendships and partnerships are long-lasting.

## With the **Pig**

Rats and Pigs may be the same age, and yet have very little in common. Circumstances and physical attraction may have pushed these two together, but to make the partnership work the Rat needs to consider the Pig's need for stability at home.

# The Ox's companions

## With the Rat

Some of the Rat's wilder schemes are likely to cause the Ox considerable unrest, but occasionally they turn out to be surprisingly successful. This is a partnership where two opposites in character blend together magically. The Rat may be older by a year, but much younger in attitude. Children born in Rat years may exasperate their parents.

## With another Ox

These two people will live and work together steadily and comfortably. Each will be familiar with other's needs, and know what is going to please and what issues need to be avoided. What this couple lacks, however, is some outside stimulation lest their lives should be too humdrum. They need to socialize more, and be more adventurous in their holiday choices.

## With the Tiger

'One Ox can fight two Tigers' runs an old Chinese proverb. It does not bode well for the Tiger partner, who may not be used to being contradicted or rebuffed. The Ox will have to work hard to gain the Tiger's confidence. Fortunately the Ox has plenty of patience. The Tiger child will need to be led carefully.

*The Ox and Rabbit form a stable partnership which often leads to a large and happy family.*

## With the **Rabbit**

Ox and Rabbit can combine their ideas to make a stable partnership. In family life, the Rabbit will probably want to have lots of children. In a business partnership, the Rabbit will be good at ensuring that clients are satisfied. The Rabbit child will bring its parents joy in later years.

## With the **Dragon**

The Ox may be attracted to the Dragon's unusual characteristics, but may despair of ever getting any sense out of such an unpredictable partner. The Ox may not always approve of the Dragon's schemes, but may acquiesce occasionally in order to spare the Dragon's disappointment.

## With the **Snake** ★

What is so special about the Snake that the Ox finds so attractive? This is what friends and family ask themselves. The Snake seems so different in personality, yet the couples share a secret understanding. This is a very successful relationship both for romance or business. Snake children will be intelligent.

## With the Horse

According to a Chinese proverb, 'the Ox and the Horse cannot share the same stable'. Both are set in their ways and are not easily persuaded to change their minds. This can be fine if both share the same interests, but when their directions differ, it can cause frustration, sometime leading to fierce argument. They should direct their energies to their enemies, not to each other.

## With the Sheep

Astrologically, the Ox has only one real enemy – the Sheep. Although the Sheep may seem unassuming and placid, the Ox should not misjudge this outer appearance. If the partner is taken too much for granted, inner resentment will erupt and the Sheep will turn into a raging ram.

## With the Monkey

The lively Monkey is able to make some points of contact with its more sober partner. If both are able to have their independence there can be

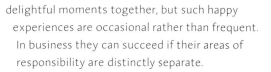

delightful moments together, but such happy experiences are occasional rather than frequent. In business they can succeed if their areas of responsibility are distinctly separate.

## With the **Rooster**★

The ideal partner for the hard-working Ox is the vibrant Rooster, who provides the touch of the exotic that the Ox needs to brighten his or her life. In business they will pool their resources and talents to make a very successful partnership. The Rooster child will be wealthier than its parents.

## With the **Dog**

The relationship is the opposite of the image of the obstinate 'dog in the manger'. It is the Ox who is obstinate, and the Dog is overruled by the Ox every time. Not the best partner for the Ox, who should care more about his or her loyal companion.

## With the **Pig**

The domestically inclined Pig is a delightful help for the industrious Ox. Together they can build a comfortable home where they can enjoy their hard-earned leisure time. In romance, there is true love. In business, these two will work diligently and earn the respect of their clients. The Pig child will be a blessing to its parents.

# The Tiger's companions

### With the **Rat**

The Rat will prove to be a loyal and witty companion, bringing a light-hearted touch to serious situations when things do not go as smoothly as they should. As a friend, the Rat will prove to be a useful ally in surprising ways, having qualities that the Tiger may not have expected.

### With the **Ox**

It is best not to get involved in arguments with this partner, since the Ox is unlikely to change his or her opinion, and discussions are likely to become heated. Romantic situations can hit impassable obstacles; at such times it is better for both to go their separate ways. In business, there is a conflict of management styles. The Ox child will be stubborn and independently minded.

### With another **Tiger**

Provided that both partners see the other as an equal, this is a favourable conjunction of like-minded people. There is no doubting the strong bonds between the members of this very stable partnership. In business, the partners work to the same goals. If there are Tiger children as well, they will be the foundation of a dynasty to continue family traditions.

## With the **Rabbit**

There is something attractively alluring about the Rabbit; the partner has all the qualities that the Tiger usually avoids and this is what makes it so much more appealing. These two make a very happy couple despite their differences. In business, since both partners tackle problems in different ways, solutions are quickly found.

## With the **Dragon**

There is a strong mutual attraction between these two lively characters. The Dragon has much to offer the Tiger, and their shared ambitions will forge a strong bond between them. In business, the partnership is a sure recipe for success, as long as the Tiger can take the leading role. The Dragon child may follow a political career and be granted honours in later life.

## With the **Snake**

Although the Tiger is drawn by the Snake's attractive manner, there is an undercurrent of insecurity which may prevent the relationship going very deeply. In business, the Snake may find it difficult to fit in with the working arrangements. The Snake child is likely to follow its own inclinations.

## With the **Horse**★

The Horse will prove to be the ideal companion for the Tiger, bringing a positive contribution to the partnership. Together they are adventurous in what they do and their life together is fulfilling. In the Horse, the Tiger sees strength of character and all the qualities the Tiger most admires. In business, they make a formidable team and can tackle rivals together ruthlessly. The Tiger parent will be proud of its Horse child.

## With the **Sheep**

Relationships will bring serenity rather than excitement; it will be a satisfactory marriage of stability. In business, the Sheep partner will work dutifully and accurately. The Sheep child will be affectionate, but may appear reserved and diffident to strangers.

## With the **Monkey**

What could have brought the Monkey into the Tiger's domain? The Monkey has such a different outlook on life and may not be afraid to voice his or her opposition to the Tiger's ideals. This can only lead to eventual disenchantment unless both partners are able to recognize that they are independent spirits. The Monkey child can bring problems into the Tiger household.

## With the **Rooster**

The Rooster has so much in common with the Tiger that there is bound to be an undercurrent of competition, if not jealousy, between them. The Tiger can see much of itself in the ambitious Rooster, which leads to occasional inner doubts regarding the direction the partnership is going. In business, the Tiger needs to exercise caution, as it is unlikely that any arrangements made will be permanent.

## With the **Dog**★

The Dog is an ideal companion for the Tiger. Not only are they immediately suited, but the Dog's loyalty and devotion will ensure that this relationship will withstand all kinds of storms. The same holds just as true of a business partnership as it does for a romantic one. The Dog child will be a great blessing to the family and a source of strength in later years.

## With the **Pig**

There may have been an initial attraction when the Pig first comes to the Tiger's notice, but the adventurous Tiger could find the Pig's natural style a little unsophisticated. And although the flame of passion occasionally dims, the Pig brings stability to an otherwise hectic home life. The Pig child will be reluctant to leave home.

*The adventurous Horse is one of the best partners and companions that the charismatic Tiger could hope for.*

# The Rabbit's companions

## With the **Rat**

The rabbit in nature does not welcome a rat into its burrow and the symbolism is no less pertinent in Chinese astrology. A quiet and serene existence is disrupted by the arrival of the smart Rat, who with suave and cunning charm inveigles itself into the Rabbit's life. Perhaps the relationship will be a firm one, but the Rabbit has to take a background role. The Rat child will be very independent.

## With the **Ox**

The Ox has much to offer the Rabbit – security, strength and stability – values that the Rabbit needs in its rapidly changing world. A reliable and firm relationship can be the result of a chance meeting, whether for the romantically inclined or for a business partnership. The Ox child will be strong and dependable.

## With the **Tiger**

Although on the face of it the Tiger seems to have very little in common with the Rabbit, this is a partnership that will be cemented by a strong bond of affection. Despite their outward differences, they share the same ambitions, even though they plan to achieve their objectives by different routes. The Tiger child will bring wealth to the family.

## With another **Rabbit**

Whether for simple friendships, social contact,
business partnerships or romantic relationships
Rabbit personalities interact very amicably.
Family ties are strong and there is a happy
ambience in the home. Wealth is not
such an important issue and
material benefits take second
place to domestic harmony.
The Rabbit child will be the
favourite in the family.

## With the **Dragon**

For once, the Rabbit's charitable
nature is turned on its head and
instead of looking after others, it
is the Rabbit's turn to be tended
by the ill-fated Dragon. Ensnared by the
gentle wiles of the Rabbit, the Dragon offers
everything, but receives little in return. The Dragon
child will need to care for its parents in old age.

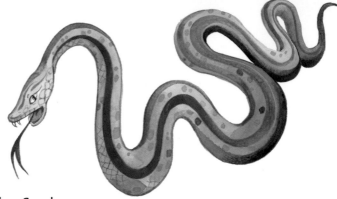

## With the **Snake**

'When the Snake meets the Rabbit, there is true happiness,' runs an old Chinese proverb. Astrologically, there is love at first sight when the Snake enters the Rabbit's life. In business relationships, mutual respect leads to commercial success. The Snake child will be well-loved.

## With the **Horse**

There is a wide gap between the Rabbit and the Horse; although the two may share a common background or upbringing, they have gone their different ways. As business partners, they may find it difficult to agree on procedure. The Horse child will leave home as soon as it is able.

## With the **Sheep**★

The Sheep is an ideal partner for the Rabbit. The Rabbit, caught up in a whirlwind of attending to other people's wants and demands, needs a stabilizing and calming influence, someone who can show him or her how to refuse persistent demands for assistance, whether these are demands on leisure time or for financial help. Meeting the Sheep will be a turning point in the Rabbit's life. The Sheep child will be warm and loving.

## With the **Monkey**

As attractive as the Monkey is, it has a destabilizing influence on the Rabbit's ordered life. A whirlwind romance will soon blow itself out, leaving the Rabbit richer in experience, but spiritually exhausted. In business, an arrangement between these two will have questionable advantages. The Monkey child will try to get it's own way and will need firm direction.

## With the **Rooster**

The Rabbit symbolizes the dawn and the Rooster the setting sun; these two have such different priorities that it is difficult to see how they can ever agree. The Rooster is only interested in the end product and cannot be burdened with the practical details of how the objectives are achieved. An exhausting partnership for the Rabbit, alas. The Rooster child will leave home early in life and be successful in business.

## With the **Dog**

The Dog is the one who gains from this partnership. This duo has its harmonious moments, but there are many discordant passages. It is better for the Dog to avoid making too many demands on the Rabbit's patience. In business, there are bound to be differences of priority. The Rabbit parent may find the Dog child too forceful and independent.

## With the **Pig** ★

This is a loving relationship, both partners being equally smitten. The Pig will enhance the Rabbit's happiness by strengthening the bonds of family life. The partners have many shared interests, and will take an active interest in each other's work. In business, the partners will be very supportive and reliable. A Pig child born to a Rabbit parent will bring blessings to the family.

# The Dragon's companions

## With the Rat ★

The Dragon is delighted when the Rat comes into his or her life. Here is someone at last who can share and enjoy the Dragon's enthusiasm for novelty and encourages the Dragon to strike out into the unknown. The successful partnership holds true whether for romance, business or both. The Rat child will study hard.

*The Rat child born to a Dragon parent will prove to be industrious and successful at school and university.*

## With the **Ox**

The Ox finds it hard to understand the way that the Dragon thinks. Often, the Ox is reluctant to fall in with the Dragon's plans, thinking that they are unworkable and doesn't want to take the risk of exploring the possibilities. The Dragon is likely to find this lack of enthusiasm a little wearisome. These two should not expect to cooperate every time. The Dragon parent will find the Ox child stubborn.

## With the **Tiger**

As long as these two people are allowed to make their own plans, this will be a stimulating and successful joining of two minds. The Tiger, perhaps from a different social background, will have respect for the Dragon's special qualities, and will lead the Dragon partner up the ladder of success. The Tiger child will be strong and wilful.

## With the **Rabbit**

'When the Rabbit appears, all the Dragon's fortune disappears,' says an old Chinese proverb. A chance meeting is fraught with problems. Wanting to help someone in need, the Dragon becomes absorbed gradually into the Rabbit's troubles, receiving very little in return Not the best start to a relationship. The Rabbit child will be indulged.

## With another **Dragon**

The double-Dragon relationship is one of the less favourable same-sign combinations. Despite the impression that they are as close as identical twins and work together as one, Dragons are independent. Concerned with the image they project, they feel resentment if they sense that they are being upstaged by their partners. The Dragon child will be a delight and bring honour to its parents.

## With the **Snake**

The Snake could be an ideal partner for the Dragon as both share similar interests while having a different approach to the solving of problems. The Snake is more of a thinker, but will leave decision making to the Dragon. The Snake child may follow in its parent's footsteps and benefit from their enthusiastic support throughout life.

## With the **Horse**

This partnership works well either as a social friendship or a business arrangement. The Horse will be from a different background to the Dragon, and because of this, can bring the Dragon a fresh approach to life. Although fascinated by the many different aspects of the Horse's life, the Dragon will not want to be too closely involved.

## With the **Sheep**

The attraction of the Sheep may be superficial, perhaps the result of initial infatuation that soon evaporates. If the partners want this relationship to last, the Dragon will have to lower his or her expectations and the Sheep will need to be more assertive. The Sheep child will need to be carefully brought up.

## With the **Monkey**★

The Monkey partner is one of the two Dragon relationships deemed to be the most successful astrologically. The Monkey brings technical expertise and practicality to the Dragon's plans. Whether planning a holiday or a house extension, the Dragon may have the ideas, but the Monkey will provide the feasibility study. In business, the Monkey is a valued member of the team without whom decisions could not be taken. The Monkey child will be industrious and enterprising.

### With the **Rooster**

The Dragon will spot the Rooster's unconventional outlook on life and realize that here is someone with whom to share views and opinions. But while the two have much in common, whether they could forge a partnership together is another matter. There is mutual admiration, but little cooperation here. At first, the Rooster child will appear hot-headed and frivolous, but be successful in later life.

### With the **Dog**

In the horoscope chart, the Dog is directly opposite the Dragon with the Dog being practical and down-to-earth while the Dragon is mystical and absent-minded. The Dragon will eventually consider the Dog to be too domesticated and banal, but maybe this is what the Dragon needs. But neither partner is going to change. The Dog child will consider its parents to be from another planet.

### With the **Pig**

While not the worst companion for the Dragon, the Pig is too much of a home-loving person to tolerate the Dragon's untidy habits and unpredictable ways. The Pig, on the other hand, seems to be taking over the Dragon's life, making decisions for them both without clearing the position with the Dragon partner first. Dragon parents may consider the Pig child to lack enthusiasm.

# The Snake's companions

## With the **Rat**

The Snake may provide intellectual stimulation in this partnership, but the Rat has a mind of his or her own. Sometimes the two are not able to agree on a course of action and the Rat may feel that he or she has to follow the Snake's lead even when the Rat's instinct goes against it. This relationship works best if the two are not obliged to agree every time.

## With the **Ox** ★

The brooding Ox stirs the Snake in a way that only romantic novelists can describe. A loving relationship is built on passion and mental stimulus; separated from the Ox, the Snake feels lost and disconsolate. Sadly, this couple is likely to have met too late for the partnership to be a material one. In business, a very successful commercial arrangement benefits both partners. The Ox child will be an achiever.

## With the **Tiger**

The Tiger brings stimulation into the Snake's life, but the initial passion is too strong and is soon burnt out. Nevertheless, memories of early love will last long into life, and the echoes of this former happiness can keep a marriage or an established relationship together. In business, the Tiger may prove intrusive and interfering. The Tiger child will be headstrong and difficult.

## With the **Rabbit**

Although astrologically this is a good, rather than a perfect relationship, according to a Chinese proverb this couple represent true happiness. There is something tender and gentle about the Rabbit that the Snake finds irresistible and the loving affection is returned. In business, it will prove to be a happy and prosperous partnership.

## With the **Dragon**

This partnership is the result of a successful bonding of two people with like minds but different attitudes. The Dragon shows emotions that the diffident Snake finds difficult to express, while the Dragon admires the Snake's assumed modesty and refinement. The Dragon child will rise to a position of authority.

## With another **Snake**

Not all couples born under the same animal sign form a successful relationship, but fortunately two Snake people form one of the happy pairs that build a lasting partnership. Love and affection are there in abundance. In business, both work to their mutual benefit.

*The bonds of affection between Snake personalities are instantly recognizable.*

## With the **Horse**

The Snake is apprehensive when he or she first encounters the Horse, as this person seems to be an intruder invading the Snake's very private world. As time passes and confidence grows, the two are drawn closer together, but for the Snake there will always be lingering doubts. In business, a rocky start, a tricky finish.

## With the **Sheep**

This partnership has all the ingredients for a long and happy lifetime together. The Sheep brings companionship and affection into a life that may have seemed to be lonely and pointless. The Sheep's openness and genuine qualities are a great comfort and the Snake will feel regenerated and more spirited. In business, a joint venture will be constructive.

## With the **Monkey**

The Monkey may be a stimulating companion at first, but this sign's irascible ways are likely to pall. In business, disputes over policy will hold back development. Whether in a personal situation or a business partnership, it is better not to hope for long term commitments. The Monkey child will need careful direction in order to instil a sense of responsibility.

## With the **Rooster**★

There is no doubting the Rooster's personal charm and magnetism, but equally, the elegant Snake can transfix the Rooster. In love, this partnership provides all the ingredients for a long and wonderfully happy relationship. It is a very good partnership for commercial enterprises, since both Snake and Rooster are sound financial manipulators. The Rooster child will be successful in business.

## With the **Dog**

The Dog will remain a faithful admirer of the Snake long after the honeymoon is over. There are aspects of the Dog's personality, however, that jar the Snake's sensitive nature. It is the Dog, sadly, who will feel let down eventually. In business, the Dog will want to change the way the concern is organized, causing resentment.

## With the **Pig**

A rather pessimistic outlook is described in an old Chinese proverb that says that the Pig eats the Snake and is then poisoned. In real life the situation is not so dire; when the Pig arrives on the scene the Snake is initially delighted to have the Pig's company. They will stay together as long as they are able to battle out their differences from time to time.

# The Horse's companions

### With the **Rat**

The Horse belongs to the Fire element, the Rat to Water. That may be why the Rat did not leave such a favourable impression on the Horse when they first met. As they got to know each other better, the Horse was able to recognize positive qualities in the Rat that were not evident originally. But there will always be something holding the Horse back from getting too deeply involved in this partnership. The Rat child may disappoint its parents by showing no interest in family affairs, but will nevertheless make its own success in life.

### With the **Ox**

As the proverb says, 'Horse and Ox do not share the same stable'. Meeting the Ox would be a surprise; the two come from different backgrounds and their partnership would grow out of the close circumstances in which they found themselves. In business, these two are more likely to be rivals than partners. The Ox child will tend to dominate the parents and demand its own way, but in later life will prove to be very supportive.

### With the **Tiger**★

Here is someone much more to the Horse's liking; they have the same opinions, ambitions and attitudes, and will readily pool their resources to achieve their objectives. Any romantic relationship is likely to develop further since in marriage, as in business, the partnership cannot be bettered. This is a formidable couple for whom success is assured. Horse parents will have many reasons to be proud of their Tiger child.

## With the **Rabbit**

This is perhaps not an ideal match, since they have little in common to share, but the Horse will be fascinated by the Rabbit's totally different attitudes to people, situations and difficult circumstances, and will feel protective of this vulnerable friend. Romance will blossom quickly. In business, however, the partnership is less promising. In later years the Rabbit child will bring many grandchildren into the family.

## With the **Dragon**

The Horse is fired by enthusiasm when it encounters the charismatic Dragon; here is someone that the Horse can relate to, someone with whom he or she can share outlandish ideas, instead of having them scorned by tedious colleagues. Soon they will be planning holidays abroad and even a move to a foreign country. In business, too, the Dragon brings stimulation and novelty. The Dragon child will be a constant source of wonder and amusement.

## With the **Snake**

The Horse rarely lets a Snake into its stable; if these two people strike up a friendship, it is not superficial infatuation that draws them together but something altogether deeper. They are close in many ways, but distant in others. In business, there may be a lack of trust that is hard to deal with successfully. The Snake child, while having many conflicting interests in life, will always retain close family ties.

## With another **Horse**

There is no mistaking the strong bonds that exist between Horse types. Friendships, romantic relationships or business partners, each partner makes his or her positive contribution to the well-being of the couple. One special benefit is that each partner is able to go his or her own way without fear of losing sight of the other. A good choice of partner.

## With the **Sheep**

Horse and Sheep belong to the same astrological house of sex and gender; that summarizes this very strong and powerful attachment between two people deeply involved in their mutual affection. Such a strong bond will last through life, even if circumstances demand that the two remain apart. In business too, it betokens a good working relationship. The Sheep child will bring benefits in later life.

## With the **Monkey**

The Horse always enjoys the conversations and antics of a lively Monkey friend, and if the relationship is a romantic one, how can the Horse fail to fall for the Monkey's outrageous charms? The Horse will be deeply attached to his or her Monkey partner, and separation, even for short periods, is painful. The Monkey child will never cease to amuse its parents.

*The Horse parent will be delighted by the antics of its Monkey child.*

## With the **Rooster**

When someone as exciting and as the Rooster enters the Horse's life, it is no surprise that the Horse is smitten. But the Rooster's independence cannot impress the Horse forever, and a failure to face up to problems can sour what had been a harmonious partnership. In business partnerships, the Rooster can be effective in finding new commercial contacts. The Rooster child may seem aloof in occasions and should never be over-indulged.

## With the **Dog** ★

The Horse immediately recognizes the Dog as a potential friend; in the field of romance, the mutual attraction will ensure that the relationship will develop into something more lasting. The Dog will have a fund of fascinating tales with which to regale the Horse during their happy times together. In the business world, this is one of the two ideal partnerships for the Horse. The Dog child will never be far from home and will be a source of great comfort in later years.

## With the **Pig**

Both partners are content with their relationship; this partnership works best when the Pig is the homemaker and the Horse the breadwinner. They live together in harmony, though the Horse may occasionally wish that the Pig was a little more adventurous. In business, this is a practical but uninspiring partner. The Pig child may be reluctant to leave the comfort of the family home.

# The Sheep's companions

## With the **Rat**

According to a Chinese proverb, Sheep and Rat soon separate. This partnership comes together after an initial period of doubt. There is something about the Rat that is fascinating, and yet the Sheep finds it difficult to know what the Rat is thinking. This would not be an ideal situation in a business partnership. Sheep parents may find it difficult to communicate with the Rat child.

## With the **Ox**

The Ox has special qualities, such as his or her reliability and determination, that are important for the Sheep. Similarly, the Ox finds that the Sheep can understand his or her deeper feelings. Perhaps this is not one of the most exciting partnerships in the world, but the qualities of character and mutual dependence bring security. In business too, a solid joint venture. The Ox child is likely to be defiant.

## With the **Tiger**

The Tiger will dominate this one-sided relationship, but if the Sheep is prepared to let the Tiger have his or her own way all the time, then the Tiger will be quite happy to continue the partnership as long as the Sheep wants. The Sheep may be happy with this arrangement, but it is not ideal. In business, the Tiger partner could prove to be a rival. The Tiger child may be wilful and fractious at times, but supportive later in life.

## With the **Rabbit**★

The Rabbit, while hardly bringing excitement into the Sheep's life, will certainly take the Sheep along paths he or she has never previously followed. This happy relationship is built on love and trust. The bonds between them are very close and mutual affection is very deep. In business, the partnership works well and prospects grow gently. The Rabbit child will be a source of joy and never fail to bring happiness into the household.

## With the **Dragon**

Friends may raise eyebrows when they see their Sheep friend in the company of this unusual character, and are likely to question the Sheep's choice. Perhaps there are doubts about the wisdom of this relationship, but only time will tell. Taking on a Dragon business partner is likely to be a short-term solution. The Dragon child will have great prospects and has the potential to do well, but will do so independently.

## With the Snake

The Snake is able to bring little luxuries, either material goods or a wealth of experience, into the Sheep's life. The Snake's prudent management and gentle persuasion lift the Sheep's spirits and widen his or her ambitions. There are promises of a new life, that with the Snake's help, can become a reality. A business partnership is equally successful. The Snake child will be thoughtful and intelligent.

## With the Horse

Since both Horse and Sheep belong to the astrological house of sex and gender, the relationship is a magnetic one. The Horse has a streak of individuality that is quite different from the Sheep's, but that is its great attraction. Despite the fixed opinion and irresolvable differences between them, this partnership has strong ties. The Horse child's career later in life will bring great satisfaction to its parents.

## With another Sheep

This smooth-running relationship toddles along in the midst of a circle of friends. Social activities are important and despite the affection that they have, they seem to have little time to spend together. Perhaps that is the reason why this relationship is so enduring – there is never time to air their differences. The Sheep child will have an artistic flair.

## With the **Monkey**

Although close astrologically, nothing could be further from the Sheep's idea of a perfect partner than this unpredictable character. The Monkey's attraction must be strong, otherwise the Sheep will see the impossibility of the situation early on. Fortunately, the Sheep has lots of patience. The Monkey child will cause its Sheep parents heartache.

## With the **Rooster**

This happy partnership works because the two partners have diverse goals. Each has their own priorities, but while these are different, the priorities do not conflict. The Rooster will bring a quality that is missing from the Sheep's life, who can as a consequence of this relationship lead a more fulfilling existence despite occasional problems. The Rooster child will make great progress in life and be a source of pride.

## With the **Dog**

When the Dog first comes into the Sheep's life, there is an initial apprehension regarding the way this relationship should continue. But a bond builds up between them and friendship grows. Provided that the Sheep is willing to follow the Dog's direction, this can be fulfilling for both. In business, however, this partnership may lead to problems. The Dog child will be happiest when it has practical tasks to perform.

## With the **Pig** ★

To ensure domestic happiness, the Pig could not be a better choice of partner for the Sheep. Astrologically, this is a relationship built on one of the strongest combinations of mutual understanding and home comfort. While it is also a sound combination for business partnerships, the prospects for a contented family life are outstanding. The Pig child will bring harmony and joy into the home.

# The Monkey's companions

## With the Rat★

This very favourable partnership is triggered by the Rat's fresh ideas and inspiration. Whether socially or in business, by teaming up with the misunderstood Monkey, the Rat will help the Monkey to relate to a wider circle of friends and direct the Monkey's energies in a more creative direction. The Rat child is rather reserved.

## With the Ox

This is not an easy partnership; although there is trust and understanding, a real or imagined barrier exists between them. Maybe a reluctance to discuss previous experiences is at the root of the problem. Do not try to solve it; the past is best left buried. The relationship works better in a business context. The Ox child will appear stubborn and recalcitrant.

*An Ox child does not readily fall in with the wishes of its Monkey parent.*

## With the **Tiger**

A romantic affair is stirred into passion very quickly, but perhaps too suddenly and dangerously. It is likely to be difficult to let the situation sail along smoothly or discuss the problems quietly and openly. In business there are obstacles and the Tiger may prove to be more of a liability than a help. Parents will need to nurture the Tiger child very carefully.

## With the **Rabbit**

This partnership is an unsteady one; the Rabbit attracts with his or her charm, but the Rabbit's intelligence must not be under-estimated. It will survive many storms and if the relationship breaks down, it will be the Rabbit who comes out of it better off. The Rabbit child will be gentle and quiet, and much less assertive than its parents.

## With the **Dragon** ★

A strange but deep affection bind these two rather special people together. This is a conjunction of like minds. The magical Dragon holds an immediate attraction for the equally eccentric Monkey. In public they appear to be a happy if unconventional couple, but what they plan together in private cannot be imagined. The Dragon child will bring excitement into the household and is likely to follow its parents' direction closely.

## With the **Snake**

An unusual couple whose relationship is due to repeated chance encounters; it can take a long time before sufficient rapport is established to take the relationship further. It is a partnership that is difficult to get into and equally difficult to escape. The relationship is more suited to business. The Snake child will be studious and diligent.

## With the **Horse**

The Monkey is always happy to be with the Horse, who will listen patiently and with understanding to the Monkey's problems. The sympathetic ear is what draws the two closer together. Far from being bored by the Monkey's sagas, the Horse finds his or her companion entertaining. A sound relationship in romance or business. The Horse child will be supportive, reliable and a good companion.

## With the **Sheep**

The Sheep is affable enough and can be a quiet companion for the Monkey. In the early stages of the relationship they would seem to have much in common, but their interests diverge with time. There is no actual conflict, but the domestic stability that the Sheep prefers will not last long in this household. The Sheep child may seem distant and awkward and prefer to be alone.

## With another **Monkey**

They consider themselves the perfect couple, but there is the problem of having to gain the confidence of someone outside the relationship. The Monkey's natural reaction is to disregard the opinions of others, but this is a special case and the other people matter. Nevertheless, despite all the difficulties, a strong bond exists between the partners. In business, team efforts are somewhat hectic but produce results. The Monkey parent should be careful to present a positive role for the Monkey child as the parents' attitude, whether positive or not, will be closely imitated.

## With the **Rooster**

It is a favourable partnership for romantic relationships, but is actually better for partnerships in the work place or in business. If business and

home life are joined, it is even better. But try to separate the two so that there is time to relax and enjoy some leisure time together. The Rooster child will leave the nest early.

## With the **Dog**

The Monkey is immediately struck by the Dog's boldness and forthright manner. The two would seem to have little in common and for this relationship to succeed there are many hurdles to overcome. But if both partners are able to follow their own inclinations and not care too much about the other, harmony can be achieved. The Dog child will be steadfast and a stabilizing influence in family life.

## With the **Pig**

A Chinese proverb holds that the Pig and Monkey are soon parted. The homely Pig has quite different priorities from the effervescent Monkey. While the Monkey wants to enjoy life outside, the Pig prefers to pool their resources in making the home a better place to live. Strife is inevitable; try to compromise. The Pig child, though seemingly aloof, will never be far from the family circle.

# The Rooster's companions

## With the **Rat**

The Rat may lack excitement, but a perceptive mind and attention to detail are qualities that the Rooster needs to accept as definite advantages in a partner. They will have

differing attitudes with regard to money matters, so to avoid confrontation they both need to manage their own budgets. The Rat makes an effective business colleague. The Rat child may be over-awed by the Rooster parent and may find it difficult to discuss problems.

## With the **Ox**★

Why it should be that such wildly different personalities can be drawn together so closely will always be a mystery to their friends, but this relationship is firm and solid. The Ox not only brings stability and cohesion into the Rooster's erratic life, but helps the Rooster to direct his or her energies in productive ways. A favourable relationship on all counts. The Ox child will be a great joy to its parents and later will bring stability and organisation to a chaotic home.

## With the **Tiger**

The Rooster sees the Tiger as a reflection of his or her own personality. They ought to be able to work and live together without any conflict of interests, but the plain fact is that envy creeps into the equation, and the Rooster may perceive the Tiger more as a rival than as a companion. A business relationship is likely to fracture because of this. The Tiger child will rival its parents in their ambitions which may cause a rift in family relations later in life.

## With the **Rabbit**

A glance at the chart of the 12 Animals will show that the Rooster and Rabbit are directly opposite, and the same is true of their personal characteristics. As a symbol of spring and the dawn, the Rabbit may lose his or her spirit of regeneration and creativity to the Rooster's pursuit of leisure. The partnership works better when the pair are business colleagues. The Rabbit child will prefer to lead its own life, rather than following the lead laid down by its parents.

## With the **Dragon**

The Rooster always wants to be the dominant figure in a relationship, and there is something about the Dragon that the Rooster secretly resents. For this partnership to work well, both need to discuss their worries and apprehensions. If there are secrets, they will surely be revealed at the least propitious moment. Either at work or socially, as the Dragon child grows older, it will begin to emerge as a rival to its parents' enterprises.

## With the **Snake**★

Chinese folklore does not regard this as a favourable match for prospective marriage partners, which is curiously at odds with the astrological forecast. The sages of old declared this to be one of the most favourable conjunctions; certainly it is ideal for colleagues working on the same project. So perhaps if the prospective couple puts their life together on a business footing there would be no slip-ups. The Snake child will be very studious.

## With the **Horse**
The Horse is determined to follow his or her own directions, and is inclined to consider the Rooster too impractical and capricious. But Rooster needs a firm, disciplined approach to life in order to succeed. Perhaps the Rooster would take sensible advice from someone with whom he or she has greater affinity, but the Horse is not that person. The Horse child will have many friends of its own and is likely to prefer the companionship of friends outside the family.

## With the **Sheep**
A great deal of love and affection wafts between these two happy people. The Sheep is able to offer the comfort and stability that the ambitious Rooster needs. Knowing that there is a steady well-managed home base, the Rooster can concentrate on developing his or her career. In business, the Sheep offers valuable assistance. In its early years the Sheep child will receive love and attention, but later in life there will not be the same commitment to family life.

## With the **Monkey**
Although this relationship is bound to have its stormy moments, it is an extremely successful one. The occasional volatile atmosphere is sparked by two highly motivated people who only want to do the best for each other. In business, this is an intriguing partnership. The Monkey child needs careful handling.

*If the Rooster wants stability and a lasting relationship, a Pig partner would be ideal.*

## With another **Rooster**

Often, individuals with the same animal sign can work together comfortably to each other's benefit. But there are exceptions and Roosters fall into this category. Confrontations result from the rivalry of two people with the same objectives and each is afraid that the other will gain the credit for the success. Unless they can work together, there will be no credit, only loss. The Rooster child will follow in its parents' footsteps and be successful in business.

## With the **Dog**

A Chinese proverb says that the Rooster breaks into tears at the sight of a Dog. Why this should be so is not made clear. Is it the unhappiness that results from the Dog wanting the Rooster to leave home? Or is it due to sadness because the Dog has to be away for such long periods. Then again, knowing the Rooster's keen dress sense, it may be the sight of the Dog's latest foray into the world of fashion. The Dog child will make its own way in the world and will not depend on its parents.

## With the **Pig**

For the Rooster who wants comfort in later years, the Pig is the perfect partner. Maybe the Pig does not offer much in the way of excitement and fast living, but on the other hand the Pig can gain a reputation for social entertainment at home that will more than make up for the absence of city life. A good, solid, reliable partnership. The Pig child will bring stability and happiness into the home.

# The Dog's companions

### With the **Rat**

There are aspects of the Rat that the Dog admires, but equally there are sides to the Rat's personality that the Dog finds really disconcerting. The Rat can bring grace and refinement into the Dog's world, but sometimes this becomes a little precious. Happily, the Dog is usually able to treat these incidents with humour. In business, the Rat will be a welcome addition to the smooth running of the firm. The Rat child will be intelligent and studious, though somewhat independently minded.

### With the **Ox**

The Dog can be exasperated by the Ox, who manages to employ obstinacy as a weapon. Often the Dog wonders whether he or she had a life before the Ox took over. Patience is the only solution to this otherwise insurmountable obstacle to their relationship. In a business situation, the Ox will work hard but will lack flexibility. There will be many disagreements between the Dog parent and the stubborn Ox child, with neither wishing to compromise.

### With the **Tiger**★

One does not usually imagine the Tiger to be a fun creature, but it brings playfulness and amusement into the Dog's life. They work in harmony together since they have the same objectives in life and their

partnership is not confined to romance. The pair will soon realize that they could be effective business partners as well. They will probably move to another country together. The Tiger child brings honour to his or her parents.

## With the **Rabbit**

The Rabbit's attraction is a physical one; although they may be tender and affectionate in private, in public the Dog scarcely acknowledges the Rabbit's presence. Naturally, this is not a satisfactory existence for the Rabbit, who will soon be looking for another field to burrow in. Sadly, the Rabbit and the Dog is an unsatisfactory partnership for business prospects. The Rabbit child will be caring and loving but is likely to cause anxiety at times.

## With the **Dragon**

The Dog's initial fascination with the magical Dragon eventually gives way to a scornful dismissal of what the Dog considers to be shallow pretence. But if the relationship founders, it will be the Dog who loses most by the break-up. Nevertheless, the Dog will become much wiser because of the experience. The Dog parent is likely to despair over the Dragon child's waywardness but nevertheless there will be causes for celebration.

## With the **Snake**

It may be the Snake's refinement, culture or even hypnotic gaze that first attracts the Dog, for there is little depth to be discovered. Not fully comprehending irony, the Dog needs to be on guard against misinterpreting the Snake's words and mannerisms. This partnership will work better in a business environment. The Snake child may prove distant and difficult, having its own priorities.

## With the **Horse**★

The Horse is with the Dog every step of the way. They make a winning team and can succeed in whatever enterprise they put their minds to. They will be highly successful at organizing social and charity events, which will bring them great respect in their community. Affection

grows and deepens with time. The Dog parent will have many reasons to be proud of their socially active Horse child.

## With the **Sheep**

This is an uncomfortable partnership, which suffers many set-backs. In love, there are tears, in business conflict. They need to assess their respective priorities, since both believe the other's aims are not the main issue. Neither will back down totally, so a compromise will have to be found. The Sheep child will feel lost at home.

## With the **Monkey**

When the Dog bounds into the Monkey's life, there is no saying what this waggish duo will get up to. Their aim will be to enjoy life to the full; whatever they are doing and wherever, at home, work or in public, their unconventional approach to any situation may cause alarm, but their plans succeed. The Monkey child will cause its parents great anxiety.

## With the **Rooster**

This is proverbially a poor relationship, but despite these two being from different backgrounds there are some points of contact that eventually draws them close. Nevertheless, there will always be an invisible barrier between the couple that prevents the Dog from fully understanding his or her baffling companion. Although early years may prove difficult, in later life the Rooster will bring honour to its parents.

## With another **Dog**

There are no secrets here; one Dog person can read another from the inside out. In this close partnership conversation seems superfluous since each knows exactly what the other is thinking. Each partner is a reflection of the other, and whatever their objectives, no matter how seemingly impractical, together they will succeed. Dog parents and dog children together make a harmonious family, bringing mutual support and shared success.

## With the **Pig**

This is a strong partnership, with both partners keen to build a safe home together. It will be their castle where they will spend many comfortable years, reaping the rewards of an industrious life, surrounded by their gifted children. The Pig child will prove to be a great blessing to the family home.

# The Pig's companions

### With the **Rat**

Pigs and Rats are contemporaries, yet they are so different in nature. The Rat is so individually minded that the Pig finds it hard to know how best to please this partner. The Pig should avoid setting rules for the relationship, as this will drive the Rat away completely. The offers are there for the Rat to take or leave as he or she chooses. The Rat child may find it difficult to confide in the Pig parent, although there is no need to worry about the Rat child's natural independent spirit.

### With the **Ox**

The Ox will bring valuable support into the Pig's household. They will form a firm friendship and the Pig will feel cherished at last. True love reigns in this happy partnership. They will work hard together and enrich their lives from year to year. In business, the Ox will prove a sound and reliable colleague. The Ox child will never be far from home.

### With the **Tiger**

The Pig may be an admirer of the Tiger before a relationship springs up, but sadly, reality rarely matches the dream. The Tiger has too many outside interests for the Pig to establish a strong rapport, and often the Pig feels shut out of the Tiger's life. In business, the Tiger may not fit in to the established scheme. The Tiger child will leave home early.

## With the **Rabbit** ★

This is a truly loving relationship. The Rabbit will bring the missing pieces into the Pig's home life. Their private life together will be rich and fulfilling, and the relationship will lead to a large family. As a business partner, the Rabbit will excel at developing fresh commercial contacts. The Rabbit child will be one of many.

## With the **Dragon**

The Pig may be disappointed that the Dragon lacks reliability and is too fond of pursuits outside the family circle. While it is pleasant to have friends in the house, the Dragon partner is blissfully oblivious to the disruption caused. These two need to sit down and take note of the other's points of view. As a business partner, the Dragon is erratic. The Dragon child will make his or her own way in the world.

## With the **Snake**

Chinese astrologers regard this partnership with caution, saying that if a Pig eats a Snake it is good for neither. In life, the Pig is attracted by the Snake's charm and wit, while the Snake is happy to share the Pig's homely wisdom. But sometimes their different views turn into arguments. They need to understand that it is their differences that make them special. The Snake child is likely to bring its parents some anxious moments.

*Whether male or female, the Horse loves to socialize, and at school will be eager to join in all kinds of activities.*

## With the **Horse**

This is a contented partnership sailing along easily. Both have much to occupy them in their own ways, although the Horse may be away from home frequently, either on business or because of some leisure pursuit. The Horse business partner will be good with client relationships. The Horse child will be popular at school.

## With the **Sheep**★

The Sheep is an ideal partner for a homemaker. There is such great contentment at home that social activities are sometimes neglected. The Pig should follow the Sheep's lead and try to mix more outside the home. In business, the Sheep's skills in dealing with female clients will serve the company well. The genial Sheep child will be happy at home and will not break home ties after marriage.

## With the **Monkey**

The Pig's Monkey partner will have many notable qualities, not all of them bad. Although the Pig is happy to welcome the Monkey into his or her life, its unpredictable nature can be very trying, not being on the spot when needed and hovering around like a parrot on the shoulder when there are more pressing things to attend to. As a business partner the Monkey could be troublesome. The Monkey child will prove to be a lively member of the household, a great source of fun and stimulation.

## With the **Rooster**

If the Pig wants someone to introduce a little sparkle into his or her life, the Rooster may be just the person. This is an arrangement that works amicably, with each partner filling the gap that was missing in the other's life. Although the relationship may be a little rocky in its earlier stages, it strengthens and develops with time. In later life the Rooster child will be able to support its parents generously.

## With the **Dog**

This is an ideal partnership for two people wanting to set up home together, who are both seeking a permanent relationship not instant gratification. They are so closely involved with each other that they will probably go into business together – a very profitable arrangement. The Dog child will be loyal and defensive.

## With another **Pig**

There is no problem so pressing that it cannot be left until tomorrow. These two people are happily wrapped up in each other, and both want to prove how deep and sincere their love is. They have many happy days ahead, their lives focusing on their home and family. In business, Pig partners cooperate closely. The Pig child will bring joy throughout life.

# The year
# ahead

Every year is ruled by a different animal sign that may bring good fortune or problems. Individuals will be affected in different ways by the effects of a particular year depending on their animal sign. In the following pages, find out what the coming years, broadly speaking, may hold for each of the 12 Animals, year by year.

# Predictions for the New Year

Come Chinese New Year, temples throughout China will be thronged with people petitioning the gods for success in the coming months. The bigger temples have their own official diviners and priests ready to unravel and expound the horoscopes of those who wish to know what the year ahead has in store. Even those who do not bother to visit the temples will turn to their newspapers at the New Year, which will always containa full-colour supplements detailing the coming year's forecasts for each of the animal signs.

## The fortunes of nations

It is not just personal horoscopes that are deemed to be important; certainly in ancient China, these were regarded as trivial matters. What was more important was whether the coming year's harvest would prosper or would fail. Would there be droughts or floods or both? What natural calamities awaited, what disasters would affect people's lives? Today, the answers to these questions and many others, are just as significant as they were 2,000 years ago. Nowadays, business people want to know what stocks will prove the best investment, which nations will be stable and which currencies will rise and fall. The answers to some of these questions are found in Chinese almanacs today.

## Analysing specific years

The following pages begin with an outline of the world events predicted
for each of the animal years in the 12-year cycle, followed by separate
forecasts for each of the animals. Look up your sign in a particular year
to see what your prospects are for that year. Some animal signs may
carry specific symbols:

★ Animal signs that will benefit from
   favourable influences that year.
✖ Animal signs that will encounter
   obstacles during a year of change.
✱ Animal signs that will need to
   take particular care during the
   course of what could be an
   adverse year.

# The Rat year

## GENERAL PROSPECTS FOR THE COMING YEAR

On the world scene, Rat years are less known for their great events than as a time when the seeds are sown which later burgeon into major changes internationally. Attention should be paid to emergent dissident groups as well as new inventions and designs that will come to have a great impact in the future. On the whole, a Rat year is a year for planning rather than action.

## For the **Rat**

The year brings fresh opportunities for changing employment or moving house. It might even mean the start of a new love affair. Finance is secure, but any unexpected gains should be put in reserve until next year, when there are likely to be further developments. The year is favourable for health matters, particularly those relating to the head.

## For the **Ox**

This is a year for consolidating past gains. It is best to complete existing projects rather than begin anything afresh, as new ventures are not likely to be enduring. This advice applies whether you plan to start a business or embark on a new romance. Sufferers from arthritis and similar complaints will find that their condition improves.

*Although this is a good year for Tiger, they should not be over-confident.*

### For the **Tiger**

There are good prospects for promotion and for expansion of business for the self-employed. Finances may seem secure, but do not take risks, as bills are likely to be much higher than estimated. Avoid too much social activity; do not deceive yourself with the excuse that it is part of your networking. Prudence will be rewarded.

### For the **Rabbit**✱

Family concerns and the welfare of children may place too great a burden on finances this year. Ensure that other people's problems are kept in proportion, and do not be persuaded to give assistance, either with time or money. You need to put your own interests first. Do not over-exert yourself in your bid to help others.

### For the **Dragon**★

This is a prosperous year, and one in which the Dragon is able to realize some long-standing ambitions. Personal gains, not merely financially, bring great satisfaction. Take advantage of whatever opportunities arise this year. A move to the south-west this year would bring many advantages. There is every possibility that a serious mistake made in the previous year can be put right.

## For the **Snake**

A year of potential progress but fraught with obstacles. It is best to tread warily; do not allow yourself to be drawn into enterprises that demand a long-term commitment from you. Try to clear up outstanding obligations.

## For the **Horse**✳

This is a troublesome year for the Horse, and will be a time when the Horse needs to follow the well-trodden path. At work, there are likely to be confrontations; do not give superiors any grounds for criticism. Watch finances carefully and avoid risks.

## For the **Sheep**

For most Sheep people this is a quiet year, a period to consolidate all the upheaval of the previous 12 months. Enjoy the opportunities to relax and to strengthen your present position, and endeavour to make improvements without any basic changes.

## For the **Monkey**★

This is an ideal time to strike out in a new direction. Your imagination will be stimulated, so act on your ideas. If you want to change your employment or move house, a location south-east of your present position would bring great advantages. In romantic matters, there are excellent prospects and a new relationship is promised.

## For the **Rooster**✹

Finances become stagnant this year and it will be necessary to dip into reserves. Your financial position comes under scrutiny, but it will not result in further action. In personal relationships, there are likely to be disputes, and money is likely to be the root of the problem.

*During the Rat year, Rooster people may find that financial difficulties put a strain on their relationships.*

## For the **Dog**

The year promises to be full of happy occasions. Although the Dog does not directly participate in them, the numerous events and social engagements to which the Dog is invited will be recalled with pleasure for many years to come. Investigate the possibilities of making major changes.

## For the **Pig**

The next 12 months have their good and bad moments. The threat that it might be necessary to make major changes fosters a general unease and a feeling of insecurity. Fortunately, next year will see the problem resolved satisfactorily. It is only necessary to remain calm and face each challenge as it is presented.

# The Ox year

## GENERAL PROSPECTS FOR THE COMING YEAR

This is a year for major urban developments such as the construction of new cities and major highways. The harvest will be difficult because of widespread drought; in particular, northern wine-growing regions will be affected, but southern vineyards will benefit. Exciting archaeological finds will be discovered.

## For the **Rat**

This is a favourable year for the Rat – many of the expected benefits of the previous Rat year now come to fruition. It helps to put the seal of approval on past actions, but do not start out on a new direction just yet. There will be a long changeover period, which may prove debilitating and costly.

## For the **Ox**

In its own year, the Ox is tempted to think afresh and begin a new life. Yet although all the opportunities seem to be there, it may not be the right time just yet. But if a change of location is inevitable, a move to the west will be favourable. Purchase of property or land will be a constructive investment.

## For the **Tiger**

The Tiger faces many obstacles in the
Ox year, with problems in his or her
social life and confrontations in
the workplace. The Tiger needs
strong allies this year, but
not from the usual circle
of friends. It is not an
appropriate time for
making radical changes,
unless the breakdown
of a relationship leaves
a gap in your life.

## For the **Rabbit**

This is a progressive year, with
positive developments in many
different aspects of life. Personal
relationships are strengthened and
additions to the family are promised.
Fears regarding health are exaggerated. If a choice lies between
expensive holidays or home improvements, choose the latter.
Gardening activities will be rewarding.

## For the **Dragon**✱

For those involved in the arts, especially theatre, this is a fallow period.
But the setbacks are not permanent, even though they may seem
completely stagnant. The favourable period is still some way off, but
nevertheless there is much to gain in the future. For the moment, stay
put and concentrate on secondary issues.

# For the **Snake**★

This is a highly productive year in which energies should be directed into the purchase of land and property, as these will prove a sound investment, especially in the west. A legacy or the maturing of some savings will be an added bonus. For those pursuing romantic relationships, this is an ideal time for making stronger ties.

# For the **Horse**

Those who are not in a hurry will get further than those people who are in a great rush. Patience, especially when dealing with obstinate people, will prevent the Horse from become too stressed in this difficult year. Next year holds much better prospects.

# For the **Sheep**✳

Although this year is filled with adversity and problems, in the end these difficulties will prove to have been merely inconvenient demands on the Sheep's time and patience. Fortunately, though time may be limited, the Sheep has ample resources of patience, which he or she will surely need during the coming months.

# For the **Monkey**

There is much that the Monkey would like to do in this year, but too many responsibilities that need attention prevent the immediate achievement of objectives. When the Monkey's plans are repeatedly thwarted because of continual obstruction, it is time to step back and rethink the situation.

# For the **Rooster**★

A renewed spirit of vitality helps the Rooster glide smoothly through this year. Major projects already underway start to

*The Ox year is a memorably happy one for people born in the year of the Snake.*

show positive results, while new opportunities are presented almost daily. If moving, choose an easterly or south-easterly location.

## For the Dog✱

Ambitious plans will have to be curtailed and made to fit with the resources available. The position at the moment is difficult and the help offered has too many strings attached to make it attractive. Since improvements are foreseen for future years, it would be advisable to wait. Do not be afraid to challenge false friends

## For the Pig

Family problems begin to be resolved. Many subtle changes add up to a major improvement in the Pig's personal life. There is a greater feeling of security now that a major source of worry has been jettisoned. Move forward confidently and begin to rebuild your life. There are greater advantages to be had by staying put, rather than moving to a different location.

# The Tiger year

## GENERAL PROSPECTS FOR THE COMING YEAR

A Tiger year suggests political instability and the likely outbreak of hostilities between former allies arising out of problems that were foreshadowed in the Rat year. An assassination or impeachment of a political leader leads to a cooling of the global economy. High-risk speculation is exactly that.

## For the **Rat**

There will be some dramatic changes this year, provided that the Rat does not sit back and wait for things to happen. In career matters, there are opportunities for a higher position, but it is up to the Rat to make the initial move. The same is true of personal relationships, with the promise of a new and stimulating partner in the Rat's life.

## For the **Ox**

Although there will be many heated exchanges and differences of opinion that cause irritating setbacks to current plans, the Ox will be able to win the arguments and proceed along his or her chosen path. Unfortunately, these hold-ups cause delays although not cancellations. Proceed with determination.

## For the **Tiger**

This year promises much and delivers its promises. Now the Tiger can assert his or her authority and lay down a few ground rules. The results will surprise the Tiger, who, not expecting such a positive response, may wish that he or she had taken this drastic action earlier. But the timing would not have been right.

## For the **Rabbit**

The Rabbit can succeed on the tail of the Tiger, since much of what the Tiger achieves in his or her own year will indirectly benefit the Rabbit. One such possibility is promotion to a position formerly held by the Tiger. Additionally, the Rabbit is able to exert his or her own influence and help others to achieve success.

## For the **Dragon**

The year ahead shows great promise for the Dragon. In business there are new opportunities and the real likelihood of promotion. Invitations to foreign countries will prove profitable. In romance, the lonely Dragon will not remain so for long. Those who aim high will reach their objectives.

## For the **Snake**✖

There is too much activity around the Snake this year for this person to be able to concentrate on his or her own problems. In the family, attention is directed at one particular member, leaving the Snake to one side. Use this fallow period for positive regeneration.

## For the **Horse**★

A productive year for those born in the year of the Horse – it will bring prospects of advancement at work and a wider of circle of friends who share the same interests and aspirations. Nevertheless, greater involvement in social activities can make an incursion into savings, even though the activity is directed at strengthening business relationships.

## For the **Sheep**

After the upheavals of the previous year, a period of comparative inactivity will be a welcome relief. Consider this year to be a buffer zone between last year and the next, and use the time constructively, because new and exciting events are foreseen.

## For the **Monkey**✳

The erratic nature of the Monkey's life takes another sharp turn during the Tiger year. There is a reversal of fortune and plans will have to be radically altered or abandoned at the last minute. When making plans, double-check to ensure that all the official regulations are properly understood and adhered to.

## For the **Rooster**

There are demands on the Rooster's time and patience from all sides and the Rooster will have to juggle family matters and business along with a new project that overshadows and consumes what little leisure time the Rooster has. Do not be disappointed if your bid for promotion is unsuccessful, since the position has already been allocated.

## For the **Dog**★

This is a very favourable year for the Dog, offering plenty of scope for developing new ideas. Relationships are sound now that

*The Tiger year is one of the most favourable for Dog people, especially for those wanting to share exciting new experiences.*

accommodation problems have been secured; if a move is contemplated, a southerly direction would be the most profitable. Those born in the Dog year will find this is a good year to undertake travel and adventure.

## For the Pig✴

This is a somewhat restless year for the Pig, with family changes causing upheavals and disruption to long-term plans. Bureaucracy reigns supreme and official interference will aggravate present problems rather than solve them. Avoid taking on extra responsibilities until the situation has resolved itself.

# The Rabbit year

## GENERAL PROSPECTS FOR THE COMING YEAR

The Rabbit year brings opportunities for earlier conflicts to be resolved; aggressors will retreat from the determined resistance of the nation under attack. A major discovery in the field of medicine will bring benefits to mothers. The year ends on an optimistic note, with better prospects for peace.

## For the Rat✖

There are difficult times ahead and the Rat will need to balance domestic and business arrangements so that they do not conflict. Earlier, it might have seemed that the prospects of the previous year would continue; they will, but not at present. There are better times ahead, but not just yet.

## For the Ox

The Ox can carry on with its plans for this year without hindrance, provided that he or she takes things at a steady pace and does not attempt to force progress forward unreasonably. By taking a gentler approach the results are likely to be better. It is a very favourable year where love and romance are concerned.

## For the **Tiger**

This is a positive year in which the gains made over the previous 12 months are consolidated. The positive trends will continue, and life will progress more smoothly. At last, long-awaited news arrives with favourable information.

## For the **Rabbit**

Happy times are ahead. Family matters are secured; worries about the home prove to be unfounded. Personal relationships are at last established on a firm footing. Opportunities to develop business interests beyond the present limits must be dealt with immediately if they are to flourish.

*There is favourable family news to be had for the Tiger in the Rabbit year.*

## For the **Dragon**

Expect setbacks and problems this year; watch finances carefully and do not rush into uncertain ventures. In personal relationships, be careful not to cause offence, no matter how unwittingly. Take a subordinate role during the current volatile period.

## For the **Snake**

Take care that your actions are not misconstrued. Be careful not to let documents fall into the hands of unscrupulous people and be vigilant when holding conversations in public places. Generally a good year.

## For the **Horse**✖

The year will plod along slowly and it may seem that you are getting nowhere in life. Personal relationships may seem shallow and your present employment tedious and lacking satisfaction. But persevere, because following this empty period are more favourable prospects ahead. Dispel gloominess by taking up some physical activity.

## For the **Sheep**★

There will be many joyous occasions this year. For once, there will be no need to worry about the expense of celebration. Personal relationships are strengthened – those considering marriage this year could not choose a more favourable time. Those hoping to improve their career prospects will have welcome news. If planning to move house, a location north-west of your present home is favourable.

## For the **Monkey**

There is less scope for the Monkey's activities this year, although prospects are still quite favourable. If full-scale changes are being considered, by all means use the present time for planning, but delay finalizing the details or putting the scheme into action until more favourable influences come into play next year. Personal relationships totter along in their usual way; business prospects remain unchanged.

## For the **Rooster**✻

This is an awkward period in which the Rooster will have difficulties in drawing any project to a close. The tendency is to hop from one idea to another without any definite notion of how to continue. It might be advantageous to list all the current activities in which you are involved in order to see which ones can be abandoned.

## For the **Dog**

There are a number of gains to be made this year, so keep a watch for unexpected opportunities, and do not let chances slip through your fingers. For the single person, there is the chance of a short-term relationship that could develop significantly. If finances permit, it is a good time to purchase land or property.

## For the **Pig**★

The year ahead focuses on family life with the likelihood of many additions to the extended family through marriages and new children. Plans to improve the home should go ahead as the improved conditions will be more beneficial than previously anticipated. If relocation is being considered, a move towards the south-west would be a favourable one.

# The Dragon year

## GENERAL PROSPECTS FOR THE COMING YEAR

The detection of massive fraud on an international scale causes the collapse of a major financial institution. Astonishing discoveries are reported from outer space, which overturn accepted theories of the nature of our galaxy. A living fossil is found in south-east Asia. Controversy over the Olympic Games prompts calls for them to be abandoned.

## For the Rat★

This turbulent year can bring many advantages for the skilful Rat. New vistas open up, and there is the promise of greater financial security, but this may not materialize until the Dragon year is nearly complete. Personal relationships are exciting and a new partnership may be forged through business connections. This is a period of intense activity, but the beneficial period will only last about two years.

## For the Ox✱

There are many hazards ahead which the Ox needs to avoid. Fortunately, the Ox is sensible enough to avoid the traps into which others are likely to fall. In business, it is important to keep your contribution clear of interference. Keep a watch on joint accounts.

## For the **Tiger**

The can be a very profitable year if the Tiger maintains firm control over his or her affairs. There are opportunities for investments bringing handsome returns, but avoid those concerns connected with the leisure industries. In the Tiger's personal life, a relationship becomes stronger and promises to be a long-term one.

## For the **Rabbit**

Keep a careful watch over your friends and close family; by all means, show them diplomatically where they are going wrong, but do not take any action yourself – your attempts to change the individual for the better will be interpreted as meddlesome interference and will rebound to your disadvantage.

## For the **Dragon**

The Dragon in a Dragon year will suggest wild schemes and adventure. Your personal life will be exciting and chaotic, with precarious personal relationships redolent of a French farce. Visits to remote and outlandish places will forge memories that will remain throughout your life. The financial position is capricious.

### For the **Snake**

The year begins to show great promise. For the Snake who is single, there is the prospect of happiness arising from a pleasant encounter. In business, the way forwards becomes clear at last. Consider the possibilities and wait; patience will be rewarded.

### For the **Horse**

There are many opportunities for finding new friends and developing new or existing relationships. Prospects for career change should be followed through, as these can lead to unexpected benefits as well as the obvious ones. It will be difficult to resist temptation, so the Horse must be vigilant.

### For the **Sheep**✖

Unfortunately, a matter that should have been cleared up has not yet been resolved, and the repercussions look set to spoil what could be a relatively peaceful year. But the problems are balanced by rewarding developments. Be prepared for emergencies by striving to be as economical as possible and do not dip into savings unnecessarily.

### For the **Monkey**★

Not that the Monkey ever needs stimulation, but this coming year will provide more than enough of it. There will be opportunities to experiment with new ideas, as well as the chance to put long-held ambitions into practice. The closing months of the year will leave the Monkey in a whirl of exhilaration; take time to review the situation.

### For the **Rooster**

Rivalry and a conflict of interests with a working colleague will tarnish the otherwise positive trends that the year has to offer. Although the main objectives will be brought to fruition, achievements will not be as satisfying as expected. But in spite of this progress will be made; do not underestimate your success.

## For the **Dog**\*

Hold on to what you have this year; trying to force change through will only result in loss. Dealings with bankers will be unfavourable at the moment. Unwelcome advice needs consideration, and a missed opportunity will prove to be a disaster avoided.

## For the **Pig**

Although much of the year is uneventful, several episodes will provide astonishment and mirth. Little that happens this year will have a lasting effect, but there will be much to remember. In general, it will be a smooth transitory period.

*During the Dragon year, there will many occasions for the Pig to celebrate, and much to laugh about.*

# The Snake year

## GENERAL PROSPECTS FOR THE COMING YEAR

A tediously long trial of world importance finally comes to an unsatisfactory end. Accusations of espionage damage relations between nations in the Southern Hemisphere and leads to international involvement. In south-east Asia, a dormant volcano erupts, causing devastation.

## For the **Rat**

It is vital to remember that we are all subject to influences beyond our personal control; there are some eventualities that cannot be foreseen. Even in our personal relationships, there are imperfections which are nobody's fault. Continue as you have planned, but be prepared to make changes at short notice.

## For the **Ox**★

At last the Ox can reap the rewards for his or her hard work and persistence; the recognition for past achievements is well deserved. Now is a good time to make lasting changes in life. Your financial position is stable and there is help and advice from an unexpected source. If a change of location is planned, a move to the west will be

advantageous. The year brings fresh
opportunities in all walks of life,
whether in career, business or
personal relationships.

## For the **Tiger**✖

Although the problems faced
by the Tiger in the year ahead
will be overcome, they intrude
into the smooth running of the
Tiger's personal life. Patience will
prove to be a better ally than
intolerance during these trying
times. Avoid getting involved in legal
wrangles; in such cases delays will be to your advantage.

## For the **Rabbit**

A chance meeting will prove extremely beneficial. There are
numerous opportunities available and several options to choose
from. Fortunately, whatever the Rabbit's decision it will be the right
one. Ignore the advice of those who are envious of your success and
follow your instincts. Make the most of the present favourable period.

## For the **Dragon**

The activities and efforts that made the previous year so hectic can now
be brought to a close, enabling the Dragon to relax and reap the rewards
of its strenuous labours. Much of what the Dragon was hoping to
achieve is at last attained; a long-standing ambition is unexpectedly
realized and there are fresh career opportunities. Use the present period
constructively and look forward to getting positive results next year.

### For the **Snake**

In its own year the Snake can look forward to fulfilling many of his or her objectives, especially those inaugurated in the past year with outside financial assistance. In personal relationships, there is a meeting of true minds and a close friendship will develop into a stronger partnership for mutual benefit.

### For the **Horse**

The Horse should tread warily this year and be wary of offending those who are of a sensitive nature. They are not as harmless as they appear, and can be ruthless enemies if their paths are crossed. Put your trust in close family members.

### For the **Sheep**

Happy times are in store for the Sheep; there are welcome chances to shine socially. A meeting with a professor or university teacher will bring you into closer contact with people who have the same interests as your own. You will be asked to give your assistance voluntarily for a charity, an invitation that you should accept at once. It will lead to friendships with influential people who can change your life.

*The Monkey's technical expertise is sorely tested during the Snake year.*

## For the **Monkey**✖

Not everything runs like clockwork this year for the Monkey. Problems with machinery or hand-held gadgets are not mere mechanical failures that can be repaired, they lead to the failure of critical meetings. With luck, appointments can be rescheduled, but confidence is shattered. Put your trust in personal contact.

## For the **Rooster**★

This is an excellent year for the creative Rooster with new ideas to share. Whether in personal life or in business matters, meetings with people will be extremely satisfactory and lead to the forging of strong relationships. If you have ever considered a change in your appearance, now is the time to experiment.

## For the **Dog**

You are close to achieving your objective, but a few worries still stand in the way. Seek advice on any problems you may have and then further advice on the direction you should take. It is not an easy time and possibly it may be better to remain as you are until the end of the year since your prospects next year are considerably better. But the Dog is resilient enough to be able to overcome adversity. Patience is certainly a virtue this year.

## For the **Pig**✳

Family harmony takes a knock this year with considerable disagreement among relatives. To outsiders, the issues involved seem trivial, but remarks are made that cause great hurt. It may be better to spend some time away from home while the atmosphere clears. Put yourself first and pay no attention to malicious gossip. It is always worth bearing in mind that this year's problems do not have lasting effect.

# The Horse year

## GENERAL PROSPECTS FOR THE COMING YEAR

The dominant topic of the year is government maladministration, over-spending and waste. The tightening world economy leads to demands for governments to be more accountable. Several high-ranking politicians with links to different states are demoted. The seasons are reversed; in the Northern Hemisphere a cool summer results in a poor harvest.

## For the Rat*

Warned in advance that this is going to be a difficult year, the astute Rat has already made several contingency plans for the next 12 months. The budget has been carefully examined and pruned; risky ventures are postponed for a more convenient time and care is taken regarding health and lifestyle. As a result, the wary Rat is able to withstand the assaults of ill-fortune and proceed successfully.

## For the Ox

An uncomfortable time for the Ox, who is not familiar with the new routines and changes that have to be dealt with. But the Ox is no stranger to hard work and will continue along his or her chosen route despite the difficulties. A close personal relationship is put under stress.

## For the **Tiger**★

There are wonderful opportunities ahead for the Tiger; exciting meetings with influential people, many new friendships, enhanced career prospects and travel to exotic places. Were that every year had such opportunities! These opportunities are there, of course, except that this year they may be more evident. Seize the chances when they arise.

## For the **Rabbit**✖

This might have been a difficult year were it not for the help provided by an old and trusted friend. There will be problems but you will soon find that they are not insurmountable. Do not worry about people for whom you feel you have a responsibility; they are clearly able to look after themselves.

## For the **Dragon**

A positive year unfolds, with personal relationships on a sounder footing and career prospects improved with the offer of a salary increase. There are advantages to be gained by joining a society that meets regularly, as you will encounter people who will help advance your business or career.

*The Rabbit is never short of friends. In a Horse year they will be there to give support at difficult times.*

## For the **Snake**

Be wary of younger colleagues who may be envious of your position. You may have to use your diplomatic skills to countermand bullying or intimidation. It can be irksome, but do not allow yourself to be goaded into counter-productive reactions. With calculated poise, you can beat the adversaries at their own game.

## For the **Horse**

Obviously, in a Horse year the Horse can gallop forwards to success. This is the time to strike out in new directions; if planning to move house, make a career change or even move to another country, the opportunities are there. Move north-east or north-west to ensure success. Do not even consider a move to the south.

## For the **Sheep**

The Sheep can enjoy a happy year with the realization of some of his or her most cherished ambitions. Much is coming your way and there may be some upheavals and changes to your lifestyle. This will all be positive, with beneficial consequences.

## For the **Monkey**

Friendships at a social level are strengthened and there are more opportunities available for meeting people from different walks of life. Any Monkey still without a life partner will meet the right person this summer. Business and career prospects are improved.

## For the **Rooster✖**

Take care not to be too ambitious and be careful that your actions do not arouse envy or contempt. Your well-meant actions may provoke the wrong response. Be more gentle in your dealings with people.

*Younger business or career rivals may cause problems for the Snake in a Horse year.*

## For the **Dog**★

There is much to be done in the year ahead, life will be full of surprises and the potential benefits enormous. If you are planning to move into new premises – home or business – you could not have chosen a better time. Moving to the east-north-east will bring the greatest advantages.

## For the **Pig**

The coming year has its share of benefits and disadvantages, but in general there is much to be gained. Male members of the family could be more supportive, but female relatives will always be ready to help.

# The Sheep year

## GENERAL PROSPECTS FOR THE COMING YEAR

Increased consumer spending indicates renewed confidence in the economy. There is greater concern for personal future security, not just through financial investment but also through mutual commitment schemes and partnership contracts, including marriage.

## For the Rat

Last year's problems begin to be resolved, and although there are some matters still lingering, for the most part, life begins to get back on track. It is a favourable time for study, for developing friendships and for participation in musical or artistic events.

## For the Ox*

The Sheep is the only real adversary of the Ox – all other opponents can be seen off swiftly. But there is something about the Sheep that antagonizes the Ox and in Sheep years, plans go awry, colleagues become distant and ideas are rejected. It is a frustrating time, but one that inevitably passes. The future is brighter.

## For the **Tiger**

The Tiger is best following his or her own instincts this year. Demands will be made on your time when people to be responsible for certain functions cannot be found. In the long run, however, when the emergency is over, you will be in a better position than before. Personal relationships move along haltingly.

## For the **Rabbit**★

For Rabbit people, the year is full of hope for the fulfilment of ambitions, which are eventually realized after the summer months. Benefits abound and there is good news nearly every month, the best saved until November. For those planning to move house or change a business address this year, the best direction is north-north-west.

*The Sheep year can have an adverse effect on the Dragon's relationships.*

## For the **Dragon**✖

The year has its hold-ups for Dragons and there are problems with your personal relationships. Arguments become heated, the main point being the perennial ones of money on the one hand and commitment to a relationship on the other. Find a compromise.

## For the **Snake**

Continued progress leads to eventual success. Use the present time well and aim to complete tasks before the end of the year. Any problems will be minor.

## For the **Horse**

This is a year when the Horse's preoccupation with work and colleagues seems less important than building up a happy personal relationship and a welcoming home. Altogether, this is a much more satisfying period giving you ample time to review your life and assess your priorities. The need for excitement gives way to wisdom.

## For the **Sheep**

Now that the cycle has turned full circle and the Sheep is in his or her own year, there is a chance to review the direction that life is taking. If ever there was a time to make major changes in life, then the time has arrived. Personal relationships should be firmly established by now and if these prove to be unsatisfactory, drastic measures need to be taken. Use the beneficial influences at work to clear out all that is stagnant.

## For the **Monkey**

The Monkey can progress successfully, following his or her own initiatives rather than being led by others. Irritating demands for your attention will have to be rejected with diplomacy; a refusal may cause offence but acceptance would lead to disaster. But an agreeable partnership can be encouraged as it may lead to better things.

## For the **Rooster**

The Rooster has much greater freedom to pursue his or her own objectives this year, with fewer calls on his or her time and fewer bothersome distractions. Personal relationships blossom, career prospects look healthy and finances are sound. If you are considering any commercial projects, the coming two-year period is favourable, but not beyond.

## For the **Dog**✱

Despite the occasional frustration with people refusing to join in with the Dog's ideas, nevertheless this is a year of continuing successes. But be careful in dealing with people; listen sympathetically, since they are important to you. A friend will need your help; give all the help you can, even though no reward is expected.

## For the **Pig**★

What a perfect year for the happy Pig! The culmination of many years of planning is at last in sight. Several pleasing events are about to unfold. Personal ambitions are realized, and the hopes you had for others prove to be justified. There are proud moments ahead and many joyful times to be recalled in later years.

# The Monkey year

## GENERAL PROSPECTS FOR THE COMING YEAR

The financial position of emergent nations is shaky, while the galloping inflation in a previously stable country hits the major currencies. Industry is held to ransom by the unpredictable price of raw materials, but the end result is favourable. After a worrying period of inertia, manufacturing regains its former thrust.

## For the Rat★

The coming year will be full of remarkable changes and improvements. Personal relationships will be complicated and you may have to be discreet in your friendships. Business opportunities flourish and there will be numerous opportunities to combine leisure travel with commercial interests. A very productive period for those studying.

## For the Ox

Unwelcome changes will not be optional. For the moment, only change what is obligatory and do not try to improve on the position just yet. Next year, when the situation has settled, you will have a clearer idea of what has to be done. The upheaval will cause plans to be postponed, but subsequent losses will be minimal.

## For the **Tiger**＊

There are many awkward moments this year that put the Tiger in an embarrassing position. His or her authority is challenged and although the Tiger will eventually regain influence, important relationships will be damaged as a consequence. It is useless to try to gather up the broken pieces, much wiser to consider how to rebuild the trust.

## For the **Rabbit**

The advance made last year begins to slow down; the quieter period will give you a chance to review the present position and see what advantages have been gained and how best they can be acted upon. Progress will remain steady.

## For the **Dragon**★

The Dragon should avoid any temptation to relax or sit back this year. There is so much to be done and if your seize your chance this year, there is a fortune to be made. But hard work, and more importantly, the ability to be flexible and change plans at the last minute, are the vital components of success. Decision making has to be quick; those who are slow to act will regret their hesitancy.

*The Monkey year is a very stimulating one for the studious Rat.*

## For the **Snake✱**

Avoid being caught in a trap. Friendship is put to the test and the Snake's good nature and honesty is exploited. Remember that promises without security are worthless. In the matter of personal relationships, a close partnership is damaged because of malicious gossip. You will eventually discover who your true friends are.

## For the **Horse**

A contented year lies ahead for the Horse. A period of loneliness at last comes to a close, as you find comfort in the companionship of a new friend. Career and business prospects are fine; if there are plans to travel to new and exotic places, the experiences will be very rewarding. You should trust your own instincts this year.

## For the **Sheep**

Although Sheep and Monkey are astrologically close neighbours, there is not much help to be obtained from this erratic influence. Events that promised improvements do the opposite, while what seemed a disaster turns out to be beneficial. Be philosophical and take life as it comes.

## For the **Monkey**

This being a Monkey year, all kinds of exciting changes are in store. It is the time for starting afresh with an idea you have been considering for a long time. If it is not followed up in this period it will never be realized. Success depends on total involvement from all partners.

## For the **Rooster**

This is an excellent period for the Rooster to plan for the future. By saving and economizing this year, and avoiding the numerous distractions and temptations to spend, the Rooster will be able to

embark on a really
ambitious scheme next
year. The goal has not
yet been reached and
much is still to come, but
sound preparation is vital.

## For the **Dog**

Help from an unexpected quarter will enable the Dog to go ahead with
plans that were on hold. Involvement in a new personal relationship will
have startling consequences. Business prospects are favourable.

## For the **Pig**✱

There is so much for the Pig to do this year that may take them away
from a main objective. There are delays and frustrations due to
mechanical breakdowns, it is important to remain patient and not
blame people for events that are not their fault. Eventually, a difficult
situation will be resolved to the Pig's advantage.

# The Rooster year

## GENERAL PROSPECTS FOR THE COMING YEAR

This is a favourable year for the leisure and entertainment industries. The uncertainty of the markets has led to hoarding of gold stocks, which has caused the price to rise significantly, along with the prices of other precious and base metals.

World political events will be eclipsed by the general public's fascination with petty trivia.

## For the Rat✖

If you haven't got those important arrangements in hand, it may well be too late. There are several things that need your urgent attention and a failure to deal with correspondence quickly will result in financial loss. Relationships are a little shaky but if you are prepared to step back from confrontation, matters may heal.

## For the Ox★

This very profitable year can see the Ox moving upwards socially. There are positive trends that should be followed, and for once you can be adventurous and take risks. Those Oxen who have decided to remain put will still benefit, though it may be difficult to make changes later.

*The Rat's financial problems will mount if correspondence is not dealt with.*

## For the **Tiger**

There are troublesome times ahead in the coming 12 months for the Tiger, but there are no problems that cannot be dealt with satisfactorily. An important visitor will make an offer that seems very attractive at first, until you examine the details. Your financial position is stronger, allowing for any increased expenditure.

## For the **Rabbit***

The creative powers of the Rabbit are put to the test this year, as many of the ideas and projects that are currently underway come up against obstacles, usually as a result of demands for these to be finished in a hurry. Do not take on too many commitments and attend to your own needs without giving in to outside pressures

## For the **Dragon**

There should be ample opportunities for Dragon expansion, but most ventures seem to be of short duration. The main problem for you could be a rival who seems to be offering more attractive proposals. Eventually, you will have to make a decision and settle for second-best. Do not hesitate for too long as third-best will be worse.

## For the **Snake** ★

This is going to be an excellent year for the Snake; for those hoping to enter into a permanent loving relationship it seems that the right partner has come along at last. Both business and career prospects are very promising. Forge ahead with confidence.

## For the **Horse** ✖

Although the Horse makes some progress this year, this period is not an easy one. The main problem is having to deal with people who are not directly concerned with the matters in hand, but are attached to people whose assistance you need. While these ancillaries are an unwelcome irritation, they will soon tire of the situation.

## For the **Sheep**

There is much to gain this year for the Sheep. Personal life is more secure and relationships bring happiness. The Sheep will make several important decisions that will bring long-term benefits and success in future years. Recognition of your special gifts leads to promotion and financial improvement.

## For the **Monkey**

Increased financial security will make this a rewarding year for the Monkey, with the assurance that there are more benefits still to come. Ideas that you have been working on for some time will now be put to the test and the results will be extremely satisfactory, although it may be some months before you are able to harvest the rewards.

## For the **Rooster**

A successful year is in the making; use these 12 months for planning and scrutinizing every detail of your ambitious project. Although this year may be too soon to launch your idea, if you are sure everything is ready then go ahead. Just because it is your own year it doesn't mean that you will always have your own way – there are other Roosters too!

## For the **Dog**

Ride the positive trends of the current year to put your ideas into practice. At the close of the year you will be astonished at the gains you have made. Successful ventures bring great personal satisfaction. Despite your business commitments, you will still find time to improve your domestic arrangements.

## For the **Pig**

The Pig would do well to forget the constraints of family life and look at different aspects of self-improvement. Expanding your cultural breadth by taking courses or reading stimulating books is one way, while attending sports centres or fitness classes is another. Be a better, fitter person and the world will be yours.

*Physical exercise and mental stimulation benefit the Pig in the Rooster year.*

# The Dog year

## GENERAL PROSPECTS FOR THE COMING YEAR

An attack on an independent state by a neighbour to its south-east will be repulsed; the prospect of a war between the two countries, though close, will be defused. Devastation is caused as buildings in the south-western district of a major city are torn apart by unprecedented gales and hurricanes. Home insurance is advised.

## For the **Rat**

Optimism is high this year and with good reason. Prospects seem better than they have been for a long time. Personal relationships move along steadily. There is considerable satisfaction with your life as it is, but there is the promise of a move that will not only be more convenient but bring you additional unexpected advantages.

## For the **Ox✖**

Many of the problems faced this year result from the Ox refusing to back down from a situation that plainly cannot continue. It is one thing to defend a principle, another to deny the advantages of the proposed changes. Compromise is necessary.

## For the **Tiger**★

Challenging times for the Tiger will be stimulating and rewarding. There is much to do and your achievements will be considerable. Those who press ahead relentlessly will succeed, but do not let it be at the expense of past friendships. The thrill of the chase must not cloud your judgement. Be prepared for major changes.

### For the **Rabbit**

Perhaps this is not destined to be an outstanding year, but nevertheless it is one in which the foundations are laid for a truly memorable year. Use your time and financial resources wisely and avoid extravagance. Next year holds exciting opportunities and you will want to celebrate and draw on your reserves. Make sure you have plenty.

159

*The sporty Horse will have several reasons to celebrate during the Dog year.*

## For the **Dragon**✳

Those who want to be unconventional and break away from a humdrum lifestyle are going to be disappointed. Various factions conspire to block the Dragon's proposals to do something awe-inspiring; the present time and setting is not appropriate. Nevertheless, continue to work on your ideas, because there will be opportunities in the future.

## For the **Snake**

Several projects that were started last year need your continued attention. If possible, bring existing plans to a satisfactory conclusion. Anything unfinished this year will remain so. You can enjoy your successes, but do not get too complacent.

## For the **Horse** ★

Those Horses who have a competitive spirit will enjoy the next few months, as there are prizes galore to aim for. Do what you can to bring more friends into your close circle. Let your holiday plans be adventurous. There is much to enjoy and celebrate.

## For the **Sheep**✖

There are new horizons for the Sheep this year. If friends and close companions appear distant, it is because they will be preoccupied with their own problems and unaware that you cherish their company. No slight was intended so avoid being resentful and diplomatically make your own approaches.

## For the **Monkey**
A favourable period lies ahead in which the Monkey can at last realize some of his or her ambitions. Not all goes smoothly however. There are sudden turns of fortune that will throw the Monkey's plans into disarray, but the final results will be superior.

## For the **Rooster**
Rivals will actively try to ruin the Rooster's ambitions; the incidents will obviously be upsetting but the conclusion will be in the Rooster's favour. Relationships will be shaky and the domestic situation precarious. But these are only temporary setbacks, akin to a sudden storm on a long voyage.

## For the **Dog**
The Dog is master in his or her own home this year and at last can get his or her own way. At home or at work, the Dog is able to put views forwards without reservation. A structured plan impresses those whose opinions matter and success in on its way. The year holds many rewards for the Dog's determined efforts to succeed.

## For the **Pig**
Now is the time to begin planning for the major changes that are not too far away. It may be the prospect of a new home, better job prospects or even a new arrival in the family. Whatever the future holds, it is important to be prepared. Time will go faster than expected. Decorating the spare room could be a start!

# The Pig year

**GENERAL PROSPECTS FOR THE COMING YEAR**

Governments are more concerned with internal matters than with pursuing hostilities and globally a more peaceful period can be expected, including the withdrawal of troops from occupied territories. Being the first of the Water element years, floods are likely in all parts of the globe.

## For the **Rat**

Since the Pig and the Rat are astrological neighbours and both belong to the element Water, one would assume that a Pig year should be a helpful period to the Rat; in fact, the Pig is reluctant to bestow any blessings on his or her astrological next-door neighbour. Money is hard to come by, but hard work will be rewarded. Personal relationships are shaky, but recover.

## For the **Ox**

A favourable time for the Ox approaches; domestic and personal life is much more relaxed and the Ox is at last able to do the things he or she wants. The Ox should not be afraid of pursuing promotion; after all, a step up is only reasonable.

*The Pig year does not bode well for those living near water: this water element year is a harbinger of floods in all parts of the world.*

## For the **Tiger**✖

Minor setbacks for the Tiger are caused by personal problems intruding into business life. This will have to be managed diplomatically, even if it means relocating away from the present situation. Travelling to the east would be a favourable solution.

## For the **Rabbit**★

A wonderful year lies ahead for the Rabbit. All the economies and savings of the previous year should have built up a reasonable reserve, which is going to be needed this year – not through any financial setbacks, but because there is cause for several celebrations. Many joyous occasions await the Rabbit's family.

## For the **Dragon**

The Dragon must be wondering when its promised fame and fortune will arrive. The answer is not quite yet. A really difficult time has passed, but major problems have been cleared up. Minor ones still remain; happily these will also be despatched soon.

## For the **Snake**＊

Adversaries may get their own way over the Snake this year, but the triumph will be short-lived. The success will rebound, but that is no help to the Snake. Let matters take their own course this year, for what seems to be adversity will turn out to be advantageous in the end.

## For the **Horse**

Progress is slow this year; achievements are a trifle disappointing. On the positive side there are fewer difficulties to unravel and no serious problems to contend with. Your social life may not have its usual gloss, but perhaps the time has come to assess your priorities. A loss of some casual acquaintances may not be a bad thing.

## For the **Sheep**★

This year will be a landmark in the Sheep's life. Not just a single event, but a whole summer's experiences will be remembered for many years. It is a favourable period where you will be able to move forwards in your life with confidence, aided by the support of friends and family.

## For the **Monkey**✖

The Monkey needs to take care that his or her actions do not cause offence. Plans, not properly thought through, will bring the Monkey problems. It is important to follow the rules and not cut corners. Attention to detail is important.

## For the **Rooster**

In an odd way, there are unexpected gains for the Rooster this year. Setting out to complete a routine activity takes a remarkable turn, resulting in a chance encounter leading to an unusual offer. It is just the kind of thing that the Rooster had been waiting for. The benefits are not only financial, but fulfilling in many other ways.

## For the **Dog**

Partnership is the keynote of the coming year. There are many ways in which the Dog succeeds in linking up with the right partner: finding the right person to tackle problems with the home; finding the right colleague to work with; and finding the right partner to embark upon a relationship. All bring concord into the Dog's life.

## For the **Pig**

The God of Time now resides in the part of the Heavens that is the Pig's domain. Blessings and honour wait for the patient and trusted Pig, who at last has reached his or her goal. Tributes and gifts are brought by respectful colleagues, while approving ancestors bestow their benefactions on the Pig and his or her family for generations to come. The close of the 12-year cycle represents the achievement of objectives and the satisfaction of having everything in perfect order.

# Calculating the hour, month and day signs

It is not only the years that have their animal signs; each month, day and hour has its own animal sign as well. Here you can uncover the harmonies and conflicts of the four animal signs that unravel the secrets of a person's inner personality.

# The Hour Animal

The animal of the hour is the second factor when calculating the horoscope. Some astrologers believe that the Hour Animal (determined by the hour of your birth) is the inner self, that part of the personality people like to keep hidden; the secret ambitions and desires that can never be realized. The Year Animal describes the yang image that people project to the outside world, the everyday personality that outsiders recognize, while the Hour Animal is a reflection of the inner yin personality that a person would like to be.

The Hour Animal also reflects the individual's relationship with children. If the astrologer is asked a question about children when looking at the full horoscope, the sign for the Hour would be examined.

## Determining the Animal Hour

To find the animal sign for the hour ought to be simplicity itself. Chinese astrology divides the day into twelve 'double-hours', but actually, the divisions are not altogether straightforward. The first or Rat double-hour doesn't begin at midnight but at 11 pm. Midnight itself is halfway through the Rat double-hour (see the table right), but after that matters are straightforward: the Ox hour lasts from 1 am to 3 am, the Tiger hour from 3 am to 5 am and so on.

*How people relate to their children is revealed by their hour animal sign.*

## Daylight Saving Time

There are one or two considerations that may pose an occasional puzzle. The first concerns Daylight Saving Time. If the time of birth is registered when Daylight Saving Time is in operation, adjustments must be made accordingly. In many cases it does not matter: someone born at 04.30 in June during Daylight Saving Time would need to subtract one hour, making the true birth time 3.30. But both 03.30 and 04.30 belong to the same double-hour of the Tiger, so there is no difference. It would make a difference, however, if the time of birth was 03.30, since subtracting an hour would mean that the hour of birth was the Ox double-hour.

## Time zones

The second consideration is the variation in local time. Some countries have a number of time

### THE ANIMAL HOURS

|     | Animal  | Hour          |
| --- | ------- | ------------- |
| I   | Rat     | 00.00– 01.00  |
| II  | Ox      | 01.00– 03.00  |
| III | Tiger   | 03.00– 05.00  |
| IV  | Rabbit  | 05.00– 07.00  |
| V   | Dragon  | 07.00– 09.00  |
| VI  | Snake   | 09.00– 11.00  |
| VII | Horse   | 11.00– 13.00  |
| VIII| Sheep   | 13.00– 15.00  |
| IX  | Monkey  | 15.00– 17.00  |
| X   | Rooster | 17.00– 19.00  |
| XI  | Dog     | 19.00– 21.00  |
| XII | Pig     | 21.00– 23.00  |
| I   | Rat     | 23.00– 24.00  |

zones: several European countries have a time one hour ahead of Universal Time (what used to be called Greenwich Mean Time) yet they cover wide areas that stretch over more than two zones. There are some strange anomalies throughout the world: China itself uses only one standard time based on Beijing in the Far East, although in reality it covers nine time zones. Russia, on the other hand, is divided into eleven time zones, one of which crosses the International Date Line. To make travel more intriguing, Russian airlines use local time for their departures and arrivals, but Russian trains only use Moscow time, even though local time may be seven or eight hours different!

## Sun solution

The answer to both of these conundrums is the same: always use the time as told by the Sun: in other words, reckon the time from when the Sun is directly overhead at noon.

If you are not sure, use a compass or some other method to check when the Sun is true south and make a note of the clock time. If the clock reads 12.00, then the clock indicates that local time is true time. If, for example, the clock reads 12.30, then subtract 30 minutes from the given time of birth to get the time that should be used for the horoscope.

The ancient Chinese, without clocks and watches, used incense sticks to record the time of a baby's birth. At the moment the baby was born, an incense stick would be lit. This would be kept burning until the dawn (if the baby was born during the night) or sunset (if born during the day), when the incense stick would be extinguished. When the family consulted the astrologer, he would measure how much of the incense had been burnt and so would be able to calculate the hour of birth.

*Even today in rural China, incense sticks are used to measure the passage of time.*

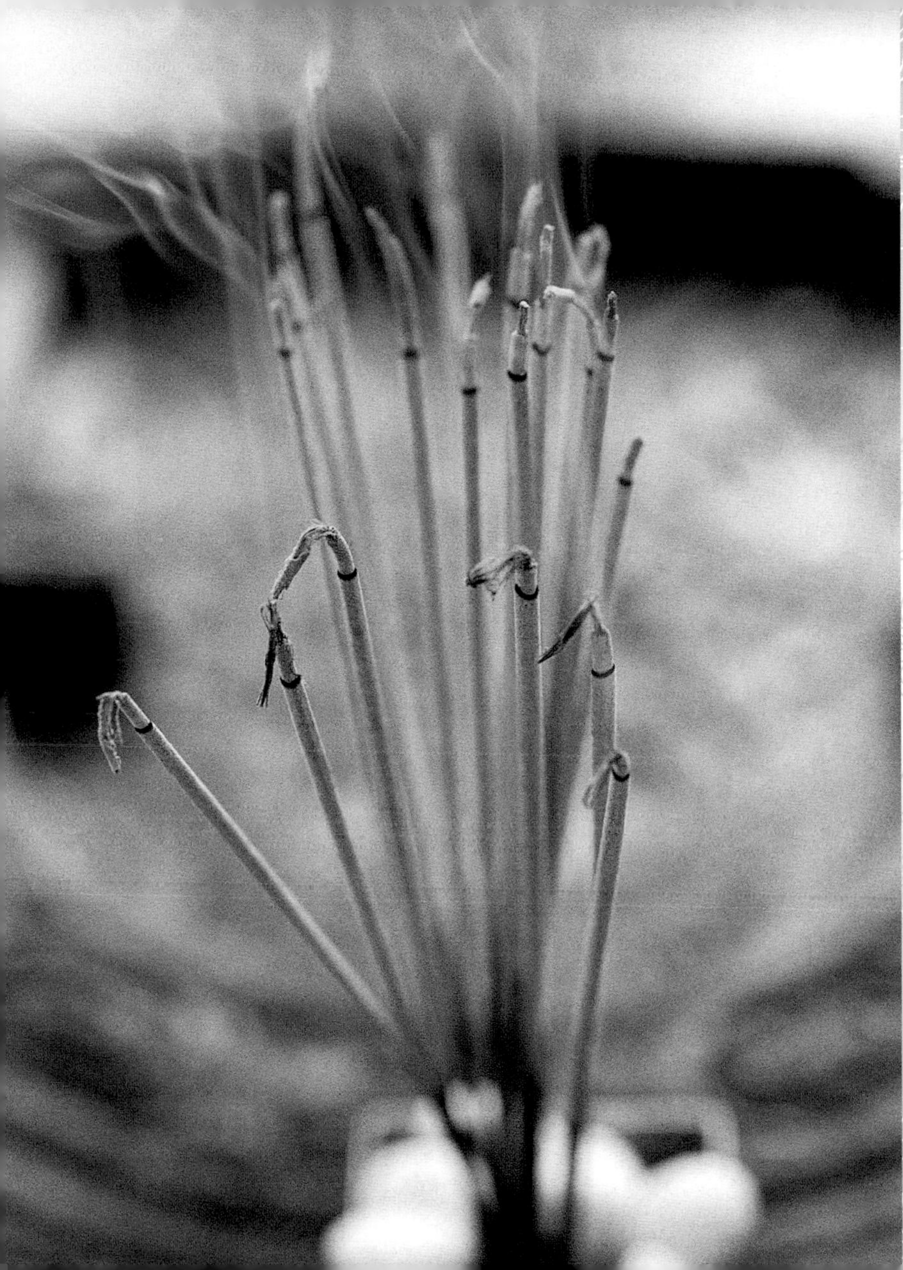

# The Month Animal

In popular Chinese astrology, more attention is given to the year of birth than the month of birth. However, when a more detailed analysis is needed, the astrologer needs to have the year, month, day and time of birth. The animal sign of the month is the second factor of the Chinese horoscope and represents the relationship between the individual and those who have responsibility for him or her – parents, teachers, and in later adult life, employers.

## Determining the Animal Month

Here we look at the way we can quickly establish the animal sign for the month, but first a word about what is meant by 'the Chinese month'. Until about 50 years ago, the Chinese used a lunar calendar that was different every year, since the first of each

### THE ANIMAL MONTHS

These are the usual dates for the start of the Chinese astrological months.

| Animal | | Month |
|--------|--------|----------|
| I | Rat | 7 Dec |
| II | Ox | 6 Jan |
| III | Tiger | 4 Feb |
| IV | Rabbit | 6 March |
| V | Dragon | 5 April |
| VI | Snake | 6 May |
| VII | Horse | 6 June |
| VIII | Sheep | 8 July |
| IX | Monkey | 8 August |
| X | Rooster | 8 Sept |
| XI | Dog | 9 Oct |
| XII | Pig | 8 Nov |

*In the Chinese-speaking world, even today many employers scan the horoscope of prospective employees to assess their suitability.*

month was the day of the New Moon. This meant that months were sometimes 29 days long and sometimes 30. It also meant that some years had 13 months, because otherwise the 'lunar' calendar would get out of step with the seasons.

Fortunately, Chinese astrology uses a quite different calendar based on the true solar year and the seasons: the first (Rat) month always has

173

the shortest day or winter solstice as its middle point; the fourth (Rabbit) month has the spring equinox as its centre; the seventh (Horse) month includes the longest day or summer solstice, while the tenth (Rooster) month is centred on the autumn equinox.

## Minor complications

For most horoscopes, the animal sign for the month is very easy to establish. There are complications when the birthday is on the junction of two Chinese months. For astronomical reasons – one being the added extra day every leap year – in some years the start of the months may be a day earlier or later.

In fact, Chinese astrological months run parallel with Western zodiac signs. The only difference is that the Chinese months start at the halfway point between two Western zodiac signs. For example, the Rat month with the winter solstice as its halfway point, starts halfway through Sagittarius and ends in the middle of Capricorn. Or to put it the other way round, Aries, which starts with the spring equinox, begins halfway through the Rabbit month.

In nearly all cases, the table on page 172 is all you need to find the animal sign of the month. But most of the time you don't even need that: all the Chinese months start between the fourth and ninth days of the Western month, so if the birthday falls on the tenth of the month or later, just add one to the Western month to find the animal sign!

For example: if the birthday was 14 June, then as June is the sixth Western month, the Chinese month would be the seventh sign, which is the Horse. If someone was born on the first, second or third day of the month, you don't need to add one, because no Chinese month begins before the fourth. For the birthday 1 January, the Month Animal will be the first sign, the Rat.

*For most people, it is simple to determine the animal sign for the month of birth.*

# The Day Animal

When Chinese astrologers delve more deeply into the Chinese horoscope, for them one of the most important factors is revealed by the day of birth. This factor is the Day Animal sign, the fourth sign along with those of the year, month and hour that goes towards building a more complete horoscope chart. The chart will reveal how the four signs relate to each other, and whether they are harmonious or clash, as will be explained in the section 'Patterns of Harmony' (see pages 181–187).

But when analysing the details for the day of birth, there are other interesting factors that come to light as well. For example, the Day animal reveals how people relate to those of their own generation: partners, brothers and sisters, work colleagues and friends. And whereas the Year Animal gives an overview of a person's personality and life prospects, the Day animal is used to give more specific information about different stages in a person's life.

## Determining the Day Animal

Finding the animal for the day is straightforward because there are none of the complications arising from the solar and lunar calendars. The downside, however, is that it does involve a short calculation based on the Western date, and specifically requires the use of tables. However, the tables are not cumbersome and can be easily copied. And this information about the Day Animal is not only used in working out a person's horoscope, it can also be used to find out the general prospects for the day. There is more about this fascinating topic in the section 'Clothes-cutting days' on pages 306– 312.

The tables and calculation to find the data for the day of birth will also give the 'element' for the day. The significance of this will be explained later on pages 202– 206, but for the moment, the animal sign is all that is needed to see if there are any Patterns of Harmony (see pages 181– 187), or even to find the prospects for any particular day. But note down the element in any case, as it will be needed later when a more detailed examination of the horoscope is made.

**Note:** A common question that arises is what happens if someone is born before the Chinese New Year? Should that person be considered to belong to the previous year? The answer is NO! Remember that the calculation is based on the Western date of birth; whether or not the birthday came before or after the Chinese New Year is irrelevant.

*How people relate to their colleagues is revealed by the animal sign for the day.*

# To find Chinese astrology factors for the day

Follow these few steps to find the Animal Sign for any day from 1931 to 2030. The result will give an 'element' for the day as well. This should be noted for future reference.

1 First look up the code number for the year in Table A (see page 179).
2 Then find the code number for the month from Table B (see page 179).
3 Now add together the two code numbers, plus the date of the month.
4 If the year is a leap year (the last two digits of the year can be divided by 4) AND the date is from March onwards, add 1 more to account for the fact that there are 29 days in February in leap years.
5 If the total is more than 60, subtract 60, or if it is more than 120, subtract 120.
6 From Table C (see page 180), look up the number and find the required information.

**Example:** What is the animal sign for 25 June 2010?
1 *From Table A, the code number for 2010 is 47.*
2 *From Table B, the code number for June is 31.*
3 *Code number A = 47; code number B = 31; date = 25.*

$$47 + 31 + 25 = 103$$

4 *2010 was not a leap year; so no need to add 1.*
5 *Total is more than 60, so subtract 60.*

$$103 - 60 = 43$$

6 *Therefore, 25 June 2010 is a (Fire) Horse day.*

## TABLE A

| Year | Code | Year | Code | Year | Code | Year | Code |
|------|------|------|------|------|------|------|------|
| 1931 | 52 | 1956 | 3 | 1981 | 18 | 2006 | 26 |
| 1932 | 57 | 1957 | 9 | 1982 | 20 | 2007 | 31 |
| 1933 | 3 | 1958 | 14 | 1983 | 25 | 2008 | 36 |
| 1934 | 8 | 1959 | 19 | 1984 | 30 | 2009 | 42 |
| 1935 | 13 | 1960 | 24 | 1985 | 36 | 2010 | 47 |
| 1936 | 18 | 1961 | 30 | 1986 | 41 | 2011 | 52 |
| 1937 | 24 | 1962 | 35 | 1987 | 46 | 2012 | 57 |
| 1938 | 29 | 1963 | 40 | 1988 | 51 | 2013 | 3 |
| 1939 | 34 | 1964 | 45 | 1989 | 57 | 2014 | 8 |
| 1940 | 39 | 1965 | 51 | 1990 | 2 | 2015 | 13 |
| 1941 | 45 | 1966 | 56 | 1991 | 7 | 2016 | 18 |
| 1942 | 50 | 1967 | 1 | 1992 | 12 | 2017 | 24 |
| 1943 | 55 | 1968 | 6 | 1993 | 18 | 2018 | 29 |
| 1944 | 0 | 1969 | 12 | 1994 | 23 | 2019 | 34 |
| 1945 | 6 | 1970 | 17 | 1995 | 28 | 2020 | 39 |
| 1946 | 11 | 1971 | 22 | 1996 | 33 | 2021 | 45 |
| 1947 | 16 | 1972 | 27 | 1997 | 39 | 2022 | 50 |
| 1948 | 21 | 1973 | 33 | 1998 | 44 | 2023 | 55 |
| 1949 | 27 | 1974 | 38 | 1999 | 49 | 2024 | 60 |
| 1950 | 32 | 1975 | 43 | 2000 | 54 | 2025 | 6 |
| 1951 | 37 | 1976 | 48 | 2001 | 0 | 2026 | 11 |
| 1952 | 42 | 1977 | 54 | 2002 | 5 | 2027 | 16 |
| 1953 | 48 | 1978 | 59 | 2003 | 10 | 2028 | 21 |
| 1954 | 53 | 1979 | 4 | 2004 | 15 | 2029 | 27 |
| 1955 | 58 | 1980 | 9 | 2005 | 21 | 2030 | 33 |

## TABLE B

| Month | Jan | Feb | Mar | Apr | May | Jun | Jul | Aug | Sep | Oct | Nov | Dec |
|-------|-----|-----|-----|-----|-----|-----|-----|-----|-----|-----|-----|-----|
| Code | 0 | 31 | 59 | 30 | 0 | 31 | 1 | 32 | 3 | 33 | 4 | 34 |

## TABLE C

| Code | Element | Animal | Code | Element | Animal | Code | Element | Animal |
|------|---------|--------|------|---------|--------|------|---------|--------|
| 1 | Wood | Rat | 21 | Wood | Monkey | 41 | Wood | Dragon |
| 2 | Wood | Ox | 22 | Wood | Rooster | 42 | Wood | Snake |
| 3 | Fire | Tiger | 23 | Fire | Dog | 43 | Fire | Horse |
| 4 | Fire | Rabbit | 24 | Fire | Pig | 44 | Fire | Sheep |
| 5 | Earth | Dragon | 25 | Earth | Rat | 45 | Earth | Monkey |
| 6 | Earth | Snake | 26 | Earth | Ox | 46 | Earth | Rooster |
| 7 | Metal | Horse | 27 | Metal | Tiger | 47 | Metal | Dog |
| 8 | Metal | Sheep | 28 | Metal | Rabbit | 48 | Metal | Pig |
| 9 | Water | Monkey | 29 | Water | Dragon | 49 | Water | Rat |
| 10 | Water | Rooster | 30 | Water | Snake | 50 | Water | Ox |
| 11 | Wood | Dog | 31 | Wood | Horse | 51 | Wood | Tiger |
| 12 | Wood | Pig | 32 | Wood | Sheep | 52 | Wood | Rabbit |
| 13 | Fire | Rat | 33 | Fire | Monkey | 53 | Fire | Dragon |
| 14 | Fire | Ox | 34 | Fire | Rooster | 54 | Fire | Snake |
| 15 | Earth | Tiger | 35 | Earth | Dog | 55 | Earth | Horse |
| 16 | Earth | Rabbit | 36 | Earth | Pig | 56 | Earth | Sheep |
| 17 | Metal | Dragon | 37 | Metal | Rat | 57 | Metal | Monkey |
| 18 | Metal | Snake | 38 | Metal | Ox | 58 | Metal | Rooster |
| 19 | Water | Horse | 39 | Water | Tiger | 59 | Water | Dog |
| 20 | Water | Sheep | 40 | Water | Rabbit | 60 | Water | Pig |

# Patterns of Harmony

Now the four animals of the horoscope have been found –
one each for the hour, day, month and year of birth. The
first step in looking at a Chinese horoscope is to see whether
these four animals are harmonious or in conflict. A chart with
the 12 Animals arranged around a clock face is a convenient
way to show the relationships.

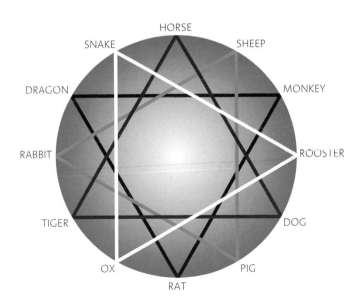

The circular diagram on page 181 shows four triangles. A glance at Table C on page 180 will show that the triangles link up the three animal signs that are always on the same row in the table. These Four Triangles of Harmony show the animals that have the best relationships with each other. Any two animal signs from a particular triangle group make a harmonious pair. These triangles show which animals make the most favourable partnership and also show which years, months, days and even times are favourable for different people, their various activities and which directions of travel are the most likely to ensure success.

## Seasons and directions

Because the four animals Rat, Rabbit, Horse and Rooster are also associated with the seasons and the seasons with the four compass directions, the triangles are sometimes known as the North (Rat), East (Rabbit), South (Horse) and West (Rooster) triangles, and sometime by the associated element, of which more later.

When three animals are combined together, they produce another dimension which provides the horoscope with important information. The four groupings of animal signs and the qualities of each of the signs in a group shows that their names were not chosen at random. For example, the Horse, Tiger and Dog are all associated with hunting and have masculine qualities. In contrast, the Rabbit, Sheep and Pig are all connected with family life and have an essentially feminine quality.

 ## North or Water Triangle
### Rat, Dragon, Monkey – Creativity

This is the creative triangle associated with discovery and invention. The Rat quality formulates ideas, the dexterity of the Monkey fashions the idea into something more tangible while the Dragon adds the sparkle and attractive quality to make the project workable.

## East or Wood Triangle
### Rabbit, Sheep and Pig – Family

The Rabbit is associated with children and caring for the vulnerable; the Sheep, from the House of Sex and Gender, is associated with romantic relationships, physical love and marriage or life partnerships; the Pig's domain is the home's interior and domestic comfort. These three animal signs construct the triangle of family happiness.

## South or Fire Triangle
### Horse, Dog and Tiger – Ambition

As all three signs are associated with hunting, this is the triangle of ambition, competition and sportsmanship. When these three signs come together in a horoscope, it reveals a person with purpose and self-fulfilment, who aims to reach the top of his or her profession.

## West or Metal Triangle
### Rooster, Ox and Snake – Commerce

These signs present the three aspects necessary to run a successful business: a flair for spotting trends and commercial possibilities is the Rooster's particular talent; the hard, diligent work needed to keep a business running is supplied by the Ox; and the necessary financial sensitivity is the Snake's special ability.

## Completing a triangle

If two of the signs from any of the triangles are present in a horoscope this is obviously a positive aspect, since any two signs from a group are a favourable pair. But it also gives a clue to the role in life that a person might take, and shows what factor might be missing and how it could be replaced. For example, suppose someone who had Rooster and Ox in a chart wanted to go into business. Although that person had good commercial ideas and was a hard worker, the business did not take off as successfully as was hoped. What is lacking from the horoscope is the Snake, the financial management side. This extra factor might be provided by a partner who was born in a Snake year, or alternatively, perhaps the business would turn out to be more profitable during a Snake year.

## Other favourable pairs of signs

In addition to pairs of signs from one of the Four Triangles, the intermediate signs, those that are next-but-one in sequence such as Ox and Rabbit, are also favourable. Often the intermediary signs help to soften unfavourable aspects elsewhere in the chart.

Signs that are in the same 'house' are favourable and strengthen the influence of the house quality. Thus, Rat and Ox strengthen creativity; Tiger and Rabbit strengthen progress and development; Dragon and Snake emphasize the spiritual, mystical side of life; Horse and Sheep strengthen partnership; Monkey and Rooster emphasize technical mastery; and Dog and Pig strengthen home security. But signs that are next to each other in the chart, but not in the same house are not so favourable. A well-known example is Rabbit and Dragon – the Dragon loses all its good luck when the Rabbit appears.

## Unfavourable signs

The less fortunate combinations of signs are those that are either directly opposite each other in the chart, such as Pig and Snake, and those that are 90° apart, such as the Snake and the Monkey. When two signs are 90° apart, the animal sign of the longer period adversely affects the sign of the shorter one. For example, a person who was born in a Rabbit month at a Horse hour would find that the Horse quality is overruled by the Rabbit.

# The Three Crosses

The three very important exceptions to the above occur when all four animal signs form a cross. All the bad influences are neutralized and combine to form a very strong beneficial influence.
The Three Crosses have practical and poetic names.

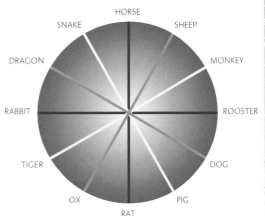

### The Four Compass Points or Four Flowers of Love

Made up of Rat, Rabbit, Horse and Rooster, each animal sign indicates a point of the compass. This combination indicates power and fame, someone who is destined to be remembered. 'Four Flowers of Love' suggests that someone in such an exalted position will never be short of lovers!

### The Four Earths or Literary Cross

Composed of Ox, Dragon, Sheep and Dog, each animal sign represents the end of a season. All four of these signs together indicates the presence of artistic gifts.

### The Four Elements or Coaching Posts

Made up of Pig, Tiger, Snake and Monkey, each animal sign represents the first month of a season. The coaching posts were inns where horses were changed on a long journey. It shows that the person will leave home to live in a foreign country.

# The missing fourth animal sign

When three of the animal signs of a cross are in the horoscope chart, but the fourth horoscope animal does not complete the cross, its absence is just as significant as one that is present. It means that the quality associated with that sign needs to be strengthened. For example, the Rabbit is associated with children; if a horoscope held the signs of the Rat, Rooster and Horse but no Rabbit, it could mean problems in dealing with one's children, or perhaps employees. The likely prospects suggested by each 'missing arm' are given below.

## Incomplete Four Flowers Cross

**Rat missing:** Decision-making takes a long time. It is difficult to get started on a project without additional help to push this person forwards. The horoscope shows a reluctance to start afresh or make important changes.

**Rabbit missing:** The management of children or employees may create problems, possibly through lack of understanding. The younger

generation seem to be from another planet.

**Horse missing:** Close involvement in family and career mean that it is not easy to have an active social life. Without the stimulation of friendly company there is a danger of stagnation.

**Rooster missing:** As the Rooster hour represents the close of the

*The absence of a sign is often more significant than one which is present.*

working day, its absence means that such a person cannot leave work behind. An over-active schedule results in restlessness and fatigue.

## Incomplete Literary Cross

**Ox missing:** The missing quotient is stamina and endurance. Frequent breaks and pauses cannot be conducive to a smooth-running life. Meditation is needed.

**Dragon missing:** Hesitancy and shyness result from this absence in the horoscope. Sparkle and excitement are needed to charge this individual's life.

**Sheep missing:** Partnerships suffer when the Sheep is missing. Relationships may not last long and will remain fragile until the right partner is found.

**Dog missing:** As the Dog represents the structure of the home, a horoscope without it reveals a nomadic quality, someone who prefers to be on the move, but longs for a stable environment.

## Incomplete Coaching Posts Cross

**Tiger missing:** A missing Tiger shows a lack of authority. Such a horoscope reveals someone who has difficulties being assertive and who is reluctant to make demands.

**Snake missing:** The horoscope signifies someone involved in legal tangles. Travel may not be possible because of lack of documentation.

**Monkey missing:** Verbal and technical skills are indicated by the Monkey, and if this sign is missing, the main problems are not people but things – inanimate objects that seem to have a will of their own.

**Pig missing:** A happy and comfortable home may seem a dream that can only be achieved with difficulty, and even then it is not completely satisfactory. Such a person is never satisfied with his or her surroundings and forever wants to make changes to the home.

# The broader horoscope

This section shows how to construct a Chinese horoscope revealing the high and low phases in a person's life. Two methods are described: the Ming Shu, which gives a quick overview of life's course; and the Life Cycle, which provides a more detailed account in ten-yearly periods.

# Constructing a Chinese horoscope

The four essential factors of a horoscope – the hour, day, month and year – have now been looked at from the perspective of the animal sign. With only these four pieces of information, it is possible to give an overview of a person's horoscope and chances of success in life. The Year Animal gives a broad picture of personality and partnership compatibility. It can be matched with the animal of any coming year to give the prospects for the next 12 months or even to find the most favourable months in the year ahead. With the extra information given by the Hour, Day and Month animals, it is a straightforward matter to construct a chart that shows further aspects of personality.

It can also reveal weak or absent animal signs that can be compensated for by the choice of a suitable colleague, friend or partner who embodies the missing signs; compensation can also take place symbolically by moving in a particular direction or even by carrying a lucky token of the missing animal.

But the four animal signs are only part – although an important part – of the Chinese horoscope. Over the next few pages, further details derived from the birth date will show how the horoscope can be expanded to reveal when the fortunate and unfavourable phases in a person's life are most likely to occur.

# The four Columns

At the core of the Chinese horoscope is a table which Chinese astrologers call the Four Columns. For example, a Chinese horoscope for sunset on 22 April 1999 (and, incidentally, for 27 April 1939) would have these signs in a box like this.

| EXAMPLE A | | | | |
| --- | --- | --- | --- | --- |
| | Hour | Day | Month | Year |
| Stem | 癸 | 甲 | 戊 | 己 |
| Branch | 酉 | 午 | 辰 | 卯 |

The Chinese use the word 'columns' the same way as us to mean columns of text, as in a newspaper, although some writers use the term 'pillars'. As each column has two parts, with a Chinese sign above and below, making eight Chinese characters in total, the Four Columns are often called the Eight Characters (*bazi* in Chinese). 'Four Columns' refers to the table and *bazi* or 'Eight Characters' (*ba* = 8, *zi* = Chinese character) to the signs themselves, although in practice the terms are interchangeable. In recent years the term *bazi* has become more common.

## Stems and Branches

Each column consists of two signs called the Stem and Branch respectively – the upper sign being the 'Stem' and the lower one the 'Branch'. The Branches have already been covered in the earlier sections under a different name – the 12 Animal signs. There are no differences in the function or application of the branches and the animals; only the names have changed. The box below shows the 'branches' replaced by animal signs. It is often more convenient when compiling Four Columns charts to follow the convention of representing the branches or animal signs with Roman numerals; thus Rat, Ox and Tiger become I, II, III and so on (see page 205 for a list of the animals with their Roman numerals).

As for the top half of the Four Columns, one of the 'stems' has already been glimpsed; in the example for calculating the animal sign for the day (see pages 178–180), an extra piece of information was added: 25 June 2010 was not just a Horse day; it was a Fire Horse day. Although 'Fire' is not a stem in itself, the stem for that particular day belonged to the Fire element. Many Western followers of Chinese astrology refer to the stems simply by the element they belong to, but it is just as important to know what the actual stem is. The stems and elements are not interchangeable, as the branches and animal signs are.

| **EXAMPLE A** | | | | |
|---|---|---|---|---|
| | Hour | Day | Month | Year |
| Stem | 癸 | 甲 | 戊 | 己 |
| Branch | Rooster | Horse | Dragon | Rabbit |

# The Ten Stems

Before the seven-day week was introduced to China, the Chinese used a week of ten days. Each day had a special name and collectively were known as the 'Heavenly Stems'. The description 'heavenly' sounds very dramatic, but actually derives from the fact that the word for a day (*tian*) is the same as the word for 'sky' or 'heaven'. The proper translation should perhaps be 'Daily Stems', except that for more than 1,500 years the stems have been applied to years, months and hours as well. (In contrast, the 12 Branches are often termed the 'Earthly Branches'.)

The original meanings of the Ten Stems are obscured by time – they were probably the names of gods, just as Western weekdays are named after Norse or Roman planetary deities: the Sun; the Moon; Tiw or Mars; Woden or Mercury; Thor or Jupiter; Freya or Venus; and Saturn. The probable original meanings of the Ten Stems are presented in the box on page 195.

From early on in Chinese history, probably since the Bronze Age, the days were reckoned not only by the ten 'daily' Stems, but were also combined with 12 other signs – the 'Branches' – to make a continuous cycle of 60 stem-and-branch days. This reckoning has gone on uninterrupted for thousands of years. The system is remarkable in that it enables historians to date an event with precise accuracy.

## TEN STEM MEANINGS

| Number | Chinese character | Chinese word | Meaning |
|--------|-------------------|--------------|---------|
| 1 | 甲 | jia | A flag; leadership |
| 2 | 乙 | yi | A sprout; continuation |
| 3 | 丙 | bing | A fire in a cave |
| 4 | 丁 | ding | A nail; construction |
| 5 | 戊 | wu | A man holding a knife or spear; defence, attack |
| 6 | 己 | ji | A thread; weaving; needlework, tailoring |
| 7 | 庚 | geng | A mortar and pestle; grinding and harvesting |
| 8 | 辛 | xin | A flower; a bitter medicinal herb. Healing power |
| 9 | 壬 | ren | Carrying a load. Transport, logistics |
| 10 | 癸 | gui | Two hands clasped in prayer. A symbol of spirituality |

Then at some point, less than 2,000 years ago, the same system of stems-and-branches was applied to the years as well. From that point, it was a short step to labelling the months and hours of the day by the same system, and that's how the calendar was reckoned when Marco Polo made his epic journey to China in the 13th century.

## How to find the Stem for the year

1 Take the Western year date. If the horoscope is for someone born before the start of the Chinese year, take the previous year.
2 Take the last digit of the year and if it is 4 or more, subtract 3. If the last digit is 3 or less, add 7. The result is the Stem of the year.

**Example:** What is the Stem for the year 2010?
1 *The Western year date is 2010.*
2 *The last digit of 2010 is less than 3, so add 7.*
*Therefore 7 is the Stem of the year.*

## How to find the Stem for the day

1 From the calculation to find the animal sign for the day, take the final total arrived at before turning to Table C (see pages 178–180).
2 The last figure of the total is the Stem (or if 0, then the Stem is 10).

**Example:** What is the Stem for the day for 25 June 2010?
1 *The final total after step 3 of the calculation for finding the animal sign was 103.*
2 *The last figure of the total is 3.*
*Therefore the Stem for the day is therefore 3.*

## How to find the Stem for the month

1 Using the Stem of the year and the animal sign of the month (see

## TABLE TO FIND THE STEM FOR THE MONTH

| Branch | Stem of Year Month | 1 or 6 | 2 or 7 | 3 or 8 | 4 or 9 | 5 or 10 |
|---|---|---|---|---|---|---|
| III | Tiger | 3 | 5 | 7 | 9 | 1 |
| IV | Rabbit | 4 | 6 | 8 | 10 | 2 |
| V | Dragon | 5 | 7 | 9 | 1 | 3 |
| VI | Snake | 6 | 8 | 10 | 2 | 4 |
| VII | Horse | 7 | 9 | 1 | 3 | 5 |
| VIII | Sheep | 8 | 10 | 2 | 4 | 6 |
| IX | Monkey | 9 | 1 | 3 | 5 | 7 |
| X | Rooster | 10 | 2 | 4 | 6 | 8 |
| XI | Dog | 1 | 3 | 5 | 7 | 9 |
| XII | Pig | 2 | 4 | 6 | 8 | 10 |
| I | Rat | 3 | 5 | 7 | 9 | 1 |
| II | Ox | 4 | 6 | 8 | 10 | 2 |

page 172), refer to the table above to find the Stem for the month. Note that the Chinese year starts with the Tiger month beginning on 4 February; Rat and Ox dates belong to the previous year.

**Example:** What is the Stem for the month for 25 June 2010?
*1   The Stem for the year is 7 and the animal sign for June is Horse. Therefore the Stem for the month is 9.*

## TABLE TO FIND THE STEM FOR THE HOUR

| Branch | Stem of day Hour | 1 or 6 | 2 or 7 | 3 or 8 | 4 or 9 | 5 or 10 |
|---|---|---|---|---|---|---|
| I | Rat | 1 | 3 | 5 | 7 | 9 |
| II | Ox | 2 | 4 | 6 | 8 | 10 |
| III | Tiger | 3 | 5 | 7 | 9 | 1 |
| IV | Rabbit | 4 | 6 | 8 | 10 | 2 |
| V | Dragon | 5 | 7 | 9 | 1 | 3 |
| VI | Snake | 6 | 8 | 10 | 2 | 4 |
| VII | Horse | 7 | 9 | 1 | 3 | 5 |
| VIII | Sheep | 8 | 10 | 2 | 4 | 6 |
| IX | Monkey | 9 | 1 | 3 | 5 | 7 |
| X | Rooster | 10 | 2 | 4 | 6 | 8 |
| XI | Dog | 1 | 3 | 5 | 7 | 9 |
| XII | Pig | 2 | 4 | 6 | 8 | 10 |

## How to find the Stem for the hour

1 Using the Stem of the day and the animal sign of the hour (see page 169), refer to the table above to find the Stem for the hour.

Once you have gathered all the above information you will be ready to convert a Western date into the Four Columns.

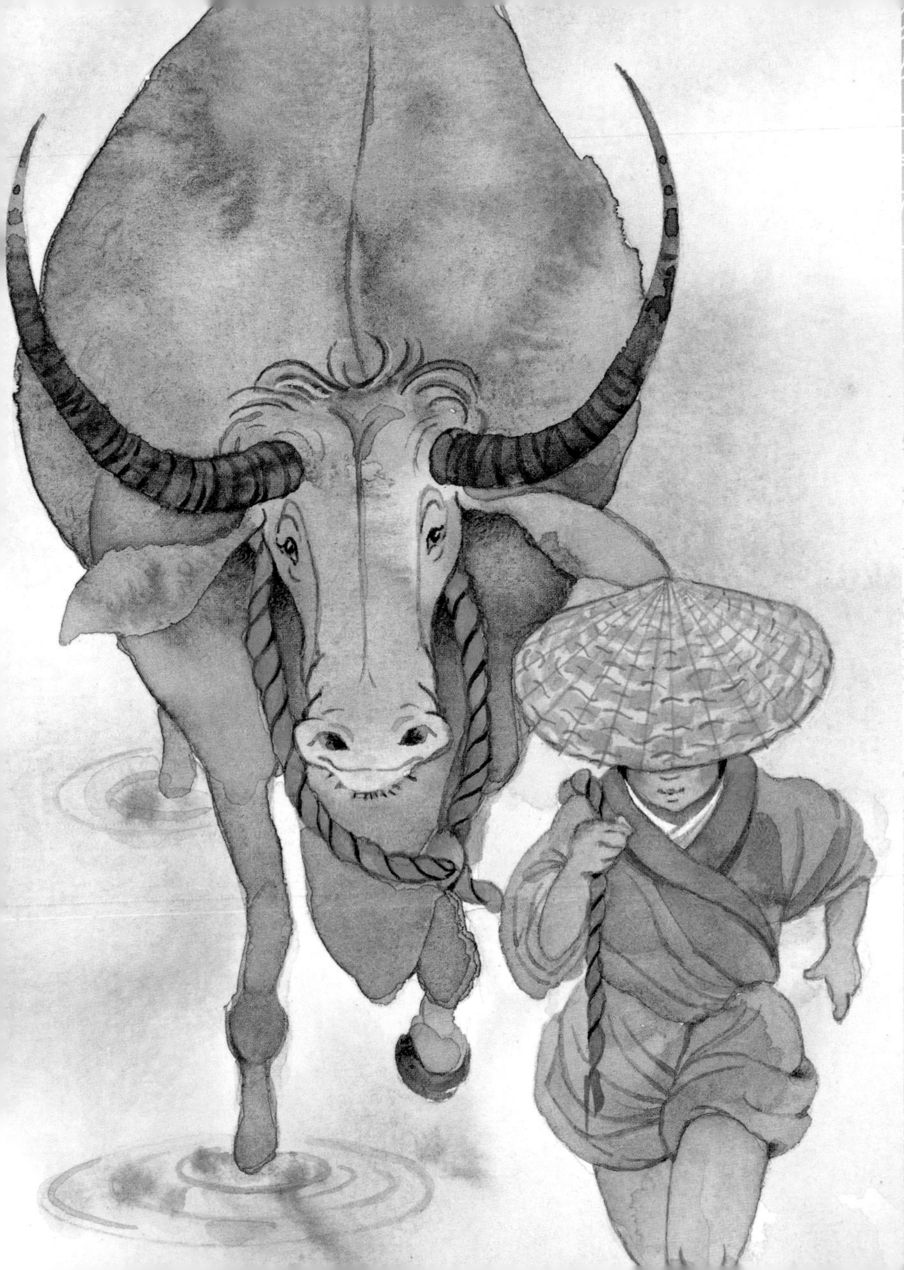

# Building the Four Columns

The following guide shows how the Four Columns chart is constructed. The same example as before, 25 June 2010, is used. As the time factor is needed, we shall use 06.30.

## How to construct the Four Columns chart

Follow these steps to build a Four Columns chart.

1 **Year Branch** Use the chart on page 36 to find the animal sign of the year. Then refer to page 172 to find the Roman numeral that represents that year.

2 **Year Stem** Use the instructions on page 196 to find the digit for the Stem of the year.

3 **Branch of the Hour** Use the chart on page 169 and the accompanying notes to identify the animal sign of the hour and its Roman numeral.

4 **Branch of the Month** Use the chart on page 172 and the notes that accompany it to identify the animal sign of the month and its Roman numeral.

5 **Stem and Branch of the Day** Use the instructions on page 178 to find the animal sign for the day and use the chart on page 172 to note the Roman numeral for that animal.
Use the instructions on page 196 to find the digit for the Stem of the day.

6 **Stem of the Month** Use the text and chart on page 196– 197 to identify the Stem of the month.

7 **Stem of the Hour** Use the text and chart on page 198 to identify the Stem of the hour.

**Example:** How to build the Four Columns chart for 06.30, 25 June 2010?

1   *2010 is a Tiger or Branch III year; insert III in the chart.*
2   *The last digit of 2010 is 0, so 0 + 7 = 7; insert 7 in the chart.*
3   *The hour is 06.30 (Daylight Saving Time) which is 05.30 local time. This is the Rabbit Hour, Branch IV; insert IV in the chart.*
4   *June is a Horse or Branch VII month; insert VII in the chart.*
5   *25 June 2010 is a Horse or Branch VII month; insert VII in the chart. The Stem for 25 June 2010 is 3; insert 3 in the chart.*
6   *The month is Horse (VII) and the Year Stem 7. From the Month table on page 197 the Stem for the Month is 9; insert 9 in the chart.*
7   *The Stem of the Day is 3 and the animal is Rabbit. From the table on page 198 the Stem of the Hour is 8; insert 8 in the chart.*

| **EXAMPLE A** | | | | |
|---|---|---|---|---|
| | **Hour** | **Day** | **Month** | **Year** |
| **Stem** | 8 | 3 | 9 | 7 |
| **Branch** | IV | VII | VII | III |

# The Five Elements

In the section that showed how to find the animal sign for the day, the calculation also revealed some other facts. One of these was the Stem of the Day, but in addition the description 'Fire' was added to the Horse. Fire along with Wood, Earth, Metal and Water make up what is now known as the Five Elements. This is a clumsy way to translate the original Chinese word, which means 'to go'. It came about because three of the names are so similar to the Aristotelian elements that early commentators on Chinese philosophy assumed that that was what they were.

But more significant than the categorization of the 'Ten Thousand Things' (a Chinese expression meaning everything) according to the Five-Element Plan, is the way that the Five Elements follow each other in diligent succession and cause friction and obstruction when the order is thwarted.

## Two sequences

There are two principal ways in which the Five Elements may be listed. The first is the productive sequence, in which each element is said to be the parent of the next in the series. Thus the productive order is Wood, Fire, Earth, Metal, Water, Wood, and so on. It can be said that Wood burns producing Fire, which leaves ash or Earth behind, from which

Metal is mined, and that under heat melts and flows like Water, which is needed to nourish the growing plants.

When two things represent two elements – say some grass (Wood element) and a horse (Fire) – which are next to each other in the series, one is said to be the parent of the other, and there is harmony between them. In this example Wood nourishes Fire as grass nourishes a horse.

## Destructive sequence

The second series, the destructive sequence, has alternate elements of the productive sequence follow in series: for example, Wood, Earth, Water, Fire, Metal, Wood. In this instance, growing plants (Wood) drain the Earth of its nutrients; Earth pollutes Water, making it unfit for drinking or cleansing; Water quenches Fire; Fire melts Metal; and Metal chops down Wood.

When two things occur as represented by elements in the destructive sequence, they are in danger of collapse, unless some intermediary element can act as a buffer between them. Thus after the wheat has grown and taken nourishment from the ground, farmers set fire to the stubble and the ground is re-fertilized

The ways in which one element 'conquers' another are quite different. When Wood drains Earth of nourishment, the Earth can be replenished. Metal loses its strength when it is melted by Fire, but regains its solidity when the Fire is taken away. Earth pollutes Water, but given time, the Earth settles, leaving the Water pure again. Metal chops down Wood, but it is nearly always a constructive process in order to produce something. But when Fire puts out Fire, that is the end of the Fire.

# Elements in the Chinese horoscope

In the Chinese horoscope, each of the stems and branches has an element. The Ten Stems follow the productive sequence in five yang-yin pairs:

Note that if the ten stems are arranged in a circle in the same way as the 12 Animals (see page 181), stems that are opposite each other, such as Stem 1 and Stem 6, are not adverse, as is the case with the animal signs or branches, but are attracted to each other like the poles of a magnet.

The 12 Branches follow the order of the seasons: Water associated with Winter, Wood with Spring, Fire with Summer and Metal with Autumn. The third month of each season is considered to belong to the Earth element. That is why in the Three Crosses (see page 185) the Literary Cross is called the Four Earths.

## 10 STEMS AND THEIR ELEMENTS

| Stem | Yang/Yin | Element |
|------|----------|---------|
| 1 | yang | Wood |
| 2 | yin | Wood |
| 3 | yang | Fire |
| 4 | yin | Fire |
| 5 | yang | Earth |
| 6 | yin | Earth |
| 7 | yang | Metal |
| 8 | yin | Metal |
| 9 | yang | Water |
| 10 | yin | Water |

## 12 BRANCHES AND THEIR ELEMENTS

| Branch | Animal | Yang/Yin | Element |
|--------|--------|----------|---------|
| I | Rat | yang | Water |
| II | Ox | yin | Earth |
| III | Tiger | yang | Wood |
| IV | Rabbit | yin | Wood |
| V | Dragon | yang | Earth |
| VI | Snake | yin | Fire |
| VII | Horse | yang | Fire |
| VIII | Sheep | yin | Earth |
| IX | Monkey | yang | Metal |
| X | Rooster | yin | Metal |
| XI | Dog | yang | Earth |
| XII | Pig | yin | Water |

# Adding the Elements to the Four Columns

Whatever way the horoscope is prepared, it is necessary to know the element qualities as well. The way to show these is to extend the Four Columns chart.

Using the example of the Four Columns (page 201), we can add the elements. From the table of '10 Stems and their Elements' on the opposite page, the element corresponding to Stem 8 (the stem of the hour) is Metal. From the table of '12 Branches and their Elements' (see left), the element corresponding to Branch IV is Wood. We can now do the same for the other three columns (Day, Month, and Year) as follows:

## EXAMPLE

|  | Hour | Day | Month | Year |
|--|------|-----|-------|------|
| Stem | 8 | 3 | 9 | 7 |
| Branch | IV | VII | VII | III |
| Stem Element | Metal | Fire | Water | Metal |
| Branch Element | Wood | Fire | Fire | Wood |

# Attributes of the Elements

The Five Elements and their qualities come to bear in the horoscope and there are specialist astrologers who look into the horoscope to detect the likelihood of illness, while Chinese doctors often adjust their prescriptions accordingly.

## FIVE ELEMENTS AND THEIR ATTRIBUTES

| Element | Wood | Fire | Earth | Metal | Water |
|---|---|---|---|---|---|
| Planet | Jupiter | Mars | Saturn | Venus | Mercury |
| Colour | Green | Red | Yellow | White | Black |
| Shape | Columnar | Triangular | Square | Round | Irregular |
| Season | Spring | Summer | | Autumn | Winter |
| Direction | East | South | Centre | West | North |
| Commodities | Plants | Livestock | Land | Wealth | Health |
| Life | Family | Career | Home | Commerce | Travel |
| Taste | Sour | Bitter | Sweet | Spicy | Savoury |
| Necessities | Light | Heat | Food | Air | Water |
| Age | Babyhood | Youth | Adulthood | Maturity | Retirement |
| Body | Liver | Heart | Stomach | Lungs | Bladder |
| Quality | Arts | Sport | Estate | Machinery | Media |
| Mood | Anger | Laughter | Introspection | Sadness | Fear |

# Understanding the horoscope

Ming Shu or Fate Calculation, is one of many methods used by Chinese astrologers to construct an overview of someone's prospects in life from the Four Columns and their component elements. It is an ideal way for beginners to gain an insight into the way that a horoscope can be interpreted. The essential data is provided by the Four Columns.

- A person's life is divided into Five Periods – babyhood, youth, adulthood, maturity and retirement – following each other in order.
- The Five Elements follow in their usual productive sequence – Wood, Fire, Earth, Metal, Water – and are attached to the Five Periods, but the starting point depends on the element of the *guandai* or 'cap-and-sash'. This is equivalent to the point in life where a person ceases to be a child, and becomes an adult with responsibilities, and therefore matches the 'Adulthood' period. The element of the *guandai* depends on the Year Stem and the Month Branch.
- There are also five qualities – Fate, Seal, Official, Wealth and Opportunity – which follow in sequence, but the beginning of the sequence depends on the element of the Year Branch.
- Finally, the quantity of each element that is revealed in the horoscope shows the extent of the influence of that element, and thus the quality it is attached to, and ultimately, the period in life when it has effect.

# How to construct a Ming Shu horoscope

Here is a step-by-step guide to the assembly of a Ming Shu horoscope using the example of page 205. Some suggestions on interpretation are given at the end of this section.

1 Once you have calculated the Four Columns and their associated elements (see pages 200– 205), find the *guandai* for the Year Stem and the Month Branch from the chart on page 209.

2 Write the name of the *guandai* element (in this case, Earth) at the top of the chart, in the 'Adulthood' position.

3 From the normal productive sequence of the elements, (Wood, Fire, Earth, Metal, Water) write the two elements which follow the *guandai* element in the Maturity and Retirement boxes, and the two elements which precede the Guandai Element in the Babyhood and Youth boxes.

4 Now find the Fate element, which is the element of the Branch of the year (in this case Wood). Write the Fate element in the chart under the aspect ruled by the Year Branch element.

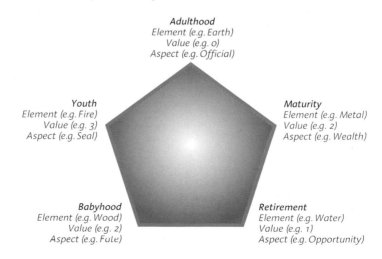

*Adulthood*
*Element (e.g. Earth)*
*Value (e.g. 0)*
*Aspect (e.g. Official)*

*Youth*
*Element (e.g. Fire)*
*Value (e.g. 3)*
*Aspect (e.g. Seal)*

*Maturity*
*Element (e.g. Metal)*
*Value (e.g. 2)*
*Aspect (e.g. Wealth)*

*Babyhood*
*Element (e.g. Wood)*
*Value (e.g. 2)*
*Aspect (e.g. Fate)*

*Retirement*
*Element (e.g. Water)*
*Value (e.g. 1)*
*Aspect (e.g. Opportunity)*

5 Following the Fate, and moving round the chart clockwise, write the remaining four aspects: Seal, Official, Wealth and Opportunity in the Aspect boxes.

6 Now in the 'Value' boxes, write the number of times each element appears in the Four Columns chart.

7 You are now ready to study and interpret the chart. Suggestions for ways to do this are given from pages 218 onward.

| *GUANDAI* TABLE | | | | | | | | | |
|---|---|---|---|---|---|---|---|---|---|
| Month/Branch | **Year Stem** | | | | | | | | |
| | 1 | 2 | 3 | 4 | 5 | 6 | 7 | 8 | 9 | 10 |
| I | Wood | Wood | Fire | Fire | Earth | Earth | Metal | Metal | Water | Water |
| II | Water | Wood | Wood | Fire | Fire | Earth | Earth | Metal | Metal | Water |
| III | Water | Wood | Wood | Fire | Fire | Earth | Earth | Metal | Metal | Water |
| IV | Water | Wood | Wood | Fire | Fire | Earth | Earth | Metal | Metal | Water |
| V | Water | Water | Wood | Wood | Fire | Fire | Earth | Earth | Metal | Metal |
| VI | Water | Water | Wood | Wood | Fire | Fire | Earth | Earth | Metal | Metal |
| VII | Water | Water | Wood | Wood | Fire | Fire | Earth | Earth | Metal | Metal |
| VIII | Water | Water | Wood | Wood | Fire | Fire | Earth | Earth | Metal | Metal |
| IX | Metal | Water | Water | Wood | Wood | Fire | Fire | Earth | Earth | Metal |
| X | Metal | Water | Water | Wood | Wood | Fire | Fire | Earth | Earth | Metal |
| XI | Metal | Water | Water | Wood | Wood | Fire | Fire | Earth | Earth | Metal |
| XII | Metal | Metal | Water | Water | Wood | Wood | Fire | Fire | Earth | Earth |

# Interpreting the Ming Shu horoscope

## The Five Qualities

In Ming Shu, these qualities are listed as the Fate, Seal, Official, Wealth and Opportunity elements.

**The Fate element** is taken from the Branch of the year; in other words, the element of the year animal. No matter whether all of the elements are present in the chart or only one repeated eight times, there will always be a Fate element. The more times the Fate element appears in the horoscope, the greater is the self-dependence. Someone with only one example of the element will be subject to the vagaries of circumstances and will be faced with difficult choices throughout life.

The Fate element can occur at any stage of life, from babyhood to retirement. It is best when the Fate element occurs at a time when something can be done about it, in adulthood or maturity, rather than in babyhood or retirement.

**The Seal** is the satisfaction and happiness which comes from a productive and fulfilling life. It is favourable when this is in retirement. If it occurs in youth or adulthood it signifies successful achievements at school or college; in maturity honours for a distinguished career. In babyhood its role has little significance and it is best if the associated element is absent.

**The Official** refers to career and promotion. Its most favourable positions are the same as those for the Seal, although it is rather late for it to be of any help in life if it appears in retirement.

**Wealth** is self-evident. If the Wealth element is strong, it should appear towards the end of life. If it is weak or absent it is best to be at the beginning.

**Opportunity** is a chance to change one's life for the better. It is best when this occurs early in life, but not too early. If it occurs in babyhood, it is best if there is no element with it. If the element is strong, it indicates a change in circumstances during early childhood. In retirement, it suggests a move to a better location.

The Five Elements give a clue to the nature of the Five Qualities: Wood is the natural element for health and family happiness; Fire for success in competitions; Earth represents land and property; Metal is the element for commerce and trade while Water is the element for travel and communication.

## Interpreting the example

The individual's babyhood is marked by a strong wood element, signifying good health and a happy family background. The schooldays were successful and showed great promise, with the person excelling in

## EXAMPLE

### Guandai

| Wood | Fire | Earth | Metal | Water |
|------|------|-------|-------|-------|
| 2 | 3 | 0 | 2 | 1 |
| Babyhood | Youth | Adulthood | Maturity | Retirement |
| Fate | Seal | Official | Wealth | Opportunity |

sporting activities rather than academic work (the competitive Fire is stronger than the creative Wood) This is perhaps the reason why college courses were postponed; there is no evidence of success in early adult years. Early adulthood would find this person without definite plans for a permanent place to live (lack of Earth element). However, the Metal element in Wealth is very significant, showing the accumulation of money and material goods throughout the working life. Opportunities come too late in life for them to be of real use, but retirement is comfortable enough, with sufficient financial resources and time available for enjoyable holidays abroad, revealed by the Water element (travel and communication).

# The Life Cycle chart

One of the great advantages of Chinese astrology is that it lends itself very easily to a method that shows how a life can be mapped out in ten-year periods. These are sometimes also called the 'Luck Pillars' and although the term is clumsy, it is better than 'Decennial Fate Periods', which is the academic translation.

The theory behind the ten-year periods is that it is similar to the 12-year periods of the Chinese zodiac. Just as each of the 12 years in the zodiac cycle represents one Branch of the Great Year, so each of the ten-year periods represents one Stem in a person's lifetime.

Compiling the ten-year periods is straightforward; it is only the interpretation that is difficult. Knowledge comes with practice. As with any form of Chinese astrology, compiling a horoscope chart begins with the Four Columns box (see example below).

### THE FOUR COLUMNS EXAMPLE

|  | Hour | Day | Month | Year |
|---|---|---|---|---|
| Stem | 8 | 3 | 9 | 7 |
| Branch | IV | VII | VII | III |

# Direction

The first thing to know is whether the horoscope will read forwards or backwards (the direction). For males (yang) born in a yang year or for females (yin) born in a yin year, the direction is forwards; otherwise (yang + yin) the direction is backwards. Whether the year is yang or yin is shown by the stem or branch of the year (see pages 204–205).

# The Natal Column

The Natal Column is a ten-year period which includes the date of birth. It is identical to the Month Column, with the same Stem, Branch and related elements. Next, a table of ten-year periods is compiled, the first of which is the Natal Column. It is conventional to write these in Chinese fashion, from right to left (as shown below). The seven periods of ten years covers an average life span.

## THE NATAL COLUMN

| 7th period | 6th period | 5th period | 4th period | 3rd period | 2nd period | 1st period | Natal Column |
|---|---|---|---|---|---|---|---|
| | | | | | | | Month Stem |
| | | | | | | | Month Branch |
| | | | | | | | Month Stem Element |
| | | | | | | | Month Branch Element |

| EXAMPLE A | | |
|---|---|---|
| 2nd period | 1st period | Natal Column |
| 2 | 3 | 4 |
| IV | V | VI |

Once the Natal column is established, the Stems and Branches of the ten-year periods follow in sequence: if the direction is forwards, the number for each stem-and-branch will increase, but if the direction is backwards, they will decrease. For example, if in the Four Columns box (see above) the Month Stem and Branch was 4– VI. Then for a male born in a yang year, the direction is forwards, as it would be for a female born in a yin year as in Example B. For a female born in a yang year or a male born in a yin year the progression would go in reverse (Example A).

## The Ages for the Ten-year Periods

Now we need to know the age at which the ten-year periods start. As there are approximately 30 days in a month and one month in real terms represents a ten-year period, it follows that three days of life must represent one year of a ten-year period. See page 174 for Western dates for the beginnings of Chinese astrological months.

1   If the direction of the horoscope is forwards, count the number of days from the birthday to the start of the next astrological month. Or, if the direction is backwards, count the number of days from the birthday to the start of current astrological month.
2   Divide this number by 3 to find the age at which the ten-year period begins  (Round the figure up or down if necessary.)

**Example:** How to find the age at which the ten-year periods start.

*1   Thus, if the birthday was 11 May and the direction forwards, the number of days to 6 June would be counted (26 days). If the direction was backwards, the number of days would be counted back to 6 May (5 days).*

*2   In the first case  26 ÷ 3 = 9, in the second 5 ÷ 3 = 2.*

The first ten-year period after the Natal Column begins at that age and the other periods follow suit. When the elements associated with the Stems and Branches are added, the Life Cycle Chart is complete.

### EXAMPLE B

| Age 39 | Age 29 | Age 19 | Age 9 | Natal Column |
|--------|--------|--------|-------|--------------|
| 8      | 7      | 6      | 5     | 4            |
| X      | IX     | VIII   | VII   | VI           |

### LIFE CYCLE CHART EXAMPLE

| Age 69 | Age 59 | Age 49 | Age 39 | Age 29 | Age 19 | Age 9 | Natal Column |
|--------|--------|--------|--------|--------|--------|-------|--------------|
| 1      | 10     | 9      | 8      | 7      | 6      | 5     | 4            |
| I      | XII    | XI     | X      | IX     | VIII   | VII   | VI           |
| Wood   | Water  | Water  | Metal  | Metal  | Earth  | Earth | Fire         |
| Water  | Water  | Earth  | Metal  | Metal  | Earth  | Fire  | Fire         |

# Interpreting the Life Cycle chart

In the Life Cycle chart, the key factor is the element of the Stem of the Day. This is the Self and represents the individual in the horoscope; the whole process of interpreting the horoscope is essentially a case of looking at all the elements which surround the Self, to see if they are helpful or adverse.

The element that produces the Self is beneficial; the element that destroys it is harmful. If the Self is Wood, then the aspects of the Four Columns that contain Water would be favourable; aspects that contain Metal would be unfavourable. In the latter case, an exception is if the destructive element is opposite in polarity: such as yin Metal with yang Wood.

## Relationships

One key to the interpretation of the horoscope lies in family relationships. The key element is the Stem of the Day. The Year Column represents the ancestors and grandparents and gives an indication of the origins of family circumstances. The Month Column represents the generation above: parents, uncles and aunts, and those who have authority such as teachers and employers. As the Day Stem is the Self, the Day Branch (or animal) represents the same generation – the spouse, siblings, friends and colleagues. And of course, the Hour Stem-and-Branch represents the generation below – children and employees.

# Elements in the horoscope

The Four Columns should have an even balance of elements, and if any are missing it is important when these appear in the ten-year periods. Too much of a particular element can be destructive; if an element appears in the Four Columns three or more times, it is seen as unfavourable when the same element appears again in a ten-year period.

The strokes of good fortune or ill-luck that might be revealed in the ten-year periods can be related to the type of element. Some of the beneficial qualities of the elements can be found in the table on page 206.

In general, the beneficial qualities are:
- Wood – health and family happiness
- Fire – career success
- Earth – land and residence
- Metal – wealth and commerce
- Water – travel and correspondence.

Adverse strokes of ill-fortune might be:
- Wood – illness
- Fire – loss or theft
- Earth – scandal
- Metal – accident
- Water – frightening circumstances.

**Example:**
We can look at a hypothetical example for a girl born at 06.30 on 25 June 2010. The Four Columns were calculated in the Building the Four Columns section (see pages 200– 205).

## FOUR COLUMNS EXAMPLE

|  | Hour | Day | Month | Year |
|---|---|---|---|---|
| Stem | 8 | 3 | 9 | 7 |
| Branch | IV | VII | VII | III |
|  | Metal | Fire | Water | Metal |
|  | Wood | Fire | Fire | Wood |

Since the year of birth (Tiger) is yang and the horoscope is for a female, the ten-year period will move in reverse. The Natal Column, taken from the month, is 9– VII. Counting backwards from 25 June to 6 June is 19 days; 19 ÷ 3 = 6; so the first period begins at age 6.

The Stem of the Day is 3– Fire, which is the Self element. Of the Four Columns elements, Fire (3 times) is dominant; Metal (2) strong; Earth (1) fair; Wood (1) fair; Water (1) fair. Fire, the Self, is so prominent that its

## LIFE CYCLE CHART EXAMPLE

| Age 66 | Age 56 | Age 46 | Age 36 | Age 26 | Age 16 | Age 6 | Natal Column |
|---|---|---|---|---|---|---|---|
| 2 | 3 | 4 | 5 | 6 | 7 | 8 | 9 |
| XII | I | II | III | IV | V | VI | VII |
|  |  | Ox | Tiger | Rabbit | Dragon | Snake |  |
| Wood | Fire | Fire | Earth | Earth | Metal | Metal | Water |
| Water | Water | Earth | Wood | Wood | Earth | Metal | Fire |

appearance in the ten-year period signifies problems and loss. The two periods beginning at the ages of 26 and 36 reveal the element that produces Fire: Wood; and the element that receives it: Earth. This period is therefore likely to be the most successful in life.

At the age of 46 the success is halted; there is too much Fire, but fortunately there is also Earth to receive it, otherwise it could indicate severe loss. The presence of Earth suggests that any losses were discovered and acted upon before they became too great, although they would probably put paid to any future plans for expansion. At the age of 56 the ten-year period encounters Water, which could be a debilitating factor in the horoscope, save that it is backed by more Fire.

## Further analysis

In addition to the analysis of the Natal Column by looking at the elements, it is also helpful to see which animal signs are present in the ten-year periods, and see how these might affect the overall picture. The section on how each animal sign is affected by the animal of the year can be read as how each animal sign is affected by the animal of the ten year period. In the example, the Year Animal was the Tiger: the ten-year periods beginning at ages 26 and 36 are respectively ruled by the Rabbit and Tiger, two favourable signs for expansion. This actually affirms the previous analysis that these are favourable periods. But when the ten-year period beginning at age 46 approaches, the ten-year period is ruled by the Ox – and 'one Ox can fight two Tigers' indicates that this is when the favourable period comes to an end.

But the combinations of stems and branches have their own interpretations. The next section deals with the general prospects for each stem-and-branch combination. Their influences are of a global nature; whether they are beneficial or otherwise is another dimension that can be added to the interpretation of the horoscope.

# The 60 stems
## and branches

For at least 5,000 years the Chinese have carefully reckoned the prospects of every day by a double sequence of numbers called the Stems and Branches. There are 60 possible combinations of Stems and Branches and each combination has its own special name and prospects for fortune. These prospects can provide additional insights when interpreting a completed horoscope.

# Understanding the Stem and Branch

The Chinese zodiac sign for the year of birth gives an overall impression of the character and qualities of the individual belonging to that animal sign. However, for each animal there are five different types, according to the element of the year. In Chinese astrological terms, the supplementary element represents the 'Stem' of the year, while the animal sign represents the 'Branch' of the year.

## Two elements for every year

It follows that every year must have two elements: one for the Stem (the 'supplementary' element) and one for the Branch. Remember that each animal has its own element peculiar to itself – for example, the Rat, associated with midnight and winter, belongs to the Water element. These would be the Branch elements for those years. When an animal sign is combined with the supplementary Stem element, an extra quality is added. Thus in 1984 the Wood Rat (the first in the series of 60 pairs) combines its own Branch element (Water) with the supplementary element or Stem – in this case Wood. This is a favourable combination since Water is the element that feeds Wood, so the two elements are harmonious. This is not always the case. Chinese families regard people born in the year of the Fire Horse (1966) with great suspicion, because it has 'double Fire'. As the Horse is associated with midday and summer, its own Branch element is Fire, and 1966

*An adult and a child may have the same animal sign, but different elements.*

being a Fire year, the Fire Horse candidate has two supplies of Fire in its horoscope, ready to burn up anyone who crosses its path!

It's useful to take a look at the two years either side of the Fire Horse as well. The Sheep year 1967 was also a Fire Year, but as the Sheep's element is Earth, the combination produces the harmonious pair of Fire supporting Earth. The Snake year 1965 was a Wood year, although the Snake itself is Fire. But again, the combination is favourable because Wood supports Fire.

## Introducing poetic licence

About 600 years ago, an alternative way of classifying the animal signs was devised, which replaced the Stem elements with vivid descriptions of the Twelve Animals. For example, the Wood Rat became known as the Rat on the Roof, and so on. There does not appear to be any logical scheme in the classification, so no doubt these poetic titles were based on the experience of professional astrologers rather than a set formula.

So, the Chinese year can be expressed in four different ways:

- The technical Chinese term; for example, the first of the 60 Stem-and-Branch pairs is called *jia-zi*.
- Non-Chinese identification with a Year cycle number (from 1–60), followed by the Stem and Branch expressed as a number from 1 to 10 for the Stem and a Roman numeral from I to XII for the Branch.
- In popular astrology, using the name of the element in combination with the name of the animal; for example, Wood Rat.
- Some versions of Chinese astrology, the year would be given its poetic name; in this example the Rat on the Roof.

# Year cycle 1 Stem 1 Branch I

**Poetic name** Rat on the Roof
**Element name** Wood Rat
**Prospects** Gold from the Sea
**Years** 1924, 1984

The first of the 60 Stem-and-Branch combinations is King Rat, who surveys the world from his elevated position on the roof. The Stem 1 belongs to the Wood element and the Rat to Water; Wood and Water are in sequence, so this is a favourable combination indicating that the Wood Rat will never go short of material goods in life. The double first (Stem 1 and Branch I) shows that with effort, the Wood Rat could aim

for a high post in politics or government. Such a person has a creative and artistic streak that needs to be channelled positively if the eminent position in life is to be achieved. This is one of two pairs of signs known as 'Gold from the Sea', which indicates the finding of hidden treasure – a legacy later in life, or a successful partnership with someone already wealthy. Traditional Chinese authors say that the Wood Rat is likely to marry later in life and to an older partner.

*The Wood Rat prefers to wait until career matters are settled before marrying.*

## Year cycle 2  Stem 2  Branch II

**Poetic name** Ox from the Sea
**Element name** Wood Ox
**Prospects** Gold from the Sea
**Years** 1925, 1985

This is the second pair of signs called 'Gold from the Sea'. Hard work is more than amply rewarded, and the Wood Ox will enjoy many benefits denied to others. There is much to be gained by being close to the sea, which will be a source of wealth. The Ox will be on familiar terms with people in high places, and though most Ox types are conservative and reluctant to make changes, this Ox is likely to have artistic talents and a determination to improve continually. An ancient Chinese tradition says that the Ox from the Sea lives a virtuous and peaceful life.

## Year cycle 3  Stem 3  Branch III

**Poetic name** Tiger in the Forest
**Element name** Fire Tiger
**Prospects** Fiery Furnace
**Years** 1926, 1986

One of two signs labelled 'Fiery Furnace', this could be the Tiger of which the poet Blake wrote 'Tiger, Tiger, burning bright, in the forests of the night'. Powerful, determined and intolerant of opposition, Fire Tiger types will succeed in whatever sphere of life revolves around them, until, that is, they meet with the kind of non-aggressive opposition for which they are unprepared. Such people are intelligent in many ways; if not academically, then in less conventional ways. They see opportunities all around them, and are able to benefit from challenges.

# Year cycle 4  Stem 4
## Branch IV

**Poetic name** Rabbit dreaming
of the Moon
**Element name** Fire Rabbit
**Prospects** Fiery Furnace
**Years** 1927, 1987

When Chinese children look
at the Moon, they don't see the
face of the 'Man in the Moon'
but the Moon Rabbit. This
particular Rabbit has not yet
achieved its ambition of getting
to the Moon, however, so there
are many unfulfilled ambitions
that may lead to a suppressed
feeling of dissatisfaction with
the world. This combination
(known also as the Fiery Furnace)
produces a very unusual character
whose motives and inclinations
are never clear to outsiders. Fire
Rabbits are likely to have sudden

*The Fire Rabbit may appear distant and
aloof, but is deep in concentration.*

mood changes, being sometimes quiet and unresponsive, and at other
times surprisingly outspoken – so much so that it might cause offence.
Often thought to be withdrawn, the Fire Rabbit is actually a deep
thinker – it is when these ideas are translated into activity that the
problems (for others) arise. There is no stopping the Fire Rabbit when it
embarks on one of its ingenious plans.

## Year cycle 5  Stem 5  Branch V

**Poetic name** Dragon of Pure Virtue
**Element name** Earth Dragon
**Prospects** Forest Wood
**Years** 1928, 1988

Dragons are generally thought of as wild and extrovert, with a touch of magic about them. But this Dragon is much more restrained; the double Earth (Dragon belongs to the Earth element) reveals an inclination towards meditation and contemplation. There is a greater affinity with the younger generation than with older ones, and they may feel that their upbringing was not what they would wish on their own children. They will be respected by their neighbours, particularly for their charitable desire to help those less fortunate than themselves.

## Year cycle 6  Stem 6  Branch VI

**Poetic name** Snake of Happiness
**Element name** Earth Snake
**Prospects** Forest Wood
**Years** 1929, 1989

People born in Earth Snake years have a reputation for wisdom. They live in harmony with their neighbours and are respected members of their communities. They will enjoy happiness and contentment, preferring the simpler pleasures of life, quietly disapproving those who squander their resources on lavish lifestyles and entertainments. They are fond of making things for themselves, have inventive minds and will find ingenious and often unconventional solutions to the banal problems that everyone has to face from time to time.

## Year cycle 7  Stem 7  Branch VII

**Poetic name** Palace Horse
**Element name** Metal Horse
**Prospects** Ditch Earth
**Years** 1930, 1990

The Metal Horse is associated with wealth and is characterized by the emperor's own horse or a horse belonging to one of the royal guards. People born in the Palace Horse year will have contact with the highest authority in the land, perhaps receiving recognition for achievements that have benefitted society. They are very private people, perhaps aloof and wary of strangers, due to the two signs combining to form 'Ditch Earth', which puts a protective cordon around their family life. In business they will succeed in any matters to do with security.

## Year cycle 8  Stem 8  Branch VIII

**Poetic name** Lucky Sheep
**Element name** Metal Sheep
**Prospects** Ditch Earth
**Years** 1931, 1991

Of all the Sheep personalities, this is the one most likely to succeed in business. Some may be envious of the Sheep's successes, which seem to be due more to good luck than good management, but this is because the Happy or Lucky Sheep does not draw attention to all the hard work that goes on behind the scenes. When people comment on the smooth running of the Metal Sheep's life, the Sheep will merely smile and think 'If only they knew!'. The Lucky Sheep always takes care to look elegant in a casual, seemingly effortless way.

*The Metal Horse is essentially a private person, and will do well in a career associated with security matters.*

## Year cycle 9  Stem 9  Branch IX

**Poetic name** Elegant Monkey
**Element name** Water Monkey
**Prospects** Sharp Sword
**Years** 1932, 1992

All Monkeys are complex characters, but the Water or Elegant Monkey is one of the most difficult to understand. The elements of Stem and Branch combined produce the Sharp Sword, giving the Water Monkey a slightly aggressive streak that the Elegant Monkey tries to subjugate. In times of stress, however, it can suddenly surface and cause outbursts of anger that are immediately regretted. The Water element prompts the Monkey to travel frequently and if this urge is frustrated, much time will be spent in other methods of communication by mail or telephone. Such a person would succeed as a manager in a manufacturing company.

*The Water Rooster tends to be impulsive – 'Do now, think later' could be its motto!*

## Year cycle 10  Stem 10  Branch X

**Poetic name** Barnyard Rooster
**Element name** Water Rooster
**Prospects** Sharp Sword
**Years** 1933, 1993

The elements of Stem and Branch combine to make a sharp sword used to cut through knots without waiting to unravel them. This Rooster is very much a practical person, the sort who likes to get on with assembling a flat-pack piece of furniture before reading the instructions. Such a one can't be bothered with the niceties and time-consuming subtleties of diplomacy, preferring to get on with the job in hand. While others discuss what has to be done, the Barnyard Rooster does it. Obviously, this approach does not appeal to everyone and Barnyard Roosters are bound to be controversial, especially since they usually end up being right all along. Such people relax by taking activity holidays and enjoy long-distance travel.

## Year cycle 11  Stem 1  Branch XI

**Poetic name** Guard Dog
**Element name** Wood Dog
**Prospects** Volcano Fire
**Years** 1934, 1994

The 60-year cycle includes two security dogs: this one and the 'Watch Dog' or Water Dog, number 59 in the series. Perhaps surprisingly, since the Wood element usually lends a gentle caring quality to whatever it is associated with, the Wood Dog can be aggressively protective. In Chinese medicine, Wood is associated with anger and this may be at the root of the Wood Dog's fiery defensiveness, but the elements of Stem and Branch also combine to produce Volcano Fire. This quality will stand the Guard Dog in good stead both in home life and in business. Family ties are very strong and in career terms there are prospects of promotion in midlife.

## Year cycle 12  Stem 2  Branch XII

**Poetic name** Travelling Pig
**Element name** Wood Pig
**Prospects** Volcano Fire
**Years** 1935, 1995

In Chinese popular fiction, a pig was one of the companions who accompanied the monk who brought the Buddhist scriptures from India to China. The Travelling Pig is therefore associated with pilgrimage, conscientiousness and a determination to fulfil obligations. As adults, Wood Pigs will be keen to set examples to their children, not just taking care that they come to no harm at the hands of others, but also to ensure that they live exemplary lives, perhaps because they had had difficult times as children themselves, experiencing deprivation and loss. But their early hardship is more than adequately balanced by the comforts awaiting in late middle age, a period of great happiness.

## Year cycle 13  Stem 3  Branch I

**Poetic name** Rat in the Field
**Element name** Fire Rat
**Prospects** Channelled Water
**Years** 1936, 1996

The Fire Rat's life is full of opportunities, but it is up to the Fire Rat to take advantage of them. When outside constraints prevent this Rat from seizing the moment, it can lead to an inner resentment that may be regretted for several years. There will be highs and lows in life; sometimes envious heights will be attained, but circumstances change rapidly, sometimes throwing the Fire Rat into despair. The two elements of Stem and Branch combine to form Channelled Water, and it is the channelling and harnessing of resources that this Rat has to learn. Fame awaits, but not in the way that was expected.

## Year cycle 14  Stem 4  Branch II

**Poetic name** Ox in the Lake
**Element name** Fire Ox
**Prospects** Channelled Water
**Years** 1937, 1997

There is success in store for the Fire Ox who is able to persevere with patience and build on whatever resources are available. Carefully treading through a humdrum and ordered early life, the astute Fire Ox slowly builds up an arsenal of experience and skills that will prove extremely useful when the decisive change of direction is taken in later life. But it is easy for judgement to be clouded; while it is charitable to help others, it is also wise to make provision for times of hardship.

# Year cycle 15 Stem 5 Branch III

**Poetic name** Tiger Climbs the Mountain
**Element name** Earth Tiger
**Prospects** Rampart Earth
**Years** 1938, 1998

The Tiger's usual abode is in the forest where its own stripes merge with the foliage to provide the camouflage it needs when hunting. But on the Mountain, the Tiger is exposed and becomes the prey itself – the hunter hunted indeed. This Earth Tiger therefore needs to make a careful assessment of his or her situation in public and private life. There is a danger that circumstances may appear to be comfortable and assured, but rash and ill-considered actions can lead to the need to make unwanted changes. Risky investments should be avoided; in one's personal life, if friends do not approve of the choice of partner, their advice will be worth serious consideration.

## Year cycle 16  Stem 6  Branch IV

**Poetic name** Rabbit of Woods and Mountains
**Element name** Earth Rabbit
**Prospects** Rampart Earth
**Years** 1939, 1999

The Earth Rabbit strives to lead a quiet and contemplative life,
but circumstances dictate otherwise. No sooner is the Earth Rabbit
settled in one place than the pressures of either family life or
career possibilities result in an urgent need to move or travel,
even so far as moving to another country. If Earth Rabbit people
have not moved themselves, then their children will emigrate,
resulting in occasional long trips to the other side of the world
to be reunited, perhaps temporarily, with their families. Hardships that
were endured in early life, however, are balanced by a comfortable
retirement in a dream home.

## Year cycle 17  Stem 7  Branch V

**Poetic name** Dragon of Patience
**Element name** Metal Dragon
**Prospects** Cast Metal
**Years** 1940, 2000

The Dragon is traditionally associated with money, represented by
the Metal element. Here, not only does the Stem-element Metal
enhance the prospects of wealth, but also the combination of Stem
and Branch produces Cast Metal, meaning metal that has been made
into coins, ingots or jewellery. But while the prospects for financial
gain are extremely potent, the negative aspect is that so much Metal

presents an indication of health problems, especially with regards to the lungs and bronchial passages. Those who seek to make a fortune must avoid tobacco.

## Year cycle 18 Stem 8 Branch VI

**Poetic name** Hibernating Snake
**Element name** Metal Snake
**Prospects** Cast Metal
**Years** 1941, 2001

The Snake belongs to the Fire element, which melts Metal, so the Snake born in a Metal year devours all the financial resources available. Fortunately, the combination of Metal Stem with the Fire Branch produces more Metal, which means that Metal, representing financial resources, can be replaced as fast as it is consumed. But if wealth is to be accumulated, the Metal Snake has to rein in a tendency for luxury spending. By stepping back, which is symbolized by a snake in hibernation, and letting things take their course and not interfering, both personal relationships and business matters might proceed favourably.

*The Metal Snake tends to invest in things which can be enjoyed and seen.*

## Year cycle 19  Stem 9  Branch VII

**Poetic name** War Horse
**Element name** Water Horse
**Prospects** Pliant Wood
**Years** 1942, 2002

The Water Horse combines the opposing elements of Fire and Water, always a danger signal. It produces an unpredictable temperament of rapidly changing moods, which causes outsiders to treat the Water Horse with caution. But since the combination of the conflicting Stem and Branch produces Pliant Wood, it renders the Water Horse susceptible to gentle coercion and the aggressive exterior is only a veneer to mask an inner lack of confidence. The interplay of robustness and flexibility can be used to great advantage when dealing with business matters, but may turn out to be a liability where personal relationships are concerned.

## Year cycle 20  Stem 10  Branch VIII

**Poetic name** Sheep in the Flock
**Element name** Water Sheep
**Prospects** Pliant Wood
**Years** 1943, 2003

Ancient astrologers chose the Sheep to represent the eighth branch because it represented the yin or receptive force, and as flocks of sheep are all female it was an appropriate sign to represent the feminine side of nature. The Water Sheep, therefore, represents the gentler side of human nature, the arts rather than the sciences, particularly music, dancing and romantic fiction. In personal relationships, the focus is on

*The Water Sheep loves marriage so much that one wedding may not be enough!*

marriage and weddings, and whether the Water Sheep is a man or a woman, it is likely that the number of personal commitments (whether they are established marriages or long-term partnerships) in the Water Sheep's life will be greater than one.

## Year cycle 21  Stem 1  Branch IX

**Poetic name** Tree Monkey
**Element name** Wood Monkey
**Prospects** Rains and Springs
**Years** 1944, 2004

A tree is an appropriate environment for a Monkey and thus with the Wood Monkeys we have people who are at home with their surroundings – uncomplicated, gentle and eager to make friends. Instead of the wild uncontrollable mischief-maker, the Wood Monkey has special skills and knows how to put them to beneficial use. This very creative character is full of ideas and has manual skills to produce things that bring pleasure to the fortunate receiver of the Wood Monkey's handiwork. The Stem and Branch combine to create the Water element, the element of communication, making the Wood Monkey a persuasive and diplomatic communicator who, with charm and humour, is often able to settle disputes among friends and colleagues.

## Year cycle 22  Stem 2  Branch X

**Poetic name** Rooster Crowing at Noon
**Element name** Wood Rooster
**Prospects** Rains and Springs
**Years** 1945, 2005

Why should a Rooster crow at noon? A false alarm can cause insecurity and the Wood Rooster may go through life bearing the weight of phobias, which outsiders fail to understand. These can be the result of being coerced into accepting situations that are unwelcome, or being forced into tight corners where there seems no possibility of escape. But the courageous Wood Rooster, having determined to defy authority at the last possible moment, will nevertheless feel guilty about making that momentous decision. Unnecessarily so, for the action is a positive step in creating a new and challenging life.

## Year cycle 23  Stem 3  Branch XI

**Poetic name** Sleeping Dog
**Element name** Fire Dog
**Prospects** Rooftop Slates
**Years** 1946, 2006

The Sleeping Dog is a sign that all is secure; the Stem and Branch elements combine to form Rooftop Slates, the surest protection against storms. Nevertheless, the Sleeping Dog should not be too complacent; the unexpected happens and it is important to have contingency resources that can be drawn upon when unforeseen circumstances arise. It is important not to rely too much on others, for their assistance may not be forthcoming when most needed.

*The words 'Fire Pig' may not immediately suggest meditation and piety, but in fact this is one of the most spiritual of the 60 signs.*

## Year cycle 24  Stem 4  Branch XII

**Poetic name** Pig Crossing a Mountain
**Element name** Fire Pig
**Prospects** Rooftop Slates
**Years** 1947, 2007

The Fire Pig is on a quest to find the things that will improve life. Whether this is for material advantage for the family or for something more uplifting such as spiritual enlightenment, the Fire Pig is constantly searching to discover ways in which human wellbeing and happiness and the enjoyment of life can be improved. If this is at the cost of some personal sacrifice, the Fire Pig is unconcerned, for the eventual benefits are more important than present comforts.

## Year cycle 25  Stem 5  Branch I

**Poetic name** Rat in the Granary
**Element name** Earth Rat
**Prospects** Lightning Fire
**Years** 1948, 2008

Although the Rat in the Granary may not be the King Rat, at least he has discovered the ideal location! People born in the year of the Earth Rat often find themselves by happy chance in unexpectedly beneficial situations, not through subscribing to the lottery or games of chance, but through chance meetings with influential people – being in the right place at the right time. But they should be careful of becoming too reliant on these fortunate circumstances. The combination of the Stem-and-Branch elements produces Lightning Fire, a warning that sudden disaster may strike at any moment. Be prepared for all eventualities.

## Year cycle 26  Stem 6  Branch II

**Poetic name** Ox in the Byre
**Element name** Earth Ox
**Prospects** Lightning Fire
**Years** 1949, 2009

The Earth Ox or Ox in the Byre signifies the Ox who is at rest in his or her own environment. It signifies satisfaction with one's circumstances, whether these might be considered by others to be favourable or otherwise. All things are in moderation, and life is neither too hectic nor too slow. When catastrophes arise, as predicted by the Stem and Branch creating Lightning Fire, the Ox is unconcerned, for ample provision has been made against any untoward eventuality. Its foresight and practicality earn the respect of the community and family life is happy, no matter how complicated.

## Year cycle 27  Stem 7 Branch III

**Poetic name** Tiger Leaves the Mountain
**Element name** Metal Tiger
**Prospects** Hardwood
**Years** 1950, 2010

The Stem and Branch of Metal and Wood combine to make Hardwood, difficult to hew, but possessing strength and permanence. Thus the Metal Tiger symbolizes the fruits of a successful career, which will bring rich rewards for determination and careful management of

*The Metal Tiger especially will look for a partner with business acumen.*

resources. In matters of personal relationships, the Metal Tiger seeks someone who will share business or career interests as well as family life, for it is by their joint efforts that happiness and successes are assured. In matters of health, stamina and a strong constitution will overcome illness.

# Year cycle 28  Stem 8  Branch IV

**Poetic name** Rabbit in the Burrow
**Element name** Metal Rabbit
**Prospects** Hardwood
**Years** 1951, 2011

The Metal Rabbit is able to combine a happy home life with successful career and business prospects. The favourable factors that provide this fortunate environment are that the Rabbit in the Burrow is in its own environment and everything is in place where it should be. The Rabbit itself belonging to the Wood element is a sign that relationships with the younger generation are harmonious; the combination of the Stem element Metal with the Rabbit's Wood produces Hardwood giving added strength and vigour to aid the Rabbit in all enterprises.

*The Metal Rabbit has the greatest chance of combining a prosperous business with a happy family and home life.*

# Year cycle 29 Stem 9 Branch V

**Poetic name** Rain Dragon
**Element name** Water Dragon
**Prospects** Flowing Water
**Years** 1952, 2012

When the Dragon constellation appears in
the sky, it signifies the beginning of the rainy
season; Chinese Dragons live in the water, so the Water Dragon is happy
in its favoured environment. The spring rains are vital for watering the
crops and filling the ponds and streams, and in Chinese parlance, Water
is synonymous with wealth, so the arrival of the Rain Dragon signifies
monetary gains. Flowing Water underlines the financial gains to be made
from those who are prepared to travel and change their residence often.

# Year cycle 30 Stem 10 Branch VI

**Poetic name** Snake in the Grass
**Element name** Water Snake
**Prospects** Flowing Water
**Years** 1953, 2013

The Snake person born in a Water year is not, paradoxically, a snake that
lives in the water. That particular snake is the Fire Snake, number 54 in
the 60-year sequence. Instead, this snake lives in the grass where it
hides to avoid capture and also to catch the careless traveller unawares.
People born in the Water Snake year tend to be very reserved, keep their
own counsel and are excellent at keeping secrets. They like to travel but
to unusual destinations; holidays are taken well away from the beaten
track and culture is more important than camaraderie.

## Year cycle 31  Stem 1  Branch VII

**Poetic name** Horse in the Clouds
**Element name** Wood Horse
**Prospects** Excavated Metal
**Years** 1954, 2014

The Wood element associated with the year gives this Horse imagination and artistic leanings, as well as ambition that is not always realistic. The Horse in the Clouds juggles a life between what is practicable and what might be. Always in company with friends and colleagues, nevertheless, this type often has a faraway look, as if belonging to another world. Indeed, while the feet are firmly planted on the ground, thoughts are in another sphere. Given the chance to develop inventive talents, and with hard work and determination the Horse in the Clouds can make a fortune.

## Year cycle 32  Stem 2 Branch VIII

**Poetic name** Serious Sheep
**Element name** Wood Sheep
**Prospects** Excavated Metal
**Years** 1955, 2015

The Stem and Branches combine to produce Excavated Metal, wealth that is obtained only

*The creative Wood Sheep will work hard, but acquire wealth through labour.*

246

through hard work and determined effort. Gold miners make a fortune with their lucky finds, but the harder they work, the luckier they get. This is why this particular sheep is so serious; career and business are weighty matters. And only when finances are not only secure but surplus to what is necessary can the family be considered comfortably well off. As is often the case with Sheep personalities, there may be unnecessary worries about the children's upbringing. Time, however, will sort things out.

## Year cycle 33  Stem 3  Branch IX

**Poetic name** Monkey on the Mountain
**Element name** Fire Monkey
**Prospects** Foothill Fire
**Years** 1956, 2016

The Stem and Branch combine to form Foothill Fire, a campfire at the base of a mountain where explorers rest and revive before setting off on an expedition. This is the adventurous Monkey, always willing to tackle a new venture and is not averse to taking risks. Consequently, because of his or her somewhat reckless nature, this might be a dangerous companion to take along on a hazardous journey. Nevertheless, when there are real problems, the Mountain Monkey will come to the rescue. An interesting life lies ahead with many challenges to be faced but these are eventually overcome.

## Year cycle 34  Stem 4
## Branch X

**Poetic name** Solitary Rooster
**Element name** Fire Rooster
**Prospects** Foothill Fire
**Years** 1957, 2017

This Rooster works best alone; there are too many special ideas that only this Rooster can deal with adequately. It is pointless trying to delegate, because other people are quite incompetent and will only ruin plans. At least, that is what the Solitary Rooster believes. Past experience has often proved this Rooster's belief to be correct, but fortunately it is not always so; life will become so much easier when the Fire Rooster comes to terms with the reality that sometimes one has to make do with second-best. The Stem and Branch combination *dingyou* sounds like the Chinese for 'spiced wine' so there are some luxuries this Solitary Rooster can enjoy!

## Year cycle 35  Stem 5  Branch XI

**Poetic name** Dog on the Mountain
**Element name** Earth Dog
**Prospects** Scrubland Twigs
**Years** 1958, 2018

It is a hard life living on a mountain and without food and shelter life can be difficult. But this is the life that the Dog on the Mountain has chosen. It indicates someone who will volunteer to help others, no matter how inconvenient, even when it entails great cost or personal sacrifice. The Dog on the Mountain is adept at making do with whatever is at hand and knows that the most trivial items may some day have a vital use. But such untiring efforts bring the Dog on the Mountain considerable respect and earns such a dedicated personality an honoured place in the community.

## Year cycle 36  Stem 6  Branch XII

**Poetic name** Monastic Pig
**Element name** Earth Pig
**Prospects** Scrubland Twigs
**Years** 1959, 2019

The Wood Pig (number 12 in the 60-year cycle) set off on a pilgrimage, the Fire Pig (number 24) encountered hardship and now the Monastic Pig has succeeded in his or her quest. Although the Earth Pig may not gain material riches, this person will achieve their ambitions in many

different spheres, receiving awards and plaudits for many successes. The humbler the Monastic Pig's situation, the greater will be the individual's standing in society. In family life, the Monastic Pig will be an authoritative parent, in personal relationships, faithful and true.

*The protective Earth Pig has the qualities to be a firm but understanding parent.*

## Year cycle 37 Stem 7 Branch I

**Poetic name** Rat on the Crossbeam
**Element name** Metal Rat
**Prospects** Earthen Walls
**Years** 1960, 2020

Although not as highly placed as the Rat on the Roof (the first animal in the 60-year cycle) the Rat on the Crossbeam is closer to where the action is. Such people are the go-betweens linking ordinary folk to the more privileged, and naturally such people make ideal agents and public relations consultants. They are able to find something profitable in whatever is around them and can quickly assess a promising situation and take advantage of it. In personal relationships, they need to take care that they do not take their partners for granted.

## Year cycle 38 Stem 8 Branch II

**Poetic name** Ox on the Road
**Element name** Metal Ox
**Prospects** Earthen Walls
**Years** 1961, 2021

The Ox person born in a Metal year becomes the Ox on the Road, someone who feels that they have a goal in life which they persevere to attain. The road is not a geographical path, but rather a direction in life, the desire to realize an ambition that may take many years to achieve. But solid determination is part of the Ox person's characteristics and from small successes greater things will come. In retirement, the financial situation will be much more comfortable than it was in middle age. Strong family loyalties secure a rich home life.

*The Water Tiger likes to keep on the move; even travelling to work daily becomes a fulfilling experience rather than a chore.*

## Year cycle 39  Stem 9  Branch III

**Poetic name** Tiger in the Forest
**Element name** Water Tiger
**Prospects** Bronze Mirror
**Years** 1962, 2022

This is a mysterious sign that combines the charisma of the Tiger with the gift of prophesy. This Tiger lives in the forest, which serves to hide it from hunters as well as from its prey. But this Tiger has other gifts: Stem and Branch combine to produce the Bronze Mirror, which is not only used as a personal accessory but also as a means to look into the future. Decorated with astronomical signs the Bronze Mirror looks on another world. This Tiger is perceptive, a good judge of character and able to determine the truthful from the dishonest. Given the option between moving to another city or staying put and commuting, the Water Tiger would opt for the latter course.

## Year cycle 40  Stem 10  Branch IV

**Poetic name** Rabbit Leaving the Forest
**Element name** Water Rabbit
**Prospects** Bronze Mirror
**Years** 1963, 2023

The Stem and Branch combine to create the lucrative Metal element, revealed as a Bronze Mirror, described in the previous paragraph as a way of seeing the future. The Rabbit Leaving the Forest means that in early life home circumstances were not the most convenient or comfortable. As soon as an opportunity arose, there would be little hesitation in deciding to move to a different area. With commonsense and determination this Rabbit will lead a very successful life. Family members will be scattered to different locations in later life.

## Year cycle 41  Stem 1  Branch V

**Poetic name** Dragon in the Whirlpool
**Element name** Wood Dragon
**Prospects** Lamplight
**Years** 1964, 2024

This Dragon person combines an artistic personality with quiet restraint and good taste. Social behaviour is refined, dress elegant and the speaking voice attractive. Such a person can move forwards in society and can host occasions for which invitations are a privilege. While remaining quietly in the background, this person will mix with those celebrities who prefer the comfort of discreet soirées to lavish spectaculars.

*The creative Wood Snake can transform work into a pleasurable experience.*

## Year cycle 42  Stem 2
## Branch VI

**Poetic name**
Snake Leaves its Hole
**Element name** Wood Snake
**Prospects** Lamplight
**Years** 1965, 2025

The Wood Snake's horoscope reveals the resources of an academic researcher or a collector of fine art. Such a person would follow a career which could employ the Wood Snake's inquisitive mind, not so much in popular journalism, but in historical investigation, enjoying the excitement of unravelling mysteries of the past. Satisfaction in career is of greater value than amassing wealth. Take care not to let one's natural curiosity be mistaken for impolite intrusion into other people's affairs, interesting though they may be. The Wood Snake enjoys mental puzzles.

*In China, boys born in the turbulent year of the Fire Horse are regarded with apprehension. They are proverbially renowned for their charisma and virility.*

## Year cycle 43  Stem 3  Branch VII

**Poetic name** Travelling Horse
**Element name** Fire Horse
**Prospects** The River Han (the Milky Way)
**Years** 1966, 2026

The bad news first. The Fire Horse year is the one that Chinese families used to dread, since it was said that the children born in that year were destined to be tyrants! In not-so-ancient China, marriage prospects for baby girls born in a Fire Horse year were considered negligible and it was not uncommon for despairingly poor families to expose their children by the roadside, a practice that persisted until the early part of the last century. However, the good news is that Fire Horses are sure to achieve great successes in life with the choicest careers and splendid prospects for advancement, and gentlemen will find themselves overwhelmed by admiring ladies. Fire Horse ladies, however, must make their choice and take the initiative.

# Year cycle 44  Stem 4  Branch VIII

**Poetic name** Lost Sheep
**Element name** Fire Sheep
**Prospects** The River Han (the Milky Way)
**Years** 1967, 2027

It might not seem very complimentary to be labelled a lost sheep, but actually this animal has decided to strike out on its own instead of being one of the herd. Perhaps this Sheep has not yet decided what his or her role in life is to be, but there is only one way to find out and that is to experiment This Sheep's horoscope already contains Fire of intelligence, the stamina of Earth and Water, the River Han that flows so far that it reaches the sky. Lost, perhaps; ambitious, certainly.

# Year cycle 45  Stem 5  Branch IX

**Poetic name** Independent Monkey
**Element name** Earth Monkey
**Prospects** Roadworks Earth
**Years** 1968, 2028

Also breaking away from the common herd or troupe in this case, is the Independent Monkey. The Monkey's skills and technological gifts are supported by the Earth in the year of birth and also in the result of the combination of the Stem and Branch of the year. Earth supports Metal, symbolizing wealth, so there are ample resources for this Monkey to draw upon. By following its own road, this Monkey will reach the pinnacle of ambition. Being such a free spirit means that the Independent Monkey needs an understanding partner.

## Year cycle 46 Stem 6 Branch X

**Poetic name** Rooster Pecking for Food
**Element name** Earth Rooster
**Prospects** Roadworks Earth
**Years** 1969, 2029

This busy Rooster takes advantage of a period of plenty. The Rooster's own element is Metal and since Metal is mined from the Earth, the combination signifies that there are ample resources for the Rooster to exploit. This industrious Rooster doesn't sit in isolation on the henhouse roof but joins the workers on the ground below. Leading by example, rather than instruction, the Rooster earns respect and gratitude. Family life is harmonious when there is cooperation from all levels.

*The Earth Rooster is the most stable and sympathetic of the five types of Rooster, generating affection within the family through trust.*

## Year cycle 47  Stem 7  Branch XI

**Poetic name** Temple Dog
**Element name** Metal Dog
**Prospects** Brooch Pins
**Years** 1970, 2030

It is not easy for the Temple Dog to have so many responsibilities. Few people appreciate how things could go wrong as a result of misguided actions; the Temple Dog worries that its warnings will go unheeded and not without cause. Maybe the time has come to consider what is best for oneself and leave others to solve their own problems. Trying to help the undeserving becomes a drain on personal finances and mental assets as well. Take time to relax and let matters take their course.

## Year cycle 48  Stem 8  Branch XII

**Poetic name** Farmer Pig
**Element name** Metal Pig
**Prospects** Brooch Pins
**Years** 1971, 2031

There are two types of tiredness: on the one hand weary exhaustion and on the other the satisfaction that is gained from painstaking effort and hard work. It is this second kind of tiredness with which the happy Farmer Pig is most familiar. The combination of Stem and Branch of the year produces Brooch Pins, a minor extravagance, which signifies that the financial position is sufficiently secure to allow the Farmer Pig's family to enjoy some of the luxuries not usually associated with a rustic existence. Family life is happy, and the children well cared for and able to enjoy privileges denied to their friends.

*The Water or Mountain Rat turns its creative talents to the arts, often developing a personal specialised technique.*

## Year cycle 49 Stem 9 Branch I

**Poetic name** Rat on the Mountain
**Element name** Water Rat
**Prospects** Mulberry Wood
**Years** 1912, 1972

It seems odd that the Rat born in a Water year should be called the Rat on the Mountain. This unusual personality relishes being in different or challenging environments and often likes to get away from the usual crowd in order to do something unexpected and different. There is a special quality about this person that puzzles some people; they wonder what it is that drives the Mountain Rat to do things that are so out of the ordinary. Such people have an artistic touch and are experts in their own special field.

## Year cycle 50  Stem 10  Branch II

**Poetic name** Ox by the Gate
**Element name** Water Ox
**Prospects** Mulberry Wood
**Years** 1913, 1973

The Ox by the Gate is waiting to embark on a new direction in life; the horoscope signs suggest there will be a great change in this person's life, transforming it in an extraordinary way. Although it will come somewhat suddenly, it will be as if the Ox knew all along that there would be a great difference in his or her circumstances at some stage in life, even though there had been no tangible reason to believe so. Fortunately, the Ox is too sensible to let any apprehensions of future changes prevent leading a normal energetic life.

## Year cycle 51  Stem 1  Branch III

**Poetic name** Tiger Stands Firm
**Element name** Wood Tiger
**Prospects** Fresh Stream Water
**Years** 1914, 1974

This Tiger is blessed with a wealth of creative resources and the opportunities to travel are wide open. But for reasons best known to this Tiger, it prefers not to be dislodged from its favoured position. There are so many variables in a fast-changing world that it may seem sensible to stay with what one knows best. Whether this results in missed opportunities will never be known and it is futile to ponder what might have been. Instead of regretting taking a step into the unknown, enjoy the undoubted satisfaction of having been right all along.

## Year cycle 52  Stem 2  Branch IV

**Poetic name** Enlightened Rabbit
**Element name** Wood Rabbit
**Prospects** Fresh Stream Water
**Years** 1915, 1975

There are plenty of opportunities for the Wood Rabbit. Whatever choices are presented, the Enlightened Rabbit will take them and use the situation to advantage. Career life is likely to proceed along a zigzag path. This gives the Enlightened Rabbit experience in many aspects of life, all of which will prove to be valuable in the future. Partnerships may not be permanent, but there is no bitterness when life has to change. The Enlightened Rabbit will have great influence on the lives of others, but with none of the accountability attached.

## Year cycle 53  Stem 3  Branch V

**Poetic name** Dragon in the Sky
**Element name** Fire Dragon
**Prospects** Sand and Clay
**Years** 1916, 1976

The Stem and Branch of the year produce Sand and Clay, which is neither good for building nor for making pots. This means that the Fire Dragon has to make his or her own way in the world. It is futile to depend on others, since their promises prove to be worthless. Funds and resources that were thought to be reliable will have been over-valued. But by trusting one's own judgement rather than relying on experts, it is possible to avoid the pitfalls that overtake those who are more complacent. Imagination and intuition lead to success.

*The Fire of the Fire Snake is more illuminating than burning, and often sheds light on complex problems.*

## Year cycle 54  Stem 4  Branch VI

**Poetic name** Snake in the Pool
**Element name** Fire Snake
**Prospects** Sand and Clay
**Years** 1917, 1977

Intelligence and wisdom are revealed by the Snake born in a Fire year. As the Snake's own (Branch) element is also Fire, the Fire Snake has double Fire, like the notorious Fire Horse (number 43 in the 60-year cycle). The difference, however, is that the Fire Snake is a yin sign and therefore lacks the potential aggression that is said to be the mark of the Fire Horse. The Snake in the Pool cools its fire, directing its energies into both the contemplation of present circumstances and the planning of future strategies.

# Year cycle 55  Stem 5  Branch VII

**Poetic name** Horse in the Stable
**Element name** Earth Horse
**Prospects** Heavenly Fire
**Years** 1918, 1978

Of the five Horses in the Chinese 60-year cycle, the one born in an Earth year is the one that most fits the astrological perception of the Horse type: someone who is reliable, sociable and dependable. But here is someone also blessed with an individuality that does not continually recycle other people's ideas, but often comes up with fresh notions of great originality. The Horse in the Stable may startle colleagues with frank assessments of situations that had been taken for granted, and is not afraid to voice a controversial opinion. Family and home life are happy and harmonious.

*The Earth Horse is a dependable, hard worker whose life centres on the welfare of the family.*

## Year cycle 56  Stem 6  Branch VIII

**Poetic name** Sheep in Pasture
**Element name** Earth Sheep
**Prospects** Heavenly Fire
**Years** 1919, 1979

Like its partner Horse above, the Sheep born in an Earth year finds itself in its natural, indeed a very green, environment. No matter what happens in life, this Sheep can always find something positive and encouraging to rejoice in. An optimistic nature spreads happiness contagiously and the Earth Sheep will never be short of friends. The Stem and Branch combine to form Heavenly Fire, which some authorities take to mean artistic inspiration. Family life and personal relationships, despite the occasional setback, are satisfying and emotionally fulfilling.

## Year cycle 57  Stem 7  Branch IX

**Poetic name** Monkey Eating Fruit
**Element name** Metal Monkey
**Prospects** Pomegranate Wood
**Years** 1920, 1980

This particular Monkey personality, whose own element is Metal, was born in a Metal year, so the horoscope has an internal harmony that leads to success and personal achievement. The Monkey is associated with technical or manual skills and as Metal is associated with money, the Monkey who follows a career involving crafts or assembly work will find ample financial reward. In personal matters, to ensure a smooth running relationship, it will be helpful to avoid being too demanding and it is important to leave some decisions to the partner.

## Year cycle 58  Stem 8  Branch X

**Poetic name** Caged Rooster
**Element name** Metal Rooster
**Prospects** Pomegranate Wood
**Years** 1921, 1981

Although this Rooster, whose own Branch element is Metal, was born in
a Metal year, the combination is not as auspicious as it might be – in
Chinese, the words for the Stem and Branch of the year, *xinyou*, sound like
'bitter wine'. There is a feeling that life has much more to offer and that
the present circumstances are restricting. The artistic Rooster needs an
outlet for its creative impulses, and if denied the freedom to experiment,
will feel frustrated and anxious. Perhaps time can be set aside for the
expression of latent talents, in whatever sphere is most attractive. Do
not let a sense of disappointment spoil personal relationships.

## Year cycle 59  Stem 9  Branch XI

**Poetic name** Watch Dog
**Element name** Water Dog
**Prospects** Sea Water
**Years** 1922, 1982

This is the second of the security dogs in the
60-year cycle, the other being the Guard Dog,
number 11 in the series. Although also a guard dog,
this dog's job is merely to watch and report, rather
than taking action. Thus this Dog personality is both
alert and tactful, exercising caution and prudence
before hastily rushing into situations that can only

get more complicated. These qualities will see the Dog advancing quietly through his or her career, being recognized as a valuable asset to management, while companions, friends and those in closer personal relationships will be grateful for the Watch Dog's prudent consideration.

## Year cycle 60  Stem 10  Branch XII

**Poetic name** Pig in the Forest
**Element name** Water Pig
**Prospects** Sea Water
**Years** 1923, 1983

Whereas Chinese astrology usually considers the Pig to be a gentle, home-loving type, the Pig born in a Water year has other qualities. This is the Pig in the Forest, the Wild Boar who can be such a dangerous adversary. Defensive of home and family, the Pig in the Forest is likely to work industriously and even aggressively to provide the best environment and welfare that can be afforded. The Stem and Branch of the year combine to produce the Sea, the symbol of a vast expanse of unknown resources ready for the taking by all those who dare to venture forward.

*The final sign is symbolized by the vast resources of the Sea.*

# Exploring further

Chinese astrology isn't confined to the horoscope. This chapter offers tantalizing glimpses into the many different aspects of life touched by this subject. It shows how Chinese astrology can help you with everything from finding favourable days to the ways in which Chinese medicine is influenced by the same principles that govern Chinese astrology.

# The 28 Animals

As well as the familiar 12 Animals of the Chinese zodiac, popular almanacs occasionally refer to another set of 28 Animals. These date back to the 6th century at least, which is about the same time that the 12 zodiac animals made their first appearance. Among these 28 creatures are the familiar 12 Animals of the Chinese zodiac; the extra animals in the longer sequence have some zoological similarity to their neighbouring zodiac signs, such as Pheasant–Rooster, Monkey–Ape or Tiger–Leopard.

However, among the 28 Animals, the sequence of the original 12 Animals runs in reverse order to their usual cycle. This is because the 28 Animals originally represented constellations in the sky, a map of which is a mirror image of a geographical map. The familiar 12 Animals represent the Earthly Branches, but the 28 Animals represent stars and constellations. Thus, to avoid confusion with the 12 Animal cycle, whenever the names of the 12 'earthly' animals appear among the

28, they are prefixed with the word 'sky'. The reason for this is that the names have been added to the 28 segments of the sky into which Chinese astronomers divided the four great constellations: Dragon, Tortoise, Tiger and Bird.

## THE 28 ANIMALS AND THEIR CONSTELLATIONS

| Green Dragon of Spring | Black Tortoise of Winter | White Tiger of Autumn | Red Bird of Summer |
|---|---|---|---|
| 1 Salamander | 8 Unicorn | 15 Wolf | 22 Tapir |
| 2 Sky Dragon | 9 Sky Ox | 16 Sky Dog | 23 Sky Sheep |
| 3 Marten | 10 Bat | 17 Pheasant | 24 Roebuck |
| 4 Sky Rabbit | 11 Sky Rat | 18 Sky Rooster | 25 Sky Horse |
| 5 Fox | 12 Swallow | 19 Raven | 26 Deer |
| 6 Sky Tiger | 13 Sky Pig | 20 Sky Monkey | 27 Sky Snake |
| 7 Leopard | 14 Porcupine | 21 Ape | 28 Worm |

## Which came first?

As both menageries made their appearance at about the same time, it is difficult to say with any certainty which of the two lists came first. Was the cycle of 28 an extended version of the 12, or was the 12 a reduced version of the 28? The likelihood, though without tangible evidence to support it, is that the zodiac of 12 Animals was already established in popular culture and the 28 Animals was an elaboration of the system.

The 28 Animals were used as names of the days of a four-week period. Popular astrology determined a person's fate from the animal ruling the day on which a person was born. To find the ruling animal for any day, use the tables on the follow pages and follow the outlined steps.

# How to find the Animal of the day

The table shown opposite how to find which of the 28 Animals rules any chosen day.

1 First find the required year and note down the code number found in the right-hand column.

2 Then find the month and again note down the code number in the right-hand column.

3 Next, note down the day of the required month.

4 Add the numbers together.

5 Finally, if the year is a leap year (*marked with * in the table*) and the date is 1 March or later (in order to account for the extra day in February) add 1.

6 If the total is more than 28, subtract 28, or if more than 56, subtract 56.

7 Use the chart on page 269 and use your final number to get the Animal sign for the required day.

**Example:** What is the animal of the day for the 9 March 1960.

1 *From the table, the code for 1960 is 23.*

2 *The code for March is 2.*

3 *The day of the required month is 9.*

4 *The numbers added together (23 + 2 + 9) = 34.*

5 *As 1960 is a leap year and the date is after 1 March add 1, giving a total of 35.*

6 *As this is more than 28, subtract 28 from the total (35 − 28) = 7.*
   *Answer 7*

7 *Using the chart on page 269 we see that 7 refers to Leopard.*

## THE ANIMAL OF THE DAY

| Month | Year | | | | | Code |
|---|---|---|---|---|---|---|
| | 1920* | 1942 | | 1987 | 2009 | 1 |
| Feb, March | | 1943 | 1965 | 1988* | 2010 | 2 |
| | 1921 | 1944* | 1966 | | 2011 | 3 |
| | 1922 | | 1967 | 1989 | 2012* | 4 |
| April | 1923 | 1945 | 1968* | 1990 | | 5 |
| | 1924* | 1946 | | 1991 | 2013 | 6 |
| May | | 1947 | 1969 | 1992* | 2014 | 7 |
| | 1925 | 1948* | 1970 | | 2015 | 8 |
| | 1926 | | 1971 | 1993 | 2016* | 9 |
| June | 1927 | 1949 | 1972* | 1994 | | 10 |
| | 1928* | 1950 | | 1995 | 2017 | 11 |
| July | | 1951 | 1973 | 1996* | 2018 | 12 |
| | 1929 | 1952* | 1974 | | 2019 | 13 |
| | 1930 | | 1975 | 1997 | 2020* | 14 |
| August | 1931 | 1953 | 1976* | 1998 | | 15 |
| | 1932* | 1954 | | 1999 | 2021 | 16 |
| | | 1955 | 1977 | 2000* | 2022 | 17 |
| September | 1933 | 1956* | 1978 | | 2023 | 18 |
| | 1934 | | 1979 | 2001 | 2024* | 19 |
| October | 1935 | 1957 | 1980* | 2002 | | 20 |
| | 1936* | 1958 | | 2003 | 2025 | 21 |
| | | 1959 | 1981 | 2004* | 2026 | 22 |
| November | 1937 | 1960* | 1982 | | 2027 | 23 |
| | 1938 | | 1983 | 2005 | 2028* | 24 |
| December | 1939 | 1961 | 1984* | 2006 | | 25 |
| | 1940* | 1962 | | 2007 | 2029 | 26 |
| January | | 1963 | 1985 | 2008* | 2030 | 27 |
| | 1941 | 1964* | 1986 | | 2031 | 28 |

# Signs of the Dragon

## 1  Salamander  Thursday

The first of the 28 Animals signifies generation and growth and may lead those born under its sign, which always appears on a Thursday, to a career in garden design or agriculture. Outside the botanical world, the first sign stimulates the imagination and inventive mind, and people born under its sign are likely to be pioneers and innovators.

**Famous Salamanders** Beatles songwriter Paul McCartney; celebrated actress Sophia Loren.

## 2  Sky Dragon  Friday

The second sign warns of troubles in later life, but that good fortune comes to those who are patient and industrious. Some astrologers of old linked this sign with alchemy, in modern terms the chemical industry, perhaps because Dragons are said to breathe fire and change the composition of substances.

**Famous Dragons** Pope Benedict; singers Barbra Streisand and Shirley Bassey; American television interviewer Barbara Walters; comedian Eric Morecambe.

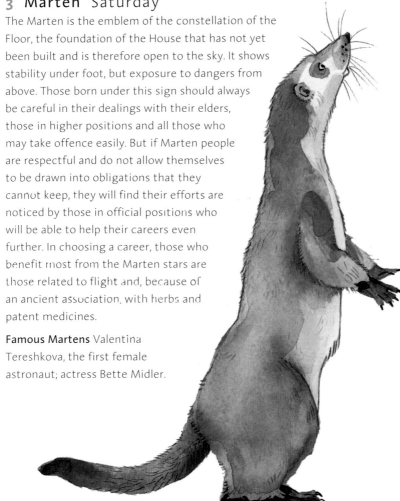

## 3 Marten Saturday

The Marten is the emblem of the constellation of the Floor, the foundation of the House that has not yet been built and is therefore open to the sky. It shows stability under foot, but exposure to dangers from above. Those born under this sign should always be careful in their dealings with their elders, those in higher positions and all those who may take offence easily. But if Marten people are respectful and do not allow themselves to be drawn into obligations that they cannot keep, they will find their efforts are noticed by those in official positions who will be able to help their careers even further. In choosing a career, those who benefit most from the Marten stars are those related to flight and, because of an ancient association, with herbs and patent medicines.

**Famous Martens** Valentina Tereshkova, the first female astronaut; actress Bette Midler.

## 4 Sky Rabbit Sunday

After the constellation of the Floor, the next group of stars comprises the finished Room, guarded by the Sky Rabbit. In ancient times, this constellation, being an 'extra room', was associated with extended families, and is a beneficial sign for all matters pertaining to surrogate parenthood. Accordingly, all those who work with interior spaces, whether in architectural design, soft furnishings or decorating will benefit from the Sky Rabbit's influence. Because of this, it is an extremely appropriate sign for those who have an interest in feng shui counselling.

**Famous Sky Rabbits** Film star and backgammon player Omar Sharif.

## 5  Fox  Monday

To succeed in business and make one's way to the front, a person needs quick wits, the ability to catch the right moment and personal charm. People born under this sign have these gifts in spades. The Fox's related constellation is the Heart of the Dragon, one of the signs associated with the emperor and a sign of promotion to high position.

**Famous Foxes** Artist Andy Warhol; the stunt rider Evel Knievel; singer Cliff Richard; composer of blockbuster musicals Andrew Lloyd Webber.

## 6  Sky Tiger  Tuesday

The royal Sky Tiger is the emblem of the emperor's heir apparent, and helps those born under this sign along the path to political office. The heir apparent implies wealth acquired through inheritance and hidden or unexpected benefits in later life. Those who apply themselves diligently to their work will succeed and earn more than they can spend.

**Famous Sky Tigers** Actor Peter Sellers; first man on the Moon, Neil Armstrong; Formula 1 racing driver Niki Lauda.

## 7  Leopard  Wednesday

The Leopard has a basketful of all the necessities of life to give to those born under this sign; and since the basket lies under the Dragon's tail, it may even be filled with gold coins. It may be the fate of some of those born under the Leopard merely to count the wealth of others, but there are many rewards awaiting those who are able to keep their own counsel and who can be trusted not to gossip or spread slander.

**Famous Leopards** Irish football star George Best; Elizabeth II.

# Signs of the Tortoise

### 8 Unicorn Thursday

In Chinese legend, the *jilin* or Unicorn was a hybrid creature with the power to discern good from evil. Thus this animal gives those under its protection the gift of foresight and the ability to detect falsehood in others. Its constellation in the sky is a group of six stars called the Southern Ladle, but when speaking of the 28 constellations, the distinction of 'southern' is usually omitted. Because of this it is often confused with the Plough, which the Chinese called the Northern Ladle. Being a ladle, it suggests the spooning out of valuable liquids such as wine or oil. Thus, people born under this sign are generally convivial and genial hosts.

**Famous Unicorns** Revolutionary Che Guevara.

### 9 Sky Ox Friday

Whether by accident or design, the emblem of the Sky Ox coincides with the constellation that includes the star Altair, the Ox-boy. He left his herd to wander while he dallied with the Weaving Maiden who appears in the next constellation. Those born under the sign of the Sky

Ox should be careful to keep their doors locked and always be insured against loss. They will find true love with the partner of their dreams, but their harmony will often be interrupted by unavoidable separation. The Ox presides over fields and land and thus is favourable for those involved in real estate.

**Famous Sky Oxen** Cuban President Fidel Castro; actress Brigitte Bardot; television interviewer David Frost; Microsoft magnate Bill Gates, singer Michael Jackson; Formula 1 driver Michael Schumacher.

## 10 **Bat** Saturday

In Chinese culture the Bat is a symbol of good fortune and is the emblem of the Weaving Maid constellation (see above). The Weaving Maid was in love with the Ox-boy but neglected her weaving to be with her lover. The gods were so angry with them that the lovers were separated, placing them on either side of the Milky Way. Now immortalized as the star Vega, she is the patroness of all seamstresses and tailors. People born under such a constellation find their lives in constant turmoil, weaving between joyful elation and depression.

**Famous Bats** Princess Diana; former athlete and member of the House of Lords Sebastian Coe; couturier Yves St Laurent; comedian Barrie Humphries better known as *alter persona* Dame Edna Everage.

### 11 Sky Rat Sunday

The Sky Rat, like his earthly counterpart, marks the midpoint of winter. But where there ought to be a star there is only emptiness. Since it marks the cold season, it suggests all processes to do with refrigeration and preservation – the frozen food industry at one end of the scale and the management of frozen assets at the other. As there are no beneficial stars to assist people born under this sign, those Sky Rats who are able to follow their instincts, take the initiative and have plenty of self-motivation are the ones most likely to succeed.

**Famous Sky Rats** Sci-fi author Erich von Daniken; interior designer Terence Conran.

### 12 Swallow Monday

This Swallow has built its nest under the Roof of the House to be found in the next constellation. While the Swallow can soar through the sky, for humans the Roof spells peril and danger. People born under this sign like challenges and excitement but are prone to take risks that others would regard as foolhardy.

**Famous Swallows** US senator Edward Kennedy; singer Julie Andrews; tennis player John McEnroe; film actor Tom Hanks.

### 13 Sky Pig Tuesday

The Sky Pig lives in a magnificent house. Two pairs of stars from this and the next constellation join together to form a bright square of four stars that shines vividly in the autumn night sky. Known to Western astronomers as the Square of Pegasus, to the Chinese it is the Builder's Star, bringing blessings on all who work in building and construction. It is the residence of the god of feng shui and offerings are made to it on the autumn equinox. It is not only builders who benefit from this constellation's positive influences, but those who live in religious houses or stately mansions are also blessed.

**Famous Sky Pigs** offspring of Queen Elizabeth II, Prince Edward and Princess Anne; former prime minister Margaret Thatcher; Russian president Vladimir Putin; musician Bob Marley; transport and music magnate Richard Branson; pianist Vladimir Ashkenazy, actor Tom Cruise; pop star Kylie Minogue.

## 14 Porcupine Wednesday

The erudite Porcupine guards the eastern wall of the House of the previous constellation, but is more concerned with the quality of the things within the building – books, paintings, sculptures, musical

instruments, in fact everything to do with the finer aspects of a cultured life. Those born under this sign will reap financial as well as intellectual rewards if their lives encompass the fine arts.

**Famous Porcupines** ballet dancer Rudolph Nureyev; playwright Alan Ayckbourn; actor-musician David Bowie.

# Signs of the Tiger

## 15 **Wolf** Thursday

The constellation Astride is symbolized by the Wolf beside the wall of the House in the previous constellations. Astride signifies the constant fear that someone may leap over the boundary, either to break into the house for some criminal purpose or else that someone belonging to the house elopes, absconds or leaves in some other undignified way. The shape of the constellation resembles a shoe and thus the Wolf watches over people born under this sign who are involved in footwear, leather goods and heavy textiles. The shoe signifies long walks, suggesting that people born under this sign will make many hard journeys.

**Famous Wolves** Actor Marlon Brando; actress Diana Dors.

## 16 **Sky Dog** Friday

The Sky Dog guards the treasure – shown by the constellation of the Mound – a heap of coins and jewels piled high, the proceeds of a wonderful harvest and a successful business. Associated with the new-found wealth are the festivities and merry-making that go with it. Those fortunate enough to be blessed by the auspicious influences of the Sky Dog will succeed in life if they surround themselves with like-minded friends who share the same interests and aim for the same targets.

**Famous Sky Dogs** Astronomer Sir Patrick Moore; actress Angela Lansbury; singer Johnny Cash; actor-comedian Dudley Moore; singer Tom Jones; actress Mia Farrow; singer-actress Jennifer Lopez.

## 17 Pheasant Saturday

The constellation of the Tiger's stomach is symbolized by the Pheasant; what has a pheasant got to do with a Tiger's stomach? Nothing; it is a misunderstanding of the term that meant the royal storehouse, an abundant granary on which no doubt a pheasant would be very pleased to sit. Thus it is a sign of accumulated wealth and symbolizes saving, hoarding and in modern parlance, banking.

**Famous Pheasants** Actress Dame Elizabeth Taylor; creator of Harry Potter, writer J. K. Rowling.

## 18 Sky Rooster Sunday

The Sky Rooster presides over the Pleiades, that beautiful constellation of the winter sky, sometimes called the Seven Sisters, though keen eyesight can discern many more than seven stars. Because it heralds the spring rains, it was associated with sad events. The Pleiades were considered by the ancient Chinese to be the ears and eyes of Heaven, and therefore ruled over inspectors, supervisors and lawmakers. People born under the auspices of the Sky Rooster are watchful and vigilant.

**Famous Sky Roosters** Prince Charles; film actors Dick van Dyke, Woody Allen, Dustin Hoffman, Johnny Depp and Leonard Nimoy; Beatle Ringo Starr; horror writer Stephen King; sportsman Michael Jordan.

## 19 Raven Monday

Not far from the Pleiades is another bouquet of stars, the Hyades, presided over by the Raven. To the Chinese eye this compact group of stars appears to be a net, spread out with the catch from the day's hunting. The Raven therefore signifies rich rewards for industriousness. The connotations of hunting suggest military activity and hence the uniformed professions, which the Raven sign favours. But for all those born under this sign, whatever their careers, there will be many occasions for rejoicing.

**Famous Ravens** Princess Grace of Monaco; actor Leonardo DiCaprio.

## 20 Sky Monkey Tuesday

The three stars that Western observers view as the head of Orion are known to Chinese astronomers as the Turtle's Beak. In the sky, it is the smallest constellation of all; it is guarded by the Sky Monkey and rules over all matters to do with animals that congregate in large numbers, whether in flocks, herds or shoals. It helps all those who need protection – children, the infirm or prisoners. Those who follow its course and help the less able and disadvantaged will receive great rewards, both in material terms and in the kinds of happiness that are impossible to put a price on.

**Famous Sky Monkeys** Celebrated tenor Placido Domingo.

## 21  Ape  Wednesday

The stars of Orion, the brightest constellation in the sky, are said to represent a human form; appropriately, the guardian spirit of this constellation is the Ape. People born under this sign, more than any other, receive in this life the rewards that they merit. The industrious are compensated generously, the idle lose what they have gained. Those who are benevolent and considerate gain honours, the mean and grasping find no friends. The studious are helped by the shining inspiration of the literary star and as a career may turn to journalism.

**Famous Apes**
Actor-comedian Rowan Atkinson; cinema director Steven Spielberg; singer Britney Spears.

# Signs of the Bird

### 22 **Tapir** Thursday

That rare animal the Tapir is the ruling emblem for the enormous expanse of sky, more than a one twelfth of it, which is the constellation of the Well. Because its breadth is so wide, its influence is dissipated and mild. As might be expected, all matters to do with water fall under its auspices and as the Water element is associated with media and communication, Tapir subjects who follow such careers will enjoy the positive benefits provided by this sign. More specifically, a widow born under this sign has good prospects for acquiring land that will gain in value, along with a second husband.

**Famous Tapirs** Beat poet Allen Ginsberg; film director Stanley Kubrick.

### 23 **Sky Sheep** Friday

The Sky Sheep guards the constellation of the Ghostly Carriage with its attendant spectral nebula, said by ancient Chinese astronomers to be the pollen blown from the catkins of the Willow in the next constellation. Much of what is written about the Ghostly Carriage is mournful, dealing with spiritual or supernatural matters. People born under the sign of the Sky Sheep may have clairvoyant abilities.

**Famous Sky Sheep** *Playboy* magazine publisher Hugh Hefner; football star David Beckham.

## 24 Roebuck Saturday

The Roebuck presides over the constellation of the Willow, which like the Sky Sheep, is a somewhat subdued sign associated with sad events. It suggests flexibility, the ability to accommodate ideas which were previously unacceptable and an ability to heal rifts in partnerships through gentle persuasion. Many of those born on a Roebuck day are bestowed with the gift of healing.

**Famous Rocbucks** tenor Luciano Pavarotti; actress Vanessa Redgrave.

## 25 Sky Horse Sunday

As the main star in this constellation originally marked the longest day and the point in the sky when the Sun has reached its highest altitude and begins its downward journey, it is associated with bridges, fords and passage-ways. When an eclipse of the Sun occurred in this constellation in 1999, Istanbul, the bridge between Europe and Asia that lay under the eclipse's path, suffered a terrible earthquake. Because the constellation bridges gaps, people born under its influence are adept at mediating between opposing signs and can be able peacemakers.

**Famous Sky Horses** Dancer Moira Shearer; film director Ken Russell; feminist writer and academic Germaine Greer.

## 26 Deer Monday

Why the Deer should suggest the garment industry, over which it rules, is explained by the shape of its associated constellation, said to look like an unfurled roll of cloth. The cloth, however, may be spread out over a table set for a feast and suggests that people born under its influence will have many reasons to celebrate festive occasions. As gifts are usually presented at such festivities, the sign suggests concord and generosity. It represents the emperor, and by extension, the head of a family or organization.

**Famous Deer** Actors Sean Connery and Larry Hagman; singer Madonna; spy writer John le Carré; George W. Bush.

## 27 Sky Snake Tuesday

The Sky Snake, representing the wings of the Red Phoenix, suggests the progress of imperial power. According to the classical texts, this constellation presided over entertainments and thus it lends inspiration to all those involved in acting and theatre. People born under this constellation are adept at presenting themselves and can subtly deflect questions during awkward situations. It instils ambition and a desire for prestige. In modern terms it could refer to air travel, unknown in ancient times, along with timeless upward mobility. This constellation rules over personal advancement and political aims, and those born under the influence of this constellation will never be satisfied with second-best.

**Famous Sky Snakes** Hair salon magnate Vidal Sassoon; the first cosmonaut to walk in space Aleksei Leonov; singer Elvis Presley.

## 28 Worm Wednesday

The final sign in this astronomical menagerie is the humble Worm, a strange choice of emblem for a constellation deemed to look like the footplate of a chariot. But perhaps ancient astrologers had already found that people born under this sign were enthusiasts for landscape and garden design, an activity that the Worm manages very well. The Chariot, its associated constellation, suggests rapid travel, many journeys and transport by road.

**Famous Worms** Ex US president Jimmy Carter; media magnate Rupert Murdoch; actor Robert Redford; Beatle John Lennon; supermodel Kate Moss; singer Robbie Williams.

# The Mansions of the Moon

The 28 constellations known as the 'Mansions of the Moon' are no longer part of mainstream Chinese astrology, but 2,000 years ago they were the foundation on which astrology and astronomical observations were based. Today, their names are preserved in the annual Chinese almanac known as the *tong shu*, and also on the outer ring of the special compass used by feng shui practitioners.

When Chinese astronomers first observed the stars and planets, the sky was divided into five areas, four of which enclosed the 'seasonal' stars that were only visible at certain times of the year, and a central area that included the stars visible at all times. The constellations of the seasonal areas were called the Dragon, Tortoise, Tiger and Bird, and the stars around the Pole Star, seen all through the year, is known as the Purple Palace. Later, when astronomical observations became more sophisticated, each of the four seasonal constellations was divided into seven, to make a total of 28. They are called 'Mansions of the Moon' (as the medieval English poet Geoffrey Chaucer refers to them in *Canterbury Tales*), because throughout the month the Moon is seen in a different mansion almost every night, until it has circulated through the Dragon, Tortoise, Tiger and Bird. The path it takes through the sky, the Yellow Road, is also followed by all the planets and neither the Moon nor the planets ever cross over into the Purple Palace. But

*The outer ring of this Chinese compass shows the 28 constellations running anti-clockwise.*

since the Moon takes rather longer than 28 days to makes its progress through the sky, knowing the true position of the Moon in the sky requires a more scientific approach, which is why the Chinese feng shui compass was invented. Sadly, nowadays only a minority of feng shui practitioners know the true origin and purpose.

## Naming the days

In the Chinese almanac, every day in a four-week period is named after one of the Mansions of the Moon. The sequence is identical to that of the 28 Animals (see pages 268– 287) Whether the constellation in question is favourable or not determines the fortune for the day, what kinds of activities are most likely to succeed and which ones would not.

The Mansion of the Moon shown in Chinese calendars has nothing to do with the Moon's actual position. The constellation-names are merely a way to list the days in a period of four weeks, each beginning with a Thursday, in order to give a general indication of whether the day will be favourable for certain enterprises or not.

To find the Moon Day, use the same method as given for finding the Day Animal (see pages 270– 271 'How to find the Animal of the day').

# Mansions of the Green Dragon

What is a dragon? Every culture seems to feature a dragon in legends. In the West, the dragon is seen as a ravaging monster usually slain by a hero-saint. In Eastern culture, the dragon is benign, brings wealth and is a symbol of virtue and power. A 'Dragon Child' is one who is talented and destined to rise to a high position in society. In Chinese astronomy, the Dragon constellation (which includes the Western constellation of the Dragon) is in the eastern part of the sky. The starting point is marked by a star called the Dragon's Horn.

## 1 the Dragon's Horn  Thursday

The first of the 28 constellations, this marks an auspicious day for beginning any new enterprise. It is particularly favourable for commencing new building works or laying foundation stones, as this will bring success and prosperity and the promise of meeting the most important people in the land. It is favourable for marriages, weddings and engagements. Conversely, sad occasions such as funerals or memorials should not be organized on a day that should be reserved for joyous celebrations.

## 2 the Dragon's Neck  Friday

The *I Ching* or *Book of Changes* opens with a description of the Dragon flying through the sky; in the autumn it dives into the sea and appears

to lose its head, which was taken to mean a reference to execution. The sign is therefore regarded as unfavourable. All building or construction should be avoided; a house built today will fall down! Whatever work is done today will be undone within ten days. Neither funerals nor marriages should be celebrated on this day.

## 3 the Floor Saturday

When ancient astronomers decided to divide the constellation of the Dragon into seven smaller sections, two groups of stars, the Floor and the Room were renamed. The unlucky nature of the Floor more or less repeats the strictures against building, weddings and funerals. If a marriage is contracted today, evil men will visit the house at night, but for what reason is not made clear. If a funeral take place, the heirs will be impoverished. It is also an unfavourable time for travelling by boat.

## 4 the Room Sunday

The previous mansion, which only had a floor and no walls, was a bad omen. But the Room is complete and shows that the day is favourable for all kinds of building. Indeed, construction or the completion of any project on this day will assure the owner of wealth and promotion. If it is necessary to organize memorial services or funeral ceremonies on this day, then the spirits of the ancestors will bring promotion and success in examinations to those attending. If a man takes a mistress on this day, a son will be born before three years are up – news that might not be regarded as favourably today as it was intended to be in Chinese imperial times!

## 5 the Dragon's Heart Monday

Many centuries ago the bright red star Antares, which the Chinese call the Dragon's Heart, would have marked the centre of this constellation, but this is no longer the case. The Dragon's Heart is therefore out of place; to disturb it further is unfavourable and if marriages are contracted today there will be problems for three years and the children of such marriages will head for trouble.

## 6 the Dragon's Tail
Tuesday

The Dragon brings wealth; pearls emerge from its mouth and gold coins and ingots from its other end. Any industrious activities will

*The almanac advises on suitable days for gardening, digging and boring for wells.*

bring success and great reward. Those who use the day for celebrations will receive rich rewards and acquire merit and distinction both for themselves and their family. Those who dig today may light upon hidden treasure and lost articles may be found.

## 7 the Basket Wednesday

Beneath the Dragon's Tail is a basket conveniently placed for gathering up all the gold which is of little use to the Dragon, but of inestimable value to mortal folk. To open new doors, physically or symbolically, will doubles one's fortunes. Those who branch out into new directions today will have a year of good fortune. Silkworms will be active: in ancient China households had to breed silkworms and pay their taxes in silk cocoons; the modern interpretation is that income will increase enough to be able to live comfortably and pay off outstanding debts.

# Mansions of the Black Tortoise

The northern part of the sky, the Tortoise, includes two stars that feature in the most loved of all Chinese folk tales, the Ox-herder and the Weaving Maid.

The Ox-herder's task was to look after the celestial dairy, while the Maid wove silk to make clothes for the gods. One day, the gods wished to pay their respects to the Queen Mother of the Western Sky on her birthday, wearing their best new clothes and taking as gifts milk from the celestial cows. But there was no milk; the Ox-herder and the Weaving Maid were too much involved with each other; he had neglected to milk the cows, so that their milk ran across the sky to make the Milky Way, while the Weaving Maid had forsaken her loom. The gods were so angry that they separated the young lovers and placed them on either side of the Milky Way, the Ox-herder as the star Altair, and the Weaving Maid as the star Vega. But their friends the birds took pity on their sadness, and every year, on the seventh day of the seventh lunar month, magpies will flock together to form a bridge across which the Weaving Maid crosses to meet her lover.

## 8 the Southern Spoon  Thursday

This constellation – not to be confused with the Northern Spoon, the seven main stars of the Great Bear – symbolizes the ladling out of oils, wine and milk in generous helpings. It is a symbol of the satisfaction

*The Ox-herded neglected his herd which incurred the wrath of the gods, who punished him with separation and sadness.*

derived from completed a task and the rewards for having done so. Silkworms thrive: a sign that a favourable financial situation ensures that taxes and dues can be paid without distress. It is a favourable day for laying the foundations of any new building or finishing the preparatory stages for any new enterprise.

## 9  the Ox-herder  Friday

As charming as is the tale of the Ox-herder and his Weaving Maid, the story ends unhappily, and so these two mansions suggest separation and sadness. There is also the additional admonition to ensure that animals are well cared for (the Ox-herder neglected his cows) and a stern reminder to keep doors locked and secure.

## 10  the Weaving Maid  Saturday

While the unfavourable aspects of the Ox-herder mansion reflect the youth's carelessness, the story seems to have little bearing on the Weaving Maid's forebodings. An inauspiciously arranged funeral today will result in epidemics, particularly diseases of the bowels, perhaps brought on by eating contaminated food at the funeral.

## 11  Emptiness  Sunday

It would have been convenient for astronomers of old if there had been an easily identifiable star to mark the centre of the winter constellation; but as there was none, the central section of the Tortoise is empty. The Chinese character for empty represents a desert – with a Tiger wandering over it. Neither of these signs is favourable, the desert suggesting famine and hardship and the Tiger danger. On such a day, any kind of digging or building work will result in heated disputes. Marriages should not be arranged on this day as the children of such marriages may head towards delinquency.

## 12  Danger  Monday

The alternative name for this mansion is the Roof, and the danger implied is that of falling off the roof of the house alluded to in the next mansion. There is a warning regarding travel by land or water. (The author can testify to the many occasions when he

*Certain days seem prone to traffic hold-ups and delays when travelling.*

was obliged, because of pressing engagements, to ignore the omen's warnings, with the inevitable consequences of mishaps and delays.) Air travel, however, seems to escape the baleful effects of this mansion's malign influences.

## 13 the House Tuesday

Four bright stars, forming a square, are very prominent in the sky at the time of the equinoxes. Together they form a box (the House) known to Western astronomers as the Square of Pegasus, and to Chinese astronomers as the Builder's Stars, and form the residence of the patron deity of Chinese builders and carpenters. The two stars on the right form the mansion of the House, and the two on the left become the next mansion of the Wall. The House, more correctly Burning House, was a model house made of wood and paper and set on fire as an offering to one's ancestors. As a result, the ancestors would reward their descendants with wealth and prospects of promotion. All activities are favourable today

## 14 the Wall Wednesday

The eastern wall of the house brings all the benefits associated with this favourable constellation. Opening new doors (either literally or figuratively) brings rich rewards. Children born of marriages contracted today will be accomplished and bring honour and joy to their parents. By being respectful to others, polite to one's family and superiors and remembering one's ancestors with devotion, wealth and promotion are assured.

# Mansions of the White Tiger

It is important to remember that the White Tiger, the constellation that embraces all the stars of the autumn sky, has nothing to do with the third animal of the Chinese zodiac. The Green Dragon and White Tiger represent the spring and autumn constellations of the sky, and in feng shui the terms are used to refer to the two sides of a building. Although white (albino) tigers are occasionally born, the White Tiger of Chinese culture is a spirit that devours the souls of the departed. In imperial times, the head of the clan acted as a magistrate for his own family and was expected to judge and punish any wrongdoers. He presided over his own family court and on his right, the tiger side, would be a door painted with a fierce tiger reserved for the most feared punishment of all – total banishment from the family.

## 15 Astride Thursday

The symbol is of someone leaping over the Tiger side wall of the previous mansion. Perhaps it is a thief running off with stolen property or a member of the family absconding. Alternatively, it could represent someone sneaking into the house at night. Whatever the meaning, it is obviously something undesirable. Be circumspect in one's actions today and pay attention to details that may be overlooked, particularly with regards to security matters.

*The Mound rules over all expressions of celebration, from triumphal arches to humble announcements in a newspaper.*

## 16 a Mound Friday

Old farm houses in country districts used to hoard all their animal manure in front of the house, not just for convenience, but as a display of wealth. Thus the interpretation is of a pile of good things – grain, goods, money – all heaped up; a very favourable sign. The old texts declare it is a good day for building triumphal arches. Although these might be seen in the Chinatowns of big cities, for more humble businesses it can refer to the publication of congratulatory messages for the opening of new premises, important business contracts or jubilees, as well as being a favourable time for family celebrations.

## 17 the Tiger's Stomach  Saturday

The Tiger is replete and settled, making this a good day for all kinds of
activities, whether commerce, physical activity or ceremony. The old
texts declare that children born of a marriage contracted today will
become favourites of the emperor; in modern terms, their talents and
achievements will be recognized by those in high authority.

## 18 the Pleiades  Sunday

The beautiful constellation of the Pleiades has always been associated
with the spring rains; by extension, the symbolism represents tears and
unhappiness. It is important to be careful that whatever is done today is
merely a continuation of what has already been started. To embark on
new ventures would lead to difficulties and challenges, and to the risk
of making hasty and ill-timed decisions. Marriages should not be
contracted today in case they lead to early separation.

## 19 the Net  Monday

A star cluster similar to the Pleiades, to the Chinese observer the
Hyades looks like a net. Whether for catching fish or game, the Net is a
sign of good fortune. With an abundance of material goods in store, the
Net promises rich rewards for whatever activities are carried out today.
It is therefore a favourable day for any kind of work with buildings or
land. Digging the ground for construction work or opening it up for
burials is favourable. As for marriages, the children of couples joined
today will have long and profitable lives.

## 20 the Turtle's Beak  Tuesday

This tiny group of stars was compiled from the stars that make the head
of Orion; thus the constellation that looks like a man who has lost his
head is a most unfavourable day. The predictions are ominous: the

necessity to sell property at a loss, punishments for wrongdoing, even execution for murder, and fatalities during a Tiger year. Fortunately, these are not inescapable prospects, but merely stern warnings to ensure that one's activities today keep within the bounds of propriety.

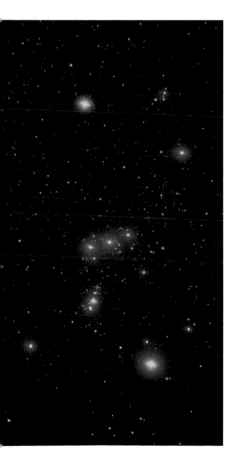

### 21 **Orion** Wednesday

The constellation of Orion, the figure of a man with his shoulders, belt and sword clearly defined, is one of the most recognizable sights in the night sky. The herb ginseng, with its branched roots looking similarly anthropomorphic, takes its name from Orion, and in fact the Chinese character for ginseng is a pictograph of the stars of Orion. It is a favourable day for building and for beginning new projects, but not for terminating existing affairs, or for ceremonies such as marriages or funerals. Industriousness brings rewards. Now, the Chinese constellation lacks the uppermost stars which form Orion's head, so it is thought by some to be an omen of impending executions.

*The constellation of Orion is one of the glories of the Winter night sky.*

# Mansions of the Red Bird

The constellation of the Red Bird occupies the part of the sky where the stars are visible during the summer and so is associated with the south. Although the constellation opposite to the Green Dragon is the White Tiger, very often the Red Bird, sometimes called the Phoenix, replaces the Tiger because of the latter's association with banishment and the devouring of souls.

At Chinese wedding banquets, embroidered banners depicting the Dragon and Phoenix are hung in prominent positions. In feng shui, while Dragon, Tiger and Tortoise represent hills surrounding a building, the Red Bird represents an open space in front in order to gather the beneficial energy and bring it through the door.

## 22 the Well Thursday

The stars forming the mansion of the Well resemble the Chinese character for the same word, but which came first is a matter for conjecture. In the *Book of Changes*, an old rhyme says, 'Up and down, up and down, the bucket goes; and finally it breaks', suggesting that there is much routine activity still to be to be completed and that one must not take anything for granted. For the student, hard work brings favourable results in examinations. The Well is the largest of the Chinese constellations, and its influence tends to fade quickly.

## 23 the Ghostly Carriage Friday

The four stars of this constellation form a box, at the centre of which is the appearance of a wispy cloud. Astronomers today know this as the Praesepe nebula, but to the ancient Chinese it looked like a chariot being driven by a ghost. Even today, the Chinese character for 'unlucky' is a pictograph of this star group – the four stars represented by a square, with a cross inside for the nebula. Not surprisingly, this mansion is regarded as a bad omen, presaging all kinds of doom. New doorways lead to disaster and marriages to separation or widowhood. But paying respects to one's ancestors will bring merit and unexpected honours.

## 24 the Willow Saturday

In some old accounts of the stars and constellations, it is said the ghostly apparition in the previous mansion is pollen blown from the willow branch next to it. The notion of the weeping willow and the fact

that willow branches were carried in funeral processions underline the unhappy omens which are associated with this mansion. But surprisingly, bearing in mind its association with funerals, it is not a favourable day for burials and memorial services of any kind. Instead, the day should be reserved for meditation and the study of uplifting literature.

*The Willow is associated with sadness, tranquillity and respectful silence.*

## 25 the Bird Star Sunday

The Bird Star itself, known as Alphard to Western astronomers, used to mark the summer solstice. Because it appeared at the central point of the year, it was considered to be the bridge from the rising yang power of the Sun to its waning, and therefore ruled over bridges. Although it no longer marks the summer solstice, but a date in early August, it still rules over matters to do with bridges. When a total eclipse of the Sun occurred in the mansion of the Bird Star in 1999, bridges across the Danube, which lay under the path of the eclipse, were destroyed, and Istanbul, the 'bridge' between Europe and Asia, was struck by a terrible earthquake. Building works are favoured today, but marriages made today would prove to be a disaster for the wife.

## 26 the Drawn Bow Monday

The bow is drawn, the arrow poised to bring down the hunter's prey. From the point of view of the bird, perhaps this is not a favourable sign, but the advice given by the almanac is for humans, not birds. The mansion therefore shows rewards for those who are careful and direct. All manner of activities are favourable and by extension of the imagery the 'bag' from the successful hunt reveals that the day is good for acquiring property of all kinds. But gardening, digging and all matters relating to the breaking of the earth are unfavourable and may lead to the wife leaving home to live with her lover.

## 27 Wings Tuesday

The bird's wings suggest flight in every sense. This is one day that should not be reserved for paying respects to one's ancestors or holding memorial services. The results are depressing: employees will leave, young girls of the household will run off with unsuitable boys and heirs of the household will emigrate. Wives who are

*The Drawn Bow is an unfavourable day for gardening, but the Chariot promises better outcomes for such pursuits.*

unfaithful to their husbands should take heed; for on such a day it is said that the men will return home to find their wives in the arms of their lovers.

## 28 the Chariot Wednesday

Weddings, funerals, digging, commercial enterprises, in fact whatever is done this day will bring success and untold benefits. Those who choose to marry today will be blessed with a Dragon child. There is great profit for those who build terraces today. These were originally raised platforms for taking tea while observing the Full Moon, but the word is now used to mean railway station platforms! Perhaps the modern interpretation would be the construction of garden patios!

# Clothes-cutting days

In addition to the days of the week, the date according to the Chinese and Western calendars, the Stem and Branch of the day, its element, and the lunar mansion, every Chinese yearly almanac lists the Clothes-cutting days. These complement the advice provided by the 28 Lunar Mansions in the selection of auspicious days for various activities such as weddings and funerals, as well as specifying days good for washing, gardening and other domestic activities.

The Clothes-cutting days, or 12 Indicators, comprise an ancient system, dating back more than 2,000 years. The system is not confined to China, and there are references from Turkistan, Central Asia and Mongolia. Some historians have suggested that the Clothes-cutting days were combined with the 28 Mansions to try and make an astronomically accurate calendar. After a few years of experimenting, when it became apparent that the mathematics didn't work, the calendar, with its associated tasks for each day and the advice for choosing suitable days for community activities, had become something more important than just a list of dates. Having everyone doing the same thing at the same appointed time was a way of keeping an empire the size of China together. Indeed, during the 19th century there was a move to abolish the Clothes-cutting days, but there was such an outcry that the emperor was petitioned to retain them, since it was believed that

*Many Chinese business people take care not to sign a contract on a day which the Chinese almanac deems unsuitable.*

without such clear-cut regulation the common people would be at a loss as to how to conduct their day-to-day lives.

## The wheels of trade

Today, many business diaries printed in Taiwan and Hong Kong will list the Clothes-cutting days, so that the wheels of trade and commerce will turn smoothly and successfully. Woe betide the Western entrepreneur who tries to get a contract signed on a day deemed an unfavourable Clothes-cutting day; the Westerner will find their Chinese counterparts strangely reticent.

Why Clothes-cutting days? The name comes from the Chinese practice of using the first two words of each chapter as the chapter's title. As the opening words of the text outlining this ancient method of establishing the favourable activities for each day began 'Cut clothes...' the phrase became the name of the method.

## Finding a suitable day

When looking for a suitable date for an event such as the opening of a shop, a wedding or some activity involving many people, begin with a date that is practical. Then check the Lunar Mansion for that day to see if it is favourable for that activity, and whether it is or not, select a few favourable days on either side of it. Then check the Clothes-cutting days in the same way and compare them until a favourable Lunar Mansion is aligned with a favourable Clothes-cutting day.

One fascinating aspect is that the Lunar Mansions and the Clothes-cutting days have one sign in common – danger. In the Chinese almanac, as one might imagine, the Lunar Mansion 12 'Danger' is marked in black to signify unlucky, but the Clothes-cutting day 'Danger' is marked in red – lucky! The reason for the apparent contradiction is that the day is considered so unfavourable for business that the best thing to do is to drink wine and be merry!

## How to find the Clothes-cutting day

The Clothes-cutting days consist of 12 Indicators that run in a cycle throughout the solar month, parallel to the 12 Animals or Branches.

However, at the month end, the Indicator for the last day of the month is also the Indicator for the first day of the new month, so that each Indicator is now paired with a different animal.

1 To find the Indicator for any day, first find the Animal sign of the solar month (see page 172) and the Animal sign for the day (see page 178– 180). Simply cross-reference the two animals in the table (see page 309) to find the Indicator.

| THE 12 INDICATORS | |
|---|---|
| a | Establish |
| b | Discard |
| c | Fullness |
| d | Even |
| e | Arrange |
| f | Grasp |
| g | Ruin |
| h | Danger |
| i | Completion |
| j | Acceptance |
| k | Open |
| l | Shut |

## FINDING THE INDICATOR

| Animal of the Month | Animal sign of the day | | | | | | | | | | | |
|---|---|---|---|---|---|---|---|---|---|---|---|---|
| beginning | Rat | Ox | Tiger | Rabbit | Dragon | Snake | Horse | Sheep | Monkey | Rooster | Dog | Pig |
| **Rat** 7 Dec | a | b | c | d | e | f | g | h | i | j | k | l |
| **Ox** 6 Jan | l | a | b | c | d | e | f | g | h | i | j | k |
| **Tiger** 4 Feb | k | l | a | b | c | d | e | f | g | h | i | j |
| **Rabbit** 6 March | j | k | l | a | b | c | d | e | f | g | h | i |
| **Dragon** 5 April | i | j | k | l | a | b | c | d | e | f | g | h |
| **Snake** 6 May | h | i | j | k | l | a | b | c | d | e | f | g |
| **Horse** 6 June | g | h | i | j | k | l | a | b | c | d | e | f |
| **Sheep** 7 July | f | g | h | i | j | k | l | a | b | c | d | e |
| **Monkey** 8 Aug | e | f | g | h | i | j | k | l | a | b | c | d |
| **Rooster** 8 Sept | d | e | f | g | h | i | j | k | l | a | b | c |
| **Dog** 9 Oct | c | d | e | f | g | h | i | j | k | l | a | b |
| **Pig** 8 Nov | b | c | d | e | f | g | h | i | j | k | l | a |

# Interpreting the 12 Indicators

Once you have found the appropriate letter in the table and the Indicator keyword in the box on the previous pages, you can interpret the 12 Indicators from the entries below.

**a Establish** 'This is the day that Ten Thousand things are generated'
*Do Cut clothes; pay bills; barter and trade; travel over land; set up positions. All positive things are favourable.*
*Don't Dig; travel by boat; dip into savings; unlock stores.*

**b Discard** 'Sweep away evil'
*Do Sweep and clean; wash and bathe; take purgatives.*
*Don't Arrange wedding ceremonies for this day. Avoid unnecessary travel. Do not open wells or arrange water features.*

**c Fullness** 'The Emperor of Heaven fills the treasuries to the brim'
*Do Organize weddings, receptions; change one's residence; go on journeys. All these are favourable.*
*Don't Cut or prune plants; dig in the garden; change the direction of water.*

**d Even** 'This is the day of Official Gathering and Equal Division'
*Do Organize weddings; change one's residence; cultivate the True Path of Enlightenment; paint walls. All these are favourable.*
*Don't Cut; plant; excavate; open water-courses.*

**e Arrange** 'The Emperor of Heaven has placed everyone in their seats. The Five Grains are in abundance'
*Do Cut; plant; organize weddings; yoke the ox and the horse; dig the ground; open up wells.*
*Don't Make accusations.*

*One of the great benefits of the almanac's Clothes-Cutting days was to ensure that the working population was able to have rest days.*

**f** **Grasp** 'The Emperor of Heaven administers the Ten Thousand Things and bestows Heaven's Blessings'

**Do** *Arrange for the opening of wells and water features; cutting and planting; wedding ceremonies.*

**Don't** *Change address; travel; open storehouses; draw on savings.*

**g** **Ruin** 'The Seven Stars of the Ladle indicate conflicts, arguments and quarrels'

**Do** *Go fishing. Punish criminals.*

**Don't** *Take part in any organized activity.*

**h Danger** 'Ascending the dangerous mountain where the wind blows fiercely there is great peril'

*Do Be joyful and drink wine. All else is of little use.*

*Don't Undertake any serious activity.*

**i Completion** 'Heaven's Annals record Ten Thousand Things'

*Do Arrange weddings; embark on long journeys; dig the earth. All these things are favourable.*

*Don't Cast aspersions!*

**j Acceptance** 'The Emperor of Heaven's precious treasures are received'

*Do Open the storehouses and granaries; carry on trading; enter college; arrange weddings; be active; dig the earth. All these things are favourable.*

*Don't Travel or arrange funerals for this day; don't take acupuncture or moxybustion treatment.*

**k Open** 'The Emperor of Heaven's Messenger is out of danger'

*Do Study arts and crafts; complete business dealings; organize wedding ceremonies; travel. All these are favourable.*

*Don't Organize funerals or interments. These are not wholesome.*

**l Shut** 'Heaven and Earth, Yang and Yin, Open and Shut. This is the day of burial and concealment'

*Do Set up notices or advertisements.*

*Don't Initiate any new projects; it is a day of misfortune and evil.*

# The Three Fates

The Chinese word *san* for 'three' consists of three lines. The top line is supposed to represent Heaven, the bottom line the Earth and the middle line ourselves. From these three lines we can see the three things that decide our fate in life. The top line, Heaven Fate, includes the Sun, Moon, planets and stars by which we regulate the calendar, and reveals the time when we are born, which is unalterable.

The bottom line, Earth Fate, shows the geographical environment, the circumstances and family conditions into which we are born. For example, nearly every composer of international renown, from classical composers Mozart, Haydn and Beethoven to today's Andrew Lloyd Webber, were not only endowed with musical creativity at birth, but were born into the families of established musicians. Their parents were able to nurture and encourage their talents that might otherwise have gone unnoticed had their backgrounds been different.

But the one major difference between Earth Fate and Heaven Fate rests in the fact that we have no say in when and where we came into the world – we cannot change the time of our birth – but we can change where we live.

The middle line, Human Fate, represents what we do with the opportunities offered to us. There are many famous people who were born at inauspicious times to poor families in depressed areas,

*Genius, like that of Mozart, is not enough. Timing is vital, too.*

but through a combination of circumstances and sheer determined efforts they were able to rise to riches, wealth and fame. Other people, born into wealthy privileged families in times of peace and prosperity, waste every opportunity and die in poverty and neglect.

## Who is in the driver's seat?

The three fates are sometimes likened to a car on a motorway. Whether it is a super sports car or an old battered wreck, both are given the Heaven Fate. The motorway is the Earth Fate, ready for the car to move along. But whether the car reaches the end of the road or stays where it is depends entirely on the Human Fate, the person who is in the driver's seat.

Our Heaven Fate is fixed; our Earth Fate can be changed, but to do so we need the action and motivation of our Human Fate to move from one location to another, and so benefit from a different environment to improve our circumstances. The Chinese refer to a location's potential for good fortune as its 'feng shui'. The literal meaning of the word is 'wind and water' and originally it merely meant a place sheltered from the weather, but today the term refers to the various qualities of a location, such as its practicality and convenience, as well other subjective aspects ranging from the aesthetic to the mystical.

# Chinese astrology and feng shui

The popular concept of feng shui is the idea that by rearranging the furniture and putting flowers, crystals and bells in the right places, or redecorating the home, you will solve all your financial problems, miraculously cure debilitating illnesses and the partner of your dreams will be at the door with tickets for a world cruise. If only this were true.

We can take into account Heaven Fate; we can change Earth Fate, but there can be no result until the Human Fate is motivated. The problem is that the sudden popularity of feng shui led to commercial exploitation on an extraordinary scale. In pre-feng shui times, people were quite happy to decorate their homes with flowers, ornaments, scented candles and whimsical trivia. But now everything is done because of the 'feng shui': the ornaments have to be Chinese, the scented candles painted with Chinese characters and the plants mustn't have pointed leaves (difficult, since almost all leaves have points). The truth of the matter is that when a place has 'good feng shui' it should look perfectly ordinary and natural, without any exotic distracting paraphernalia. It will look right and feel comfortable; what feng shui is all about is finding the criteria for creating the ideal living and working conditions.

*The use of crystals in feng shui is essentially a Western concept. Chinese connoisseurs prefer smooth stones.*

## Feng shui and the time factor

There is, however, one aspect of feng shui that does overlap with Chinese astrology – the time factor. Time does not stand still, but moves forward. For more than a century it has been realized that time is another dimension of space. More than two thousand years ago, when Chu, the King of Wei, wanted to establish the foundations of a new city, he not only took advice regarding the environment, but the precise time – 'When the Builder's stars were overhead, and the Sun had reached its proper place'. Without such considerations of matters celestial, the project would have lost the Mandate of Heaven and be doomed to fail.

# The Four Constellation Animals

From the time/space factors come the notion of direction. The four main compass points are associated with the equinoxes and solstices, as well as the times of the day (noon, midnight, sunrise and sunset) and the four celestial animals (Dragon, Bird, Tiger and Tortoise). These four great constellations are reflected on the Earth, and in feng shui are used as the terminology for the aspects of the environment surrounding a particular location. The rear of the location is termed the Tortoise; circling the site in a clockwise direction, to the side is the Dragon, at the front is the Bird, with the Tiger opposite the Dragon, thus completing the circuit. Ideally, the Tortoise should be in the north and should be the highest part of the surroundings, the Dragon the second highest, the Tiger slightly lower, while the Bird should be on level ground or lower. The configuration as a whole is often likened to an easy chair, the back of the chair being the Tortoise, the two arms the Dragon and Tiger, and the Bird a foot stool in front of the chair.

The Dragon side is regarded as masculine and the Tiger feminine; if the environment is more prominent on the Dragon side, it supports the male members of a family or organization; in the traditional Chinese family this was regarded as the most favourable configuration since it was usually male members of a family who earned the income. If the Tiger side is higher than the Dragon, this is more favourable for the female members of the household, and there are likely to be more daughters than sons, and the mother the main breadwinner.

Do not confuse the Four Constellation Animals with the 12 Animals of the Chinese zodiac; in both systems the Dragon is to the east, but the Tiger constellation is on the opposite side to the zodiac Tiger, and the Rat and Horse zodiac signs replace the Tortoise and Bird of the celestial constellations. That said, we can now take a closer look at the roles played in feng shui by the 12 Animals.

# The 12 directions

The Western compass plate first identifies four basic compass points – north, east, south and west – and then subdivides each of these to 8, 16 and 32 bearings. The naval recruit learns to 'box the compass' by reciting the points in order: north, north-nor'east, nor'east, east-nor'east, and so on.

The Chinese compass plate is divided rather differently: each of the eight main divisions (the four principal directions and the four 'corners') is subdivided into three, making 24 directions altogether. These 24 divisions form pairs of animal directions in the same way that the Chinese clock divides the day into 12 fore and aft 'double-hours'. Thus the 12 Earthly branches represent compass directions and so identify favourable and obstructive locations for living, working and sleeping. By travelling in the appropriate direction, the prevailing beneficial *qi* (roughly translated as 'life force') can be harnessed, and harmful influences turned away.

Only four of the 'animal' directions correspond to the Western compass directions: Rat to north, Rabbit to east, Horse to south and Rooster to west, but even so, these are not precise points, but rather general directions. If we use compass degrees, rather than points of the compass, the association between the 12 Animal signs and the directions becomes clearer.

## THE 12 DIRECTIONS CHART

The circular chart below shows the 12 years of the cycle, beginning in 2008 and the direction associated with each animal.

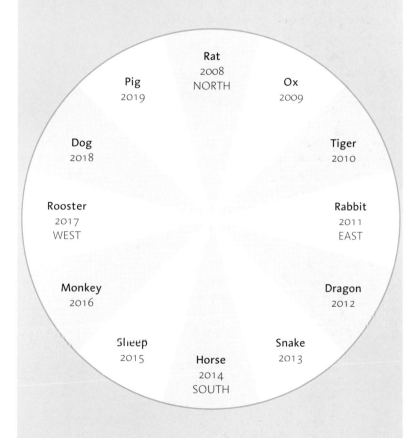

# The Tai Sui

According to ancient astrological theory, there is an influence called the Tai Sui, literally, the Great Age, orbiting the Sun every 12 years. Since the 12 years correspond to the 12 years of the Chinese zodiac, each animal sign also represents the direction from which the influence emanates. We can think of this influence like a powerful wind, blowing across the sea into the sails of a boat. It is almost impossible to sail against the wind and just as foolhardy to let the wind blow the boat wherever it will, since it may dash the boat on to the rocks.

From this image comes the concept that we do not attack the Tai Sui nor do we allow it to attack us by moving ourselves in the opposite direction to the Tai Sui, the Counter-Sui. 'Attack' in this instance means to travel in a particular direction with the object of remaining there more or less permanently. It could mean a change of employment, moving house, building an extension to one's house or generally doing anything that implied a move in that direction.

If the year is the Rat year, for example, which represents the north, it is inadvisable to 'attack' the north by moving house to a location that is directly north of the previous address, and likewise foolhardy to let the Tai Sui lead us to 'attack' the south, by moving house to the south. In the first instance, because the move north was 'attacking' the Tai Sui, there would be numerous difficulties and obstacles impeding progress at every stage, until the Tai Sui had passed to a different direction. If the move were to the south, at first everything would appear to go smoothly, but it would be too easy; matters would be rushed, resulting in carelessness, oversights, rash expenditure and lack of attention to important details, leading to difficulties later.

One should aim to travel in a direction that is favourable for the Tai Sui; that is, one which is 120° distant from the direction of the year. (These favourable directions are the same as the 12 Directions described on page 319). Thus, in the year 2010, the Tai Sui lies in the Tiger direction, making it unfavourable to travel towards the Tiger (45°– 75°) or to the opposite direction of the Monkey (225°– 255°). Since the Horse and the Dog are companions to the Tiger, it would be favourable to

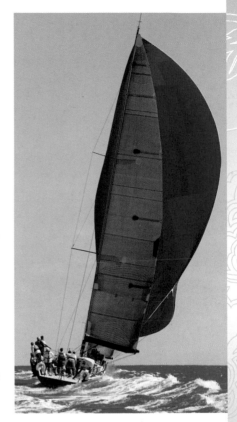

*The force of Tai Sui can be likened to a wind blowing the sails of a boat.*

travel due south (the Horse) or towards the Dog (285°– 315°). Note that traditional Chinese maps often place South, and the Horse, at the top of the chart, as seen on page 181. The following table shows which directions are favourable and unfavourable for a cycle of Tai Sui years.

## FAVOURABLE AND UNFAVOURABLE DIRECTIONS

| Year | | Tai Sui | Counter-Sui | Favourable direction | Fair direction |
|---|---|---|---|---|---|
| Rat | 2008 | Rat | Horse | Dragon, Monkey | Tiger, Dog |
| Ox | 2009 | Ox | Sheep | Snake, Rooster | Rabbit, Pig |
| Tiger | 2010 | Tiger | Monkey | Horse, Dog | Dragon, Rat |
| Rabbit | 2011 | Rabbit | Rooster | Sheep, Pig | Snake, Ox |
| Dragon | 2012 | Dragon | Dog | Monkey, Rat | Horse, Tiger |
| Snake | 2013 | Snake | Pig | Rooster, Ox | Sheep, Rabbit |
| Horse | 2014 | Horse | Rat | Dog, Tiger | Monkey, Dragon |
| Sheep | 2015 | Sheep | Ox | Pig, Rabbit | Rooster, Snake |
| Monkey | 2016 | Monkey | Tiger | Rat, Dragon | Dog, Horse |
| Rooster | 2017 | Rooster | Rabbit | Ox, Snake | Pig, Sheep |
| Dog | 2018 | Dog | Dragon | Tiger, Horse | Rat, Monkey |
| Pig | 2019 | Pig | Snake | Rabbit, Sheep | Ox, Rooster |

## Attack of the self

Unfortunately, there is another stricture that limits the directions in which one may relocate; just as it is inadvisable to 'attack' the Tai Sui or the Counter-Sui, so it is unfavourable to travel at any time in the direction of one's own animal sign of the year (Attack of the self) or in the direction opposite to this (Attack of the mind).

It is said that attacking the self results in physical injury or sickness, while attacking the mind brings mental confusion and instability.

# Short and repeated journeys

'Attacking the Tai Sui' usually means making a more or less permanent move against the direction ruled by the Tai Sui. The question is often asked whether the same problems affect short journeys or visits of only a few days. What must be remembered is that if the travelling involves a journey returning by the same route, then the outward journey attacks the Tai Sui and the return the Counter-Sui; it isn't as if the influences of the return journey cancel out the malign effects of the outward one: both are unfavourable. Short unrepeated trips are not likely to be affected by the adverse currents of the Tai Sui. However, what is regarded as inadvisable is when there might be a change of employment which will necessitate making daily journeys travelling against the Tai Sui and returning via the Counter-Sui: this is tantamount to making a permanent move in that direction.

The solution, one long practised by the Chinese for ceremonial processions at weddings and funerals, is that when the Tai Sui is unfavourably disposed to the direction of the change of location, misfortune can be avoided by making a journey which does attack the Tai Sui, but takes a detour, setting off at an angle to the Tai Sui (preferably at 120° to it), then at a suitable point along the journey, veering to the other side. It does not matter that the line joining the departure and arrival points may be, as the crow flies, in the same direction as the Tai Sui: the essential feature is that the journey itself followed a path that was in harmony with it.

# Colour

Chinese astrology teaches that there are five planetary colours: Jupiter the Wood planet is the blue-green of foliage and the sea; Mars the Fire planet is the red of cinnabar, an ore of the metal mercury; Saturn the Earth planet is the colour of the yellow ochre of central China; Venus the Metal planet, also known as the Great White, is brilliant silvery white; Mercury the Water planet with no colour of its own is deemed to be bluish-black, the colour of the night sky. The planetary colours send out specific messages:

### Red
This is the colour of blood and in the West is thought of as a danger signal, but in China the reverse is the case – lucky days are marked in red, unfavourable ones in black. Being a lucky colour, restaurants and temples in China are vividly decorated in red to welcome clients. But if a house was painted in that colour, it might suggest to the casual observer that the welcome, effusive and attentive as it might be, would be of a more personal nature.

### Green
This represents spring, health and growth, and has long been regarded as a healing colour, appropriate for the interior decoration of hospitals and clinical practices.

*In China, red is considered lucky and the preferred colour for restaurants, temples and even wedding dresses – white is reserved for funerals.*

### Yellows and browns
These symbolize stability and endurance.

### White or silvery grey
These are the colours of knife blades and money. Indeed, the oldest Chinese coinage was not round but knife shaped.

### Black or dark blue
These are the colours of flowing water, suggesting change and communication.

## Combinations of two colours
Combinations of colours represent conjunctions of the planets – when two or more planets are seen together in the sky, celestial messages are

inferred from the conjoining of their elements. Thus combinations of colours, such as black and yellow, are more informative than the particular shades on their own. Here are the hidden messages revealed by the various possible combinations of the planetary colours

## 1 Green and red
This combination links intelligence with creativity and stimulates study which is allied to practical work, and is thus favourable for a creative environment. As red and green also suggest vegetable and animal life, it is a good combination for all matters to do with farming and husbandry.

## 2 Green and yellow
A pretty and vivid combination but not a favourable one for permanent decorative schemes; the Wood element takes all the nourishment from the Earth, suggesting loss of resources and eventual distress.

## 3 Green and white
Green and white shows the element Metal chopping down Wood, so is an unfavourable combination as it suggests the onset of ill-health.

## 4 Green and black
A beneficial combination, the healing green is supported by nourishing Water. Several commercial enterprises specializing in healthy foods have used this combination successfully as their livery.

## 5 Red and yellow
A harmonious combination that suggests both activity and stability. Close-knit family groups and long-standing established firms benefit from this colour pairing.

## 6 Red and white

Fire conquers Metal, so the associated planetary colours red and white are not a harmonious combination. Many countries use these colours in their national flags, usually in commemoration of some battle or war. In some countries, a barber's pole is striped with red and white, a gory reminder of the days when the barber was also the local surgeon.

*The white on the Austrian flag is said to symbolise the line left on a bloodied shirt when a fierce warrior took his belt off.*

## 7 Red and black

Water and Fire are discordant, represented by the colours black and red. This dramatic colour combination is immediately aggressive which is effective occasionally, but has an adverse result when used too readily. Some psychologists have detected a preference for this combination in people with a tendency to bipolarity or schizophrenia.

## 8 Yellow and white

Yellow and white suggest the creation of wealth, but to the exclusion of all else. According to the rules of Western heraldry, the two colours (representing gold and silver) should never be used together on a heraldic device, except for that of the pope.

## 9 Yellow and black

Nature has its own clear danger signal: black and yellow is the colour of stinging insects, poisonous reptiles and ferocious tigers. This effective colour combination has been adopted by industry as the warning sign for hazardous materials. People who habitually adopt black and yellow as a colour combination are subconsciously sending out a message which says 'Come closer at your peril!'. These two colours represent Water and Earth, elements that are mutually discordant.

### 10 White and black

Water and Metal, black and white, harmonize like the notes on a piano keyboard. Black suggests communication and correspondence, the white suggests blank paper waiting for words to be written on it. Together the two colours suggest efficiency and economy, but a dislike of compromise.

## Heavenly colours

Violets and purples do not belong to the planetary system, but to the Heavens themselves. The north polar region of the sky, which holds the stars of the Great Bear, is known in Chinese astronomy as the

### STAR OF WONDER

A recently discovered piece of woven brocade from the 1st century BCE records the conjunction of five planets. The brocade has a repeat pattern of the four celestial animals – Dragon, Bird, Tiger and Tortoise – to represent the Heavens, and among the pattern are woven ancient Chinese characters stating 'the five stars were seen in the east, bringing good fortune to China'.

Some commentators believe that since the brocade was found in the most westerly part of China and dates from the 1st century when there actually was a conjunction of the five planets, it is possibly a reference to the 'wise men of the East' seeing the star that forecast the birth of Jesus.

*People who are involved with mysticism may be drawn to violet and purple.*

Purple Palace. People who have inclinations to clairvoyance and a connection with the spirit worlds often prefer clothes of these colours. Opposite the purple spiritual realm is the Earth, for which the associated colour is yellow. The combination of purple and yellow is rarely seen in fashionable clothing or commercial advertising because the effect is so startling, yet purple and yellow represents the harmony of Heaven and Earth.

## Harmonious triplets

Conjunctions of three planets are less common while conjunctions of four or five planets are very rare indeed. Ancient astrologers reflected on the forecasts predicted by the conjunction of three planets, and their observations can be applied to the five possible combinations of the three planetary colours. In the following remarks, the first and third colours of each triplet (the outer two) are in opposition and by themselves would be an unfavourable combination. But with the intermediary colour added as an accessory, the conflict is turned into a harmonious combination.

The outer two colours in each triplet should be the principal colours in any design and be in similar proportions. Only a hint of the binding intermediary colour (shown over the page in italics) is needed. Thus if a decorating scheme of green and white is chosen, a subtle touch of black would separate the potential conflict between Wood and Metal.

**The creative triplet** – black/dark blue, *light blue/green*, red
This combination is favourable for artists and writers or those wishing to stimulate their personal relationships or romantic life.

**The intellect triplet** – light blue/green, *touches of red*, yellow/ochre
This combination is an aid to study and gives confidence to those who need help and stamina when going through a difficult phase.

**The stability triplet** – red, *yellow/ochre*, white/cream
Inner conflict arising through dissatisfaction with existing circumstances can be resolved by calming the restlessness which mars a peaceful existence.

**The wealth triplet** – yellow/gold, *pale shades/white*, black/dark blue
Business people, in fact anyone involved in trade and commerce, can benefit from this combination of colours, which helps to sharpen negotiating skills.

**The media triplet** – white, *black/dark blue*, light blue/green
This combination deals with communication, through the written word or by travel; at a personal level it hones verbal skills and quick thinking.

## The five absences

It is not favourable to have a colour scheme involving four of the planetary colours, since one is missing, implying that one area of life's activities will be weakened. The five possible combinations are:

**Wood absent** – red, yellow, white, black
Absence of the Wood element shows lack of creativity, complacency, problems with children, weakened health and poor eyesight.

**Fire absent** – green, yellow, white, black
The absence of Fire reveals reduced intellectual capacity, loss of physical energy, poor circulation and lack of taste.

**Earth absent** – green, red, white, black
When the stabilizing Earth element is missing there is a lack of commitment to projects, places and relationships, with flawed loyalties resulting from a feeling of insecurity. When subjected to such an environment, the digestive system can be adversely affected.

*Blacks, whites, blues and greens stimulate the written and spoken word.*

**Metal absent** – green, red, yellow, black
This is an unfavourable combination for any commercial enterprise. It reveals a lack of business acumen, a reluctance to compete and a failure to empathize. Pulmonary problems and breathlessness are symptomatic of such an environment.

**Water absent** – green, red, yellow, white
The combination reveals a haphazard agglomeration of ideas in a confused situation that does not relate to real issues. In business, it results in a failure to understand the client's needs, while in personal relationships it indicates a lack of rapport between partners. This weak environment may lead to a loss of sexual vitality.

# Sound and matching houses to people

A reference in very early Chinese literature reveals that the practice of matching people to their homes was commonplace even 2,000 years ago. Unfortunately, the method described is rather vague, merely asserting that the 'sound' of the person must match the 'sound' of the house without explaining exactly what the house sound is, or what is meant by the sound of the person.

One early reference from the 1st century says that by going into the marketplace on New Year's Eve and listening to the general hum of the people milling about, the musical pitch of the overall sound will predict the general forecast for the year ahead. Perhaps the 'sound' of the house is the acoustic resonance heard in an empty building. The 'sound' of the person may be the tone of the name; unfortunately the writer of this reference is tantalizingly short of information on this point.

What we are told, however, is that if the sound of the house did not match the sound of the person, a bell of an appropriate tone would be hung up to remedy the discord. The five notes of the Chinese musical scale (the pentatonic scale, common to folk music throughout the world) were equated with the Five Elements (see pages 202– 203) and their planetary colours (see page 324) – though not in either of the more familiar sequences.

## MUSICAL NOTES, THEIR BELLS AND ELEMENTS

| Musical note | Bell name | Element |
|---|---|---|
| C | Yellow Bell House | Earth |
| D | White Bell House | Metal |
| E | Green Bell House | Wood |
| G | Red Bell House | Fire |
| A | Black Bell House | Water |

## Alernative method

Fortunately, there exists another method of finding the appropriate sound for buildings and people that does not require the expert services of an acoustic engineer. This simply relates the 'bell' sound to the year when the house was constructed rather than any audible sound, and similarly the 'bell' sound of a person is found from the person's year of birth, according to established principles of Chinese astrology. The appropriate 'sounds' can be found in the table on page 334.

## Remedy for discord

If a potential occupier wishes to know whether a prospective residence or business premises will be suitable, it is only necessary to compare the 'sounds' for the building and the potential occupier to see whether or not they are favourable together. If the combination is not a favourable one, compare the sound with the planetary colours above and introduce the intermediary colour into the decorating scheme (see pages 329–330 on Harmonious triplets), or a bell sounding the appropriate note (see small table above).

Use the table on page 334 to find a house or person note from the year the house was built or the year of birth. Find outlined below the particular house note – a, c, d, e, g – along with each kind of person (by note) and what these combinations may mean.

## FINDING THE BELL SOUNDS FOR HOUSES OR PEOPLE

| Year of house construction or year of birth | | | | | | Note |
|---|---|---|---|---|---|---|
| 1840–41 | 1870–71 | 1900–01 | 1930–31 | 1960–61 | 1990–91 | c |
| 1842–43 | 1872–73 | 1902–03 | 1932–33 | 1962–63 | 1992–93 | d |
| 1844–45 | 1874–75 | 1904–05 | 1934–35 | 1964–65 | 1994–95 | g |
| 1846–47 | 1876–77 | 1906–07 | 1936–37 | 1966–67 | 1996–97 | a |
| 1848–49 | 1878–79 | 1908–09 | 1938–39 | 1968–69 | 1998–99 | c |
| 1850–51 | 1880–81 | 1910–11 | 1940–41 | 1970–71 | 2000–01 | d |
| 1852–53 | 1882–83 | 1912–13 | 1942–43 | 1972–73 | 2002–03 | e |
| 1854–55 | 1884–85 | 1914–15 | 1944–45 | 1974–75 | 2004–05 | a |
| 1856–57 | 1886–87 | 1916–17 | 1946–47 | 1976–77 | 2006–07 | c |
| 1858–59 | 1888–89 | 1918–19 | 1948–49 | 1978–79 | 2008–09 | g |
| 1860–61 | 1890–91 | 1920–21 | 1950–51 | 1980–81 | 2010–11 | e |
| 1862–63 | 1892–93 | 1922–23 | 1952–53 | 1982–83 | 2012–13 | a |
| 1864–65 | 1894–95 | 1924–25 | 1954–55 | 1984–85 | 2014–15 | d |
| 1866–67 | 1896–97 | 1926–27 | 1956–57 | 1986–87 | 2016–17 | g |
| 1868–69 | 1898–99 | 1928–29 | 1958–59 | 1988–89 | 2018–19 | e |

## House note a  Black Bell House
### Black Bell person a

The harmony of peace. This combination favours communication and travel and cements friendships. It benefits those who work with people, the media and those in the public eye.

### Yellow Bell person c

With this combination the atmosphere is tense; there may be broken love affairs and scandal.

### White Bell person d

With this combination there is a welcome awaiting for those who spend long periods away from home.

### Green Bell person e

This combination may result in parents marrying more than once and having many children and numerous descendants to care for them in later life.

### Red Bell person g

With this combination there is a danger of accident, calamity and burglary. Make the house safe against intruders.

## House note c  Yellow Bell House

### Black Bell person a

In this combination dangers linger in hidden corners; guard against polluted water supplies. It suggests sickness, particularly with regards to the digestive or reproductive systems.

### Yellow Bell person c

The harmony of a satisfied life. This combination provides stability and contentment, and is favourable for all matters regarding real estate.

### White Bell person d

With this combination business will prosper and the residents' wealth will increase.

### Green Bell person e

With this combination there is a lack of commitment; problems are left unresolved. Indecisiveness leads to instability.

Red Bell person g

> With this combination, the Red Bell resident will be extremely happy, transform the house into a magnificent property and gain the respect of friends and family.

## House note d  White Bell House

### Black Bell person a

> With this combination the resident will travel to far-off places or marry someone from a foreign land, yet always maintain the home here.

### Yellow Bell person c

> This combination is an ideal situation if the plan is to both live and work here. Business and family life are both favoured.

### White Bell person d

> The harmony of wealth. This combination is especially favourable for males who achieve their ambitions. Females will be successful in business.

### Green Bell person e

> With this combination the prospects for health are unfavourable and eyesight may be affected.

### Red Bell person g

> With this combination it is difficult to manage finances and money leaves the house as fast as it comes in.

## House note e  Green Bell House

### Black Bell person a

> With this combination the resident will be happy and content with the house, and will not wish to move elsewhere.

*Matching the home to the person will help to provide an environment which is both stable and yet stimulating.*

### Yellow Bell person c

With this combination the resident will not feel at ease here, but lack the motivation to move on.

### White Bell person d

With this combination the notes are discordant; the house does not give any support to the resident. There is no stability, a feeling of insecurity. In health matters, there are prospects of pulmonary illnesses.

### Green Bell person e

The harmony of long life. With this combination the prospects for health, family relationships, the well-being of females and personal happiness are extremely favourable.

### Red Bell person g

With this combination the house provides security; the environment is stimulating and allows the resident to work with diligence and dedication. Enthusiastic study leads to discovery.

# House note g  Red Bell House

## Black Bell person a

With this combination the resident will not be satisfied with the surroundings and will suffer depression.

## Yellow Bell person c

With this combination the house will increase in value because of the care and attention that the dedicated resident will lavish on the property. There will be further gains of land and property.

## White Bell person d

With this combination the house will prove to be in a hazardous location and there are risks of injury and accident.

## Green Bell person e

With this combination the environment is supportive, especially if the occupier is obliged to stay at home because of family or other commitments. It is an ideal situation for study and recovery from chronic illness.

## Red Bell person g

The harmony of a virtuous life. With this combination honours, fame and the rewards for dedicated service to others await the worthy occupier whose sound matches that of the house.

# The Magic Square of Nine

The system of matching people to their homes by their 'inner sounds' is the oldest method on record, but within the past couple of decades, another Chinese technique for matching people to their homes has become widely popular in the West.

Several variations of the basic system exist, and these are known by various names such as *Luo Shu* or *Book of the River Luo* (its original name); *Ba Zhai* or the Eight House Plans; *Ba Gua* or Eight Trigrams; Flying Stars; Nine Star *Ki*, and countless other adaptations. It is even probable that the *Luo Shu* inspired the addictive sudoku puzzle, since all these topics are ultimately derived from the same simple plan: the Magic Square of Nine. There is now a whole library of books on the subject, and the following section is a very brief attempt to summarize some of the different methods in a few pages.

## Origins of the *Luo Shu*

There are numerous examples of the *Luo Shu* on artefacts from the 1st century, while more detailed texts with charts and predictions on manuscripts from the 7th century have been discovered at the cave temples of Dun Huang. Nevertheless, no references to the *Luo Shu* have been found so far in the most ancient Chinese text sources, the oracle bones from the Shang dynasty (*c.* 4,000 BCE) even though these include hundreds of references to astronomical events and related predictions.

Strictly speaking, because *Luo Shu* methods have nothing to do with the stars and planets (although *Luo Shu* numbers are referred to as 'meteors' or 'flying stars') the subject is not part of Chinese astrology at all, but the Magic Square of Nine is now so inextricably linked with Chinese astrology that it would be remiss to exclude it.

## What is *Luo Shu*?

The Magic Square of Nine, the *Book of the River Luo*, is said to have been discovered in the markings on the back of a sacred tortoise that lived in the river Luo, which flowed through the ancient capital of Luoyang. It consists of the numbers 1 to 9 arranged in such a way that each vertical, horizontal and diagonal row adds up to 15. This is the fundamental *Luo Shu* in the yang pattern.

| 4 | 9 | 2 |
|---|---|---|
| 3 | 5 | 7 |
| 8 | 1 | 6 |

Sometimes the sequence of numbers goes in reverse, making the yin pattern.

| 6 | 1 | 8 |
|---|---|---|
| 7 | 5 | 3 |
| 2 | 9 | 4 |

Readers with a logical turn of mind will realize that the mirror images of these two patterns would also form magic squares, but as yet no nine-star calculation methods using mirror-imaged patterns exist. No doubt, however, the time is ripe for some enterprising fortune-teller to develop a novel system which does so.

According to the method used, the *Luo Shu* numbers may all be increased or reduced by the same amount, depending on the number that is placed in the central position; but of course when this is done, the rows will no longer total 15 and the modified pattern is no longer a Magic Square. For example, if the rules of whatever system used stipulate that the central number should be 6, each figure in the pattern would accordingly be increased by 1. (As only nine digits are ever used in the sequence, 9 is followed by 1).

| 5 | 1 | 3 |
|---|---|---|
| 4 | **6** | 8 |
| 9 | 2 | 7 |

Because it appears that each number has 'flown' from one position to the next in the sequence, they are called 'flying stars' – a literal translation of the Chinese expression for 'meteors'. Predictions are inferred from the relation between the new pattern of numbers and the original *Luo Shu*.

But the logic behind the interpretation of the *Luo Shu* numbers is derived from another aspect of Chinese philosophy, the Eight Trigrams of Change. To understand the way in which the diviners of the *Luo Shu* arrive at their forecasts, it is first necessary to understand the relevance of the Eight Trigrams.

*Rubik's Cube and Sudoku puzzles have their origins in the Magic Square of Nine.*

# The Eight Trigrams of Change

Even those with only little familiarity with Chinese traditions cannot have escaped seeing the particularly Chinese pattern of lines, collectively known as the *bagua*, which means 'eight groups of three lines'. These groups of lines are a prototype of the binary system used in computer and digital technology, but their related *Luo Shu* numbers are not equivalent to the binary numbers known to today's mathematicians. The amount of Chinese literature devoted to the investigation of the trigrams and their philosophical application is vast, but the fundamental qualities of the trigrams are quite simple.

There are eight patterns. Each has an untranslatable Chinese name, a common name and a family member name. For example, the trigram consisting of three unbroken lines has the Chinese name *Qian*, the common name 'Heaven' and represents the father in the family. See the table opposite showing of the eight trigrams and their names.

There are more than 40,000 possible ways in which the eight trigrams could be allocated to the eight compass directions, but in practice only two are ever used:

- One usually found on feng shui *bagua* mirrors and other talismans called the 'pre-Heaven' sequence which has the trigram consisting of three yang lines (Heaven or Father) in the south position.

## THE EIGHT TRIGRAMS

| Trigram | Character | Chinese name | Common name | Family role |
|---------|-----------|--------------|-------------|-------------|
| ☰ | 乾 | qian | Heaven | Father |
| ☵ | 坎 | kan | Water | Middle son |
| ☶ | 艮 | gen | Mountain | Youngest son |
| ☳ | 辰 | zhen | Thunder | Eldest son |
| ☴ | 巽 | xun | Wind | Eldest daughter |
| ☲ | 離 | li | Fire | Middle daughter |
| ☷ | 坤 | kun | Earth | Mother |
| ☱ | 兌 | dui | Lake | Youngest daughter |

- The other sequence, known as the 'post-Heaven' sequence, is found on practical Chinese mariners' compasses and special feng shui compasses, and has the three yang lines in the north-west position.

Unfortunately mass-produced tourist souvenirs cannot be relied upon to be manufactured according to correct Chinese philosophical principles and bizarre arrangements of the diagrams will often be found on cheaply made trinkets. The only relevant sequence that need be considered is the post-Heaven sequence, which equates the Eight Directions and the Nine *Luo Shu* numbers and the Five Elements as follows:

## THE POST-HEAVEN SEQUENCE

| Trigram | Common name | Direction | Luo Shu number | Element | Qualities |
|---|---|---|---|---|---|
| | Heaven | NW | 6 | Metal | Inspiration, creativity, authority, masculinity |
| | Water | N | 1 | Water | Repeated activities, machines, circular movement, communication |
| | Mountain | NE | 8 | Earth | Youth, obstinacy, steadfastness, land and buildings |
| | Thunder | E | 3 | Wood | Movement, transport, logistics, change of residence, relocation |
| | | Centre | 5 | Earth | |
| | Wind | SE | 4 | Wood | Crafts and skills, construction and assembly, manufacture, career |
| | Fire | S | 9 | Fire | Kilns and ovens, chemical processes, friendships, non-sexual relationships, judgements, rewards and retribution |
| | Earth | SW | 2 | Earth | Nourishment, femininity, marriage, motherhood, farming and horticulture, healing |
| | Lake | W | 7 | Metal | Babyhood and old age, education. the arts and entertainment |

*Each trigram has associated qualities: the trigram Wind is associated with qualities including crafts and skills.*

Note that the number 9 represents the south and 1 the north. It is a convention, nothing more, to compile *Luo Shu* charts with south at the top, so that in the basic Magic Square, 9, representing the south, will be at the top and 1, the north, at the bottom.

Each of the trigrams has its own quality and influence (in itself neither good nor bad; the favourability or otherwise of a trigram depends on its relevance to a situation). Thus Heaven or Father in the north-west, represents both inspiration and authority. A summary of the qualities of each trigram is set out in the table opposite.

# The Ba Zhai or Eight House Plans

The most fundamental of the many systems employing the *Luo Shu* is that of the Eight House Plans, also known as the Seven Portents. It is simple and elegant in its logic and all other systems are derived from this source. In *ba zhai*, the trigram representing the direction faced by the door is compared with each of the other seven trigrams, resulting in a 'portent' for each direction other than that of the door – hence the reason for there being Eight House Plans, but only Seven Portents.

For example, suppose the door faces north-west. The door's trigram is the Heaven trigram of three unbroken or yang lines. The area to the 'dragon side' of the door will be in the west, the trigram of which is a yin or broken line on top of two yang lines. When the trigram for the door is compared with the trigram for the west, the line that changed is the top line which, as will shortly be revealed, signifies inspiration.

## Comparing trigrams

Since a trigram consists of three lines, it can be compared to the Chinese number three ☰, which represent Heaven, People and the Earth. When two trigrams are compared, there are four possibilities:

- Identical (when the trigram of the door is compared with itself)
- Complete reversals of each other
- One of the lines changes
- One line will remain the same while the other two change.

Bearing in mind that the three lines of the trigram represent Heaven, People and the Earth, the meaning of the replacement of one trigram by another becomes clear. Here are the seven possible changes.

**Top line changes:** Something comes from Heaven; inspiration. Very favourable, this conjunction is known as the Birth of Qi.

**Middle line changes:** A person's state changes from living to lifeless. Very unfavourable and known as Severed Fate.

**Bottom line changes:** The ground gives way, causing an accident. An unfavourable location called Accidents and Mishaps.

**Middle and bottom lines change, top line remains:** Favourable. Heaven is eternal; known as Celestial Unity or more usually as the Celestial Healer, this is a suitable area for invalids.

**Top and bottom lines change, middle line remains:** People are torn between responsibilities (Heaven) and desires (Earth) causing unrest and difficulties. Known as the Six Curses, this area is best reserved for routine work.

**Top and middle lines change, bottom line remains:** The body's state has changed and the Heaven line accepts the soul. Known as the Five Ghosts, this place is best reserved for spiritual matters.

**All lines change:** If everything changes, things revert to what they were; thus a cycle has ended and another one begins. This very favourable conjunction is known as Long Life.

 **No lines change:** This is the doorway; the technical term for the conjunction is 'Facing the Throne'. It is neither favourable nor unfavourable.

Although it would be a useful and instructive exercise for readers to compile their own charts of the eight possible orientations of a house, this table will serve to relieve readers of that chore.

## TABLE OF THE SEVEN PORTENTS

| If the door faces, then | NW | N | NE | E | SE | S | SW | W |
|---|---|---|---|---|---|---|---|---|
| The Celestial Healer area is in the | NE | E | NW | N | S | SE | W | SW |
| The Long Life area is in the | SW | S | W | SE | E | N | NW | NE |
| The Source of Inspiration is in the | W | SE | SW | S | N | E | NE | NW |
| The Six Curses affect the | N | NW | E | NE | W | SW | S | SE |
| Accidents and mishaps occur in the | SE | W | S | SW | NW | NE | E | N |
| The Five Ghosts lurk in the | E | NE | N | NW | SW | W | SE | S |

# Comparing *Luo Shu* numbers

Exactly the same principles apply when two numbers on a *Luo Shu* chart are compared. If we want to compare the *Luo Shu* numbers 8 and 4, for example, we only need to compare the relevant trigrams and refer to the preceding notes. *Luo Shu* Number 8 belongs to the trigram Mountain, which is a yang line atop two yin lines, whereas *Luo Shu* Number 4 belongs to the trigram Thunder, which shows two yin lines above an Earth yang line. The top and bottom lines have changed, but the inner line remains the same, producing 'Six Curses'.

The fact that we are now dealing with numbers not mystical diagrams, opens up endless possibilities, since almost anything can be represented by a number. The most obvious application for using a *Luo Shu* number is for a date; perhaps for the year that a house was built or for a person's date of birth. Thus the links between the *Luo Shu* numbers and Chinese astrology now begin to appear. Chinese calendars, even from more than a thousand years ago, identify the *Luo Shu* number for the year and month, a practice continued to this day. Indeed, some Chinese astrological calendars give the *Luo Shu* number for the day as well.

A simple formula gives the *Luo Shu* number for the year: simply add the four digits for the year and if the total is greater than 9, add the digits of the result, then subtract the final figure from 11.

For example, the year **2010**: $2 + 0 + 1 + 0 = 3; 11 - 3 = $ **8**

For the year **1976**: $1 + 9 + 7 + 6 = 23; 2 + 3 = 5, 11 - 5 = $ **6**

Note that the *Luo Shu* numbers for the years go in reverse order.

## *Luo Shu* numbers and trigrams

Having established the number to work with, this is placed in the central position of the *Luo Shu* diagram (see over the page for an example). Because each of the directions is now occupied by a guest number, we can compare the various visiting numbers with the original

*Luo Shu* number to establish which conjunctions are favourable or otherwise, exactly as is done in the case of the Eight House Plans (see pages 346–348). There is, of course, one discrepancy; there are nine *Luo Shu* numbers, but only eight trigrams. Thus, if any number other than 5 occupies the central position of the chart, it follows that 5 must take the place of one of the trigrams. In Chinese, the word *wu*, meaning 5, sounds like the Chinese word for 'not' or 'without'. Thus whatever direction is occupied by the number 5 lacks the beneficial qualities of the missing trigram. In Chinese calendars, this is called the 'Five Yellow Curse' because 5 should occupy the central position, which belongs to the Earth element whose planetary colour is the yellow of central China. To take an example, as noted in the previous paragraph, the *Luo Shu* number for the year 2010 is 8.

This number occupies the centre of the Nine Squares in place of 5, and the remaining eight numbers distributed proportionally by increasing each one by 3. Thus the original:

| 4 | 9 | 2 |
|---|---|---|
| 3 | 5 | 7 |
| 8 | 1 | 6 |

becomes:

| 7 | 3 | 5 |
|---|---|---|
| 6 | 8 | 1 |
| 2 | 4 | 9 |

Recollecting that south is at the top, the number 5 now occupies the south-west corner of the chart. Because the south-west trigram, Earth or Mother, represents motherhood and women's interests, and since it

*The direction that a house or building faces determines how favourable it can be. The date of its construction can determine how suitable it will be for an owner.*

has been displaced by 5, it would appear that 2010 would be a generally unfavourable year for women. There is, however, a beneficial effect: 5 normally resides in the centre and belongs to the Earth element, as does the trigram for the south-west. In other words, the Earth Trigram has been replaced by 5 Earth! We can interpret this to mean that any problems facing women in 2010 will reach a satisfactory solution.

Tables that give the distribution of *Luo Shu* numbers for the coming year, together with the Tai Sui (see pages 320– 323) and related influences appear on the opening pages of every Chinese almanac.

# further applications of the Luo Shu numbers

It has already been said that *Luo Shu* numerology does not strictly belong to the realm of Chinese astrology and it is beyond the scope of this book to delve much deeper into the subject than these few introductory remarks. For completeness however, it should be added that the most popular system of *Luo Shu* numerology borrows from an older method of divination known as *Qimen Dunjia*, a technical Chinese expression that defies translation.

In *Qimen Dunjia* divination, each cycle of 60 years (one for each of the combinations of the 60 Stems and Branches) is divided into three 20-year periods; each of these 20-year periods has a *Luo Shu* number allocated in ascending order (unlike the yearly numbers, which descend).

## Modern use of *Luo Shu*

Present-day feng shui practitioners reckon the 'age' of a house according to the 20-year period in which it was built. The period 8, for example, began in 2004. This is the number, which for a building, is placed in the centre of the *Luo Shu* chart. To that are added two more numbers, one based on the direction faced by the front door, called the 'Facing' or Water-star direction, and the other from the rear of the house, the 'Sitting' or Mountain-star direction. The Water-star

*The direction faced by the main door of a building is of prime importance when determining whether it has favourable feng shui or not.*

number and the Mountain-star number generate further *Luo Shu* charts that may follow in a forwards or reverse direction. When they are superimposed, they provide a trio of *Luo Shu* numbers for every direction, which the feng shui practitioner uses to discover the most favourable areas in a building and uncover potential hazards or weaknesses.

Sadly, we have already strayed beyond the bounds of astrological lore, and must leave this fascinating topic in the good hands of an adept feng shui consultant. Instead, let us leave the confines of the house, and take a stroll into the Scholar's Garden.

# food and philosophy

Some 50 years ago in the West, Chinese food was an exotic delicacy to be treated with awe and suspicion. Today it is as much a part of Western cuisine as pizza, French fries, frankfurters, chicken korma, chilli con carne and doner kebabs. Unlike these well-established dishes, however, Chinese food is the only one that comes with its own astrological accessory – the fortune cookie. Furthermore, while all these international dishes are eaten at any time of the year, Chinese cuisine is associated with a particular astronomical event – the Chinese New Year. It is then that supermarkets will stock and promote a range of Chinese-style foods in glorious red and gold packaging.

But behind these obvious displays of traditional allegiance to the Chinese calendar there are many other aspects of Chinese cuisine that stem from the basic concepts of Chinese astrological philosophy. Firstly, there is the balance of yin and yang. Every Chinese cook-book will emphasize the importance of adhering to this fundamental principle. The predominant taste, texture or colour of the main part of a dish should be balanced by a garnish opposite to it in quality. Indeed, it is generally believed that eating particular combinations of food that destroy the balance of yin and yang can have disastrous consequences.

*Fortune cookies are a fun treat at the Chinese New Year, although they are a relatively new invention.*

## The Five Elements in Chinese cuisine

The five elements, which are the outward manifestations of the five planets, play a pivotal role in the choice of ingredients. The element quality is not confined to the taste, colour and texture of the foods, but in the manner of preparation as well. The methods of cooking food relate to the Five Elements according to the degree of moistness or dryness, mild warmth or charring heat. The hotter and dryer the cooking process, the greater the Fire quality, the cooler and more moist the process, the greater the Water element. Although there are many cooking processes, they can be summarized as simmering (Water), steaming (Wood), dry-roasting (Fire), deep-frying (Earth), and stir-frying (Metal). Two of these, steaming and stir-frying, although familiar to the cuisines of nearly every culture, are particularly Chinese. Moreover, these are the most nutritious methods since they conserve more of the vital healthy qualities of the food than other culinary methods, and are also energy-saving because they make economical use of fuel resources.

# General principles

The place of the Five Elements in Chinese cookery not only refers to the ingredients themselves, but to their colours and textures as well as tastes and the five methods of cooking.

## Steamers

Chinese food-steamers are an essential part of a Chinese kitchen, and usually have three or more tiers. Only the lower two tiers can be used for cooking; the upper tiers do not become hot enough to cook and must only be used for keeping cooked food warm. Traditional steamers are made of woven bamboo, thus complementing the Wood element of the steaming process. Modern metal steamers belong to the industrial factory canteen and have no place in the domestic kitchen, at least for cooking Chinese food.

*Bamboo steamers belong to the wood element, as does steam cooking.*

## Woks

The other quintessentially Chinese method of cooking is stir-frying, and this, belonging to the Metal element, is appropriately done in the Chinese frying pan or wok. This should be made from iron, which is thick and heavy at its centre, with the sides tapering to an almost sharp edge. This construction keeps the centre of the pan at a high temperature, while the edges are so cool they can be handled without any discomfort. The diced vegetables and other ingredients can then be stir-fried in the sparsest drop of hot oil, and the whole pan lifted and shaken according to the cook's inclination and dexterity. When covered with its domed lid, the food can be left to sizzle without any danger of its burning. The food will cook under the vapour which gathers under the dome and when this begins to escape, the cooking process is complete.

## Eating utensils

Chinese people use chopsticks to eat with, and porcelain spoons from which to drink soups and sauces. Knives are not placed on the table as this is regarded as a hostile gesture. Because there are no knives handy, Chinese food is presented at the dining table already sliced so that the diners can pick up the morsels easily.

*Westerners are sometimes at a bit of a loss when faced with chopsticks!*

# The digestive system

Digestion belongs to the body's central element, which is Earth. This element governs the associated organs of digestion. Just as a kitchen prepares food for our consumption ('external cooking'), so the digestive system prepares the food for the body to use ('internal cooking'). Too much external cooking – overcooking or cooking in too much fat – creates internal cold and damp, which reduces the digestive system's ability to process the food. Too little cooking is also to be avoided. While salads and raw vegetables are essential to a healthy diet, it is important to avoid eating too many raw foods.

Do not hurry the meal; Western cuisine places several contrasting foods on one plate – the meat or other protein, the green and root vegetables and the sauce altogether. The Chinese system is for a series of dishes to be offered one by one, so that there is time to select and digest each dish in turn.

# Foods of the Five Elements

The notion of a healthy, well-balanced diet is a relatively new concept in Western culture. The Chinese, however, have been aware of the secrets of a healthy eating regime for millennia.

In the Five Element scheme, the Wood element is represented by green vegetables, Fire by meat, Earth by fruits, Metal by grains and Water by salt and other naturally occurring minerals. The associated tastes are sour (Wood); bitter or burnt as in roast meat (Fire); sweet, when fruit is ripe (Earth); spicy and sharp (Metal); and savoury or salty (Water). Since the Five Elements are also associated with the body's zones, any deficiency or excess of the elements in the diet results in the malfunction of the relevant organ. Some further remarks about food balance and its place in traditional Chinese medicine are given in the Diet in traditional Chinese medicine section (see pages 372–373).

*While fruits generally belong to the Earth element because of their sweet taste, there are many with astringent or acid tastes which are classified as Wood or even Metal.*

# The 12 Animals and Chinese cuisine

According to some historians, the 12 Animals of the Chinese zodiac were originally items of food to be offered in sacrifice to the ancestors, but it is hard to imagine a venerable grandfather being appeased by the offer of a rat sandwich for afternoon tea. And would none of the ancestors have enjoyed a nice piece of fish, for there are no fish in the zodiac? And where would those petitioning their ancestors find dragon meat?

Nevertheless, even if the animals were not items on the menu, at least one thing is sure: every Chinese New Year banquet has to find some means of representing the animal sign of the year, usually displaying or even serving it among the less prominent depictions of its 11 companions.

Many Chinese cooks are wonderfully skilled in the art of carving and shaping meats and vegetables into delightful shapes and forms, and it is not uncommon at wedding banquets for the guests' tables to be decorated with marvellous dragons carved out of cucumbers and phoenixes fashioned from giant Chinese radishes.

For people wanting to celebrate the Chinese New Year with an animal zodiac-themed dinner, Chinese confectioners offer cakes decorated with the 12 Animals. Those wanting to try something a little more adventurous, the following suggestions may prove useful. Detailed recipes and cooking methods are not given since Chinese cook-books are now so readily obtainable.

## Rat

While a cat might be delighted with a mouse soufflé, the more conventional of your guests may not be. Since the Rat, standing in the north position, occupies the position of the Tortoise and belongs to the Water element and the colour black, you might consider turtle consommé for a very special dinner, perhaps with a hint of black truffle and water chestnuts to garnish. For vegetarians, settle for a mouse-shaped offering, perhaps half a pear garnished to give it the appearance of a cheerful rodent.

*Beef, stir-fried with ginger, is a good source of the Fire element.*

## Ox

Beef should be the main dish. A favourite is strips of lean beef stir-fried with spring onions and ginger, or strips of lean beef simmered in black bean sauce. Slice the beef across the grain so that it cooks quickly and is more palatable. Vegetarians may be offered dairy products.

## Tiger

There is no need to deplete the dwindling number of endangered species even further; striped tiger prawns will serve the purpose. Vegetarians can take heart: lion dancers at Chinese celebrations are given cabbage (and banknotes) as a reward for their exertions, partly because it was popularly believed in China that lions were vegetarians, and partly because the Chinese word for cabbage (*pak choy*) sounds like 'good luck'. So with a stretch of imagination, Chinese cabbage could substitute for Tiger!

## Rabbit

For those averse to eating Mr Bunny, herbs and spring greens are an appropriate replacement for the Hare that can distil the elixir of long life.

## Dragon

The Dragon is king of all the Water creatures, so lobster, prawns and all kinds of seafood, the more dragon-like the better, are appropriate. Vegetarian or not, those with artistic flair might attempt to carve a dragon from cucumber or more simply slice a gherkin in half, making a little slit at one end for its mouth with a sliver of pimento for its tongue and two cloves for its horns.

## Snake

Snakes occasionally feature on Chinese menus: indeed, there are restaurants specializing in the delicacy, but the treat could be less acceptable in the Western world. Eel could be served as an suitable alternative, but even that is not to everyone's taste. Pasta (cannelloni) simmered with spinach and green vegetables makes a suitable substitute.

## Horse

The Horse symbolizes the Great Yang and the Sun at its highest point. If horse-meat is not available, venison is equally appropriate. The accompanying sauce should be bold red to represent the Fire element. Vegetable alternatives should be a medley of brilliant red vegetables: tomatoes, pimentos, chilli, served very hot.

## Sheep

Lamb and mutton are found more commonly in northern China, so the appropriate course would be a Mongolian dish of minced lamb balls dropped into a spicy soup base. As sheep eat grass, a green salad provides the same nourishment that the lamb acquires so you can cut out the middle man if you are vegetarian!

## Monkey

The sign of dexterity, the Monkey can be represented by an intricately fashioned confection of either meat or vegetable. The cleverer and more awe-inspiring the dish, the greater the Monkey symbolism.

## Rooster

Chicken without a doubt is the food of choice here – an excellent dish is chicken simmered with mushrooms in a coconut milk sauce and given a really exotic touch with a slight hint of star anise. Of course, for the vegetarian there are lots of ways to present eggs.

## Dog

In China, a hot dog may literally mean just that. In the Western world, however, the notion of 'hot dogs' might substitute, but those bought from a street stall are hardly appropriate for a celebration dinner. Much more suitable would be a selection of various Chinese sausages that can be obtained from Chinese supermarkets, with vegetarian sausages for those who do not eat meat.

## Pig

Pork is probably the meat most favoured by the Chinese. Since we return to the Water element that began the cycle of 12, a dish of pork stewed very slowly with black plums or prunes would be an ideal choice. For the vegetarian, aubergines in a black bean sauce, seasoned with onions and root ginger reflects the attributes of the Water element.

# Practical considerations

The purpose of the following section is to show how the principles of Chinese astrology are woven into the philosophy that underlies Chinese traditional medicine. It is certainly not intended to be an introductory manual to traditional Chinese medicine and only the general outline of the subject is set out here. The principles of cold and heat, damp and dryness owe a great deal to Greek thought and it is obvious that much of the later theory of traditional Chinese medicine stands at the juncture of two ancient philosophies: the Greek with its four humours; and the Chinese with its Five Elements, with the latter deriving much of its theory from the basic principles of Chinese astrology.

Nevertheless, the practical application of traditional Chinese medicine requires some prior understanding of physiology and acupuncture theory, and a familiarity with diseases and their symptoms – knowledge that can only be gleaned from observation and practice. Thus while this section reveals the link between Chinese astrology and traditional Chinese medicine, it cannot be a practical guide to the subject.

Indeed, established practitioners of traditional Chinese medicine may take exception to the over-simplification of the subject and to some of the terms used here (for example, referring to zones rather than organs, or the 'stomach' where the Chinese term would be 'spleen'). But it is felt that these free interpretations will more readily help introduce the newcomer to the fundamental concepts of traditional Chinese medicine.

## The Western world

Traditional Chinese medicine is becoming widely recognized in the Western world as a vehicle for several kinds of complementary medical practice, alternative therapies and diagnostics, among which are the Chinese *materia medica*, specific herbal medicines, foot massage, moxybustion and acupuncture. As in Chinese astrology, at the core of Chinese medical diagnosis and prognosis

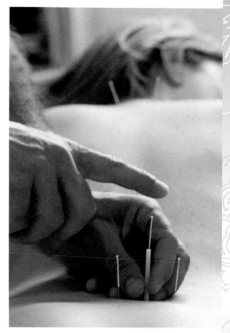

*Chinese medicine stresses the importance of acupuncture at specific times.*

lies the philosophy of the Five Elements. These relate to the zones (or organs) of the body and their attendant kinds of *Qi* or life force. In diagnosis, the Chinese doctor assesses whether the balance of the elements within the patient has been disturbed, which influences were too intense and which are weakened. Often, the doctor's deliberations take into account the seasons of the year or the times of the day when particular helpful or obstructive elements are at their zenith and the treatment will reflect these factors.

# The five Elements and the body zones

Traditional Chinese medicine refers to ten 'organs' of the body – five yang and five yin – but some of these ten 'organs', such as the pericardium (the membrane enclosing the heart) or the 'triple energizer' which has no physical existence, would not be regarded as organs in Western medicine, while other vital components, such as the brain and the uterus, are considered in Chinese medicine to be 'extraordinary functions'.

## Body zones

From the point of view of Chinese astrology, it is simpler to regard the body as being divided into five 'zones', one for each of the five elements. These are the liver (Wood); heart (Fire); stomach (Earth); lungs

### BODY ZONES AND THEIR ELEMENTS

| Element | Wood | Fire | Earth | Metal | Water |
|---------|------|------|-------|-------|-------|
| Stem | 2 | 4 | 6 | 8 | 10 |
| Yin | Liver | Heart | Spleen | Lungs | Kidneys |
| Stem | 1 | 3 | 5 | 7 | 9 |
| Yang | Gall bladder | Small intestine | Stomach | Large intestine | Bladder |

(Metal); and kidneys (Water). Further, each of these zones (regarded as yin) has a yang partner, thus establishing ten zones corresponding to the Ten Heavenly Stems.

To these are added two extra zones, the pericardium and the triple-energizer, making a total of 12. These 12 zones give rise to the 12 Meridians, paths along which the acupuncture points lie, and correspond to the 12 Earthly Branches or Chinese zodiac animals, as shown in the table below.

## TIMES OF THE DAY WHEN THE ACUPUNCTURE MERIDIANS ARE DOMINANT

| Branch | Animal | Hours | Meridian | Zone |
|--------|--------|-------|----------|------|
| I | Rat | 23.00–01.00 | Foot shao-yang | Gall bladder |
| II | Ox | 01.00–03.00 | Foot jue-yin | Liver |
| III | Tiger | 03.00–05.00 | Hand tai-yin | Lung |
| IV | Rabbit | 05.00–07.00 | Hand yang-ming | Large intestine |
| V | Dragon | 07.00–09.00 | Foot yang-ming | Stomach |
| VI | Snake | 09.00–11.00 | Foot tai-yin | Spleen |
| VII | Horse | 11.00–13.00 | Hand shao-yin | Heart |
| VIII | Sheep | 13.00–15.00 | Hand tai-yang | Small intestine |
| IX | Monkey | 15.00–17.00 | Foot tai-yang | Bladder |
| X | Rooster | 17.00–19.00 | Foot shao-yin | Kidney |
| XI | Dog | 19.00–21.00 | Hand jue-yin | Pericardium |
| XII | Pig | 21.00–23.00 | Hand shao-yang | Triple energizer |

# The five Openings

Associated with each element's zone is an opening of the face, which the Chinese doctor will study in diagnosis. The liver is associated with the eyes, which discolour and blanch when the patient is jaundiced; the heart's well-being is seen in the tongue; the malfunctioning of the digestive system is revealed in the mouth; infection of the lungs by an inflamed nose; while any imbalance in the urino-genitary system will be reflected in the state of the ears. (Other than the ears being roughly kidney-shaped, the connection between the ears and the Water element may not be immediately evident, but the association of water with sound is very ancient: the Nine Muses, river spirits, give us the word 'music', which of course goes in the ear.)

## Cross-cultural influences

It is at this point where ancient Greek medicine and Chinese medicine overlap. Related to the Five Elements are the Five Internal Symptoms, with the elements of Wood, Fire, Earth, Metal and Water manifesting themselves in Wind, Heat, Dryness, Dampness and Cold. As an example of a typical diagnosis, muscular spasms are said to derive from an excess of 'liver-wind' or disturbance of the body's Wood element; short-duration fevers with symptoms of red eyes, flushed face and irritability are due to excess heat or Fire element, while arthritis is the result of too much dampness in the body – an excess of the Metal element.

A doctor might also judge a condition by the emotionals: the Five Elements correspond to anger (liver/Wood); laughter (heart/Fire); contemplation (stomach/Earth); sadness (lungs/Metal); and fear (kidneys/Water). An unreasonable display of any of these – irrational rage, hysteria, introversion, depression or phobia – would tell the doctor that there was an excess of the element in the body. Similarly, if the emotion was lacking – complacency, showing a lack of the aggressive Wood or liver influence or a humourless disposition – would reveal a deficiency of the Fire or Heart

*Ears, eyes, nose, mouth and tongue are related to the element zones of the body.*

influence. Likewise, impulsiveness would indicate the absence of the steadying contemplative Earth element; callousness and a lack of sympathy reveals the absence of the lung-Metal element; rash heroism may be due to a lack of the cautious Water or kidney influence rather than sheer bravery.

## Cure to fit the disease

The types of therapy or cures are also related to the Five Elements: the Wood element is represented by the use of herbs; the Fire element by moxybustion and cautery (the use of heat to seal wounds); the Earth element by appropriate food; Metal by acupuncture (surgery is rarely applied); and Water by hydrotherapy.

# Diet in traditional Chinese medicine

In the previous section on Chinese food, mention was made of the fact that Chinese medicine stresses the importance of a balanced diet, particularly with regard to the role of the Five Elements. A comparison of the element of a particular food with the organ of the body associated with that element can indicate the consequence of any dietary excess or deficiency. The table below shows the various qualities associated with the Five Elements with particular relevance to diet:

| FIVE ELEMENTS, DIET AND HEALTH | | | | | |
|---|---|---|---|---|---|
| Element | Wood | Fire | Earth | Metal | Water |
| Flavour | Sour | Burnt, bitter | Sweet | Spicy | Savoury, salty |
| Food | Green vegetables | Meat, fats | Fruit, honey, sugars, grains | Herbs, spices | Salt, additives |
| Five Openings | Eyes | Tongue | Mouth | Nose | Ears |
| Body Zones | Liver | Heart | Stomach | Lungs | Kidneys |
| Emotions | Anger | Laughter | Contemplation | Sadness | Fear |

The classic text on traditional Chinese medicine, the *Yellow Emperor's Book*, compiled between the 4th and 1st centuries BCE, outlines the results of dietary excesses and deficiencies.

> *Too much salt (excess of Water element) results in a hardened pulse, watery eyes and a bluish complexion. Food which is too bitter (Fire element) causes the skin to age and results in hair loss. An excess of spicy food (Metal element) makes the muscles seize up and the nails rot. Too much sour food (Wood element) weakens the lips, hardens the flesh and wrinkles the skin. Over-indulgence in sweet foods produces weakness in the bones and incipient baldness.'*

Whenever symptoms indicate that a particular element is excessive, the situation can be alleviated by incorporating into the diet foods associated with the element that destroys the excessive element Similarly, where the symptoms suggest a particular element is deficient, the diet should include those foods that either relate to the weak element or support it.

*Honey is a natural remedy when there is a deficiency of the Earth element.*

# Applying Chinese astrology to diagnosis

Because diseases and weak functioning of the body can be attributed to the excess or deficiency of particular elements, it is possible to evaluate the elements prevailing at a particular date and time to see whether these are likely to be beneficial or otherwise. The Chinese practitioner would consider the element associated with the symptom and compare this with the patient's Four Columns (see pages 192–205), paying special attention to the Day Stem, the prevailing elements of the Day and Month, and the elements of the Life Cycle Pillars to establish whether the symptoms are likely to persist or only be of short duration.

Some acupuncture practitioners use even more sophisticated techniques in order to ensure that the patient receives the optimum benefit from the treatment. It must be stressed that what follows here is not intended to be a guide to acupuncture methods; there is much more to the study and practice of acupuncture than merely knowing the names and locations of the various points and meridians. However, those readers who have some knowledge of the subject may find this information of interest.

*The curative powers of some herbs in the Chinese pharmacopoeia were described at least two thousand years ago.*

## Time factors in acupuncture

Among the many branches of traditional Chinese medicine are two schools of thought that equate the rise and flow of different kinds of *Qi* or energy through the body to the temporal influences of the Stems and Branches, and their culmination at certain acupuncture points at specific times of the day. One such school is known as the *Zi Wu* or

*Acupuncture therapy takes many forms, some practitioners using needles of various lengths and thicknesses, others using none at all.*

'Branches I and VII' method, and the other, the *Ling Gui* or 'Mystic Tortoise' method. Both methods require the practitioner to refer to complex tables in order to find the appropriate acupuncture point according to the symptom and time of consultation.

## Branches system

Acupuncture practitioners following the *Zi Wu* system will consult tables that reveal the 'Main' acupuncture points, those open to stimulation every day, and the 'Mutual' points, which can only receive stimuli on certain days at particular times. For each of the days of the ten-day cycle there are different times when particular acupuncture points may be stimulated. Usually, there is at least one point open for every hour of each day. For example, the acupuncture point *shen men* (Spirit Gate) is open on a Stem 1 day between 05.00 and 07.00. But at noon on the same day, as no point is deemed to be particularly receptive at that time, the *shen men* point is suggested as a possible substitute. In the tables published in Chinese acupuncture manuals, about 60 different acupuncture points are listed.

## Mystic Tortoise system

In contrast, the Mystic Tortoise method concentrates on just Eight Prime acupuncture points, out of a possible 366 identified in the classical literature. These eight points are associated with the Eight Trigrams (see pages 342–345), which accounts for the method's unusual name – it derives from the quotation 'Study the Mystic Tortoise'.

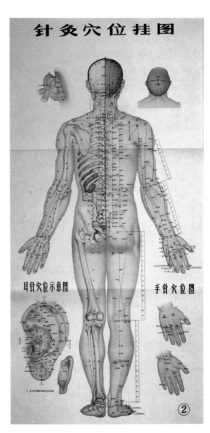

*The acupuncture points lie along certain 'meridians' below the surface of the skin.*

## LOCATION OF THE EIGHT PRIME ACUPUNCTURE POINTS

The Eight Prime acupuncture points lie on eight of the 12 Meridians, as shown in this table. (*Note: the cun is a comparative measurement used in acupuncture, being the distance between the creases of the middle finger.)

| Luo Shu number | Trigram | Chinese name of acupuncture point | Name of Meridian |
|---|---|---|---|
| 1 | Kan, Water, north | Shen mai | Bladder |
| 2 | Kun, Earth, south-west | Zhao hai | Kidney |
| 3 | Zhen, Wood | Wai guan | Triple energizer |
| 4 | Xun, Wood, south-east | Lin qi | Gall bladder |
| 5 | Qian, Metal, north-west | Gong sun | Spleen |
| 6 | Dui, Metal, west | Hou xi | Small intestine |
| 7 | Gen, Earth, north-east | Nei guan | Pericardium |
| 8 | Li, Fire, south | Lie que | Lung |

Since the Eight Trigrams have an affinity with the Five Elements, the nature of the related Trigram suggests the treatment to be followed.

When the nature of the illness is diagnosed, its related element, appropriate trigram and even the hour of consultation are taken into account when deciding which of the Eight Prime points needs to be stimulated. Since each hour of the day is also related to one of the 12 acupuncture meridians, the time for treatment depends on

**Location**

| |
|---|
| In the depression between the ankle bone and the tendon |
| Medial side of foot, tip of medial malleolus |
| Locate a point about 5 cm (2 inches) above the wrist, in the space between the arm-bones |
| Locate the depression in front of the joint of the 4th and 5th metatarsals, near the tendon of the little toe |
| Medial border of foot, anterior and inferior to end of 1st metatarsal |
| Intersection of dorso-ventral boundary of hand and ulnar end of distal palmar crease |
| Palmar side of forearm, 2 cun* above wrist crease, between tendons of long palmar muscle and wrist's radial flexor muscle |
| Radial side of forearm, proximal to styloid process, 1.5 cun* above wrist's crease |

which of the Eight Prime acupuncture points has been selected, since the meridian on which it lies will be more effective at a particular hour.

The table above gives the location of the Eight Prime acupuncture points used in Mystic Tortoise therapy. The trigrams are listed according to their positions in the Magic Square of Nine Numbers or *Luo Shu* (see pages 340 and 350), thus accounting for the strange numbering of the Eight Trigrams, which omits 5.

# Tales of Chinese astrologers

In Chinese folklore and legend, there are many stories associated with famous Chinese astrologers throughout the history of this ancient discipline. Below are a few featuring some well-known figures from the past.

## The mysterious fisherman

Many tales and legends are woven round the life of the scholar-statesman Wen Wang, the legendary author of that mysterious volume, the *Book of Changes*. As was the custom in those far-off days, before going out hunting he would cast yarrow stalks and consult the oracle to find out whether he would have a good catch that day. On one occasion, the oracle's response was that he would not catch the usual game, but something much more valuable – the teacher of a prince.

Wen Wang was perplexed by this remark, but while out hunting he met an old man fishing, not with a line and hook, but a straight piece of iron on which the fish jumped voluntarily. He realized that the angler must be the 'teacher of a prince' revealed in the prophecy, and invited him to be his adviser and counsellor, awarding the old man the title Jiang Tai Gong (Jiang the Great Duke). He had clairvoyant powers, and even today Chinese people sometimes hang up red paper scrolls on which are painted the words 'Jiang Tai Gong is here!' in order to fend off evil spirits.

## Prophecies can be dangerous

Sometimes being an astute astrologer can be dangerous. Jing Fang lived during the 1st century BCE; it was said that his clever predictions would be his downfall and so it proved. As his fame grew, he was invited to court and asked to reveal what the future held in store. He replied that there would be a terrible flood. Indeed there was a terrible flood, but instead of being praised for his foresight and warning, he was blamed for causing the flood and was thrown into prison where he died.

## Time traveller

There is a legend connected with a famous magician of the 1st century that seems to predict Einstein's theory of relativity. The magician in question, Fei Zhang Fang, was given a magic rod by his teacher, which allowed him to travel vast distances in a few moments. But when he got back from his travels, what he thought had been a journey of a day or two had actually taken many

years. Fei once told his apprentice that on the ninth day of the ninth month there would be a disaster, and to avoid it he should fill a bag with herbs and take his family for the day up to the mountains to drink wine. They did so, and when the family returned that night, they found that all their livestock and poultry were dead. Today, Chinese families still go on mountain picnics on the ninth day of the ninth lunar month.

## The undercover agents

During the 2nd century, the emperor would send undercover agents around the country to find out what people really thought about his government. At the time, there was a humble clerk called Li living in Szechuan. He was keen on astronomy and astrological implications, and one evening he noticed two new stars in the sky. He took this to mean that important visitors would soon arrive, and when the two agents called at his village, he saw through their disguises, and much to their amazement, told them so.

Some years later, one of the investigators was promoted to a high position and remembering the remarkable astronomer, decided to take him on as his adviser. This turned out to be a wise move, because shortly afterwards the governor of the province was due to marry, and all the local mandarins got ready to send their congratulations and gifts. Li, however, foresaw trouble and warned his employer not to send a gift. Despite Li's warning, the official ignored the advice and instead ordered the astronomer to deliver the wedding gift in person. But on his journey to the capital, Li deliberately wasted time and arrived too late for the wedding ceremony –

which never happened. The governor had been arrested for corruption and all the officials who had sent presents were considered to be in his pay and were promptly sacked.

## A reluctant astrologer

The astrologer Yan Cun had no desire to become rich, and though he had many followers, some of whom became renowned and rose to positions of importance, fame and fortune never appealed to him. 'Material wealth means intellectual poverty', he declared. Any prospective clients needed to get to his shop early; he considered 400 cents sufficient for his daily needs and as soon as he had earned that amount, he would put up the shutters and devote the rest of his time to study.

## The legacy

A man who had been a very skilled fortune-teller during his life realized that he was nearing the end of it. He called his wife to his bedside, handed her his copy of the *Book of Changes* and told her, 'There's going

to be a time of great famine; money will be short, but I want you to promise that you will not sell the house, no matter how much you may be tempted to do so. Then, in five years' time, in the spring, a man called Hong will visit the village; when he does, find him and give him this book. Remind him that he once owed me a great deal of money and you should ask him to repay the debt.'

The fortune-teller passed away, and just as he had foreseen, the famine came. Many times the poor widow was on the verge of selling the house, but she remembered her promise and struggled on as best she could. Then, exactly as her husband had predicted, after five years had passed there was news of a man called Hong who was passing through the village. The

widow took the book and hurried out to present it to the stranger, but when she reminded him of the debt, he said he knew nothing of it. The widow's insistence was so determined and her sincerity so obvious, that he began to wonder if he had forgotten some old debt.

But it so happened that Hong himself was a skilled diviner and when he realized that the book the widow had given him was the *Book of Changes*, he concluded that her husband had meant to convey a hidden message to him. He decided to use his divining prowess and the mystery became clear. He turned to the anxious widow, and said: 'It's true that I had no debt to your husband, but I know why he told you so, and why he asked you to present me with this book. Since he had correctly predicted that I would be coming, he also knew that I would be skilled in deciphering the *Book of Changes*. Your husband knew that there would be difficult times ahead, but was worried that if he left you all his money on his death, your family would spend it all before the hard times came. So he buried his money in the garden, in a black jar, next to the eastern wall.'

And sure enough, when the widow went home and dug in spot the stranger had said, there was the jar full of gold.

## The fitness fanatic

During the 1st century, Ren Wengong, an assistant to a local provincial governor, predicted that on the first day of the fifth month the city would be swamped by a torrential flood. But his advice went unheeded until he began to build a boat, after which Wengong's less sceptical neighbours followed his lead and constructed boats for themselves.

Despite the fact that some villagers were beginning to take precautions against an impending flood, the governor himself refused to make any emergency arrangements. On the predicted day, much to the governor's amusement not only was there no sign of rain or flood, but the was sun shining down as brightly as ever. Nevertheless, Wengong and his trusting neighbours still raced to complete their

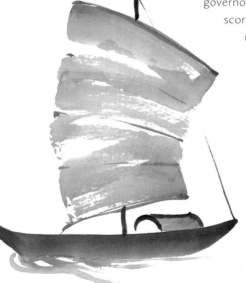

boats while further pleadings with the governor to do likewise were met with scorn. Then the storm began. The river rose 30 metres (90 ft), houses were washed away and thousands of people drowned.

Wengong's astrological skills now brought him fame and respect, so that when he ordered his family and servants to run around the house every day, carrying heavy weights on their backs, they might have thought that their master had gone mad, but no one dared question his instructions. And then came an uprising with rebel troops and marauders on every side. Most villagers tried to get away but were soon overtaken and killed by the rebels. But Wengong's strict training programme meant that his household was strong enough to escape with their possessions, carrying their luggage on their backs.

## Incompatible horoscopes

Sometimes it appears that two horoscopes are not in harmony. This little anecdote from historical records of the Han dynasty (1st century) has a special interest, because it shows that even 2,000 years ago astrologers would sometimes look for ways to get around such vexing problems.

A beautiful and intelligent girl called Du Lanxiang wanted to marry a youth of about 16 or 17 called Chang, but when she compared their horoscopes she saw that they were astrologically incompatible. As the historical records reveal, she said that 'the numbers of their lives did not correspond'. But she was well-versed in astrological lore and advised her lover that they should wait until 'the year star was in the East', which in those early days was how 'the year of the Rabbit' would have been expressed. The sign of the Rabbit would have been one that made the two opposing signs into a compatible group. They married that year, and as the story books say, lived happily ever after.

## Guan Lu

Guan Lu is one of the most celebrated of historical figures from Chinese astrology, but he appears to have been something of a character. Despite his reputation as probably the most inspired diviner in Chinese history, the account of his life in *The Records of the Three Kingdoms* describes him as being unattractive in both appearance and manner, a heavy drinker, a glutton, ill-mannered but amusing company, and tolerated rather than respected. But with regards to his prodigious talent there was never any doubt.

As a boy of eight, he would gaze at the stars, demanding to know their names, and constructed star-maps on which he drew the positions

of the Moon and planets. While still a youth he was invited to a conference of the greatest minds in the area and astonished them with his talents. He went on to study astronomy with another famous teacher of the time, Yibo, but soon exhausted the store of his teacher's knowledge and decided to rely on his own intuition.

Guan Lu's first case occurred when a local woman decided to consult him over an ox she had lost. He made a prediction and told her exactly where the ox could be found. Instead of being grateful, however, the woman claimed that Guan Lu must have stolen it and reported him to the magistrate! Fortunately, the magistrate accepted Guan Lu's explanation and knowledge of his gifts began to circulate.

An early case that attracted wide attention occurred when he was asked to make a prediction for a lady who was so close to death that the family had already prepared her coffin. Guan Lu told the husband the date and hour that she would pass on, but this was such a long time ahead that the family could scarcely believe him. Yet the lady recovered and lived for several more months, before finally relapsing and leaving this world exactly at the time he predicted.

On another occasion, he encountered a lady who was so seriously ill that there seemed to be no hope of recovery. Guan Lu told her that although he wasn't a doctor himself, a soldier in armour would soon arrive from the east, and they should ask his help. Later, when a cavalry officer in armour passed by on his way to the frontier, the lady's husband invited him into his house for refreshment. When the officer saw the invalid, he said he knew how to cure her. The lady soon recovered and convinced the officer that he would be better employed as a physician.

Guan Lu's advice was sought by all the influential people of his province and he gradually climbed the ladder of success until it seemed his position in life was assured. When he was 46, he was offered a highly remunerative position but Guan Lu sighed and said, 'If I were the Prefect of the city, I would rule it so well that money could be left by the side of the road and alarm bells would never be needed. But although Heaven has given me my ample talents, the gift of long life has been withheld. I will never see my children married, and it appears that instead of governing living people, I shall be attending to the needs of ghosts.' Sure enough, shortly after receiving the appointment as assistant treasurer to the state, Guan Lu passed on to the next realm of existence.

## Tai Yang

The astrologer Tai Yang, who lived during the latter half of the 3rd century, was so celebrated that the official history of the period devotes an entire chapter to his life and work, recording not only his predictions, but also his explanations of how he made the forecasts. According to the official history, when he was 12 years old, he was taken ill and apparently given up for dead, but five days later was restored to life. During the five days he was in a coma, he dreamed that he had climbed seven sacred mountains, where he met many immortals and learned the secrets of astrology.

He had a successful career in government administration, but did not have an official astrological position. Nevertheless, his advice was often followed even when it ran counter to that of the official astrologer. One day there was a great storm and he predicted it was a

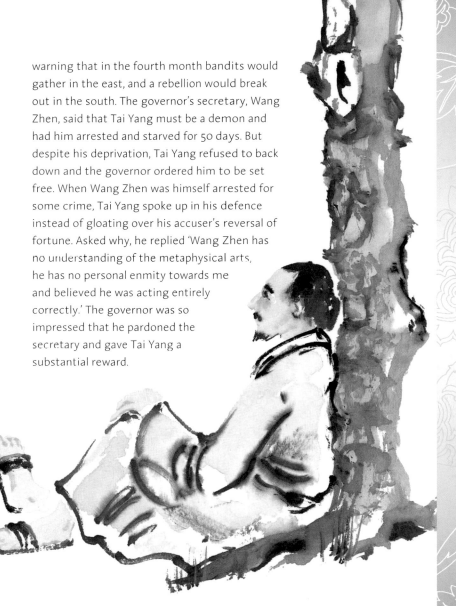

warning that in the fourth month bandits would gather in the east, and a rebellion would break out in the south. The governor's secretary, Wang Zhen, said that Tai Yang must be a demon and had him arrested and starved for 50 days. But despite his deprivation, Tai Yang refused to back down and the governor ordered him to be set free. When Wang Zhen was himself arrested for some crime, Tai Yang spoke up in his defence instead of gloating over his accuser's reversal of fortune. Asked why, he replied 'Wang Zhen has no understanding of the metaphysical arts, he has no personal enmity towards me and believed he was acting entirely correctly.' The governor was so impressed that he pardoned the secretary and gave Tai Yang a substantial reward.

# Index

# Acknowledgements

**Alamy**/Art Kowalsky 131; Jupiter Images/ Comstock Images 119; Pat Behnke 17; Tetra Images 237; Topix 299. **Bridgeman Art Library**/Chinese School (20th century)/ Private Collection, Archives Charmet 377. **Corbis UK Ltd** Abode/Beateworks 134; Brooke Fasani 105, 137; Christine Schneider/zefa 160; Fleurent/PhotoCuisine 356; Flint 239; Gabe Palmer 9; Gideon Mendel 175; Greg Hinsdale 226; Image Source 147; Jack Hollingsworth 186; Jim Craigmyle 151, Max Power 177, Misty Bedwell/Design Pics 96, moodboard 157, 337, Oscar Abrahams 232, Pinnacle Pictures 243, Randy Faris 129, Sean Justice 112, The Art Archive 314; Tim Pannell 93, 251, Tom Grill 225; Uli Wiesmeier/zefa 77. **Fotolia**/ Brebca 305, cris13 327; Daniel Budiman 325; Dmitry Pichugin 311; Jean-Yves Foy 21 bottom right; Michael Flippo 351. **Getty Images**/Jon Feingersh 376; Andrew Wong 33; Barry Yee 329; Bruce Dale 296; Daly & Newton 252; Jamie Grill 244; Jeremy Hardie 71; Jose Luis Pelaez 82; Jose Luis Pelaez 121; Richard Drury 231; STOCK4B 309; VEER/Steve Cicero 256; Wayne H Chasan 367; Wendy Ashton 143. **istockphoto.com**/ 23, 87, 163, 253, 303, 341. **Octopus Publishing Group Limited** 357; Colin Bowling 373; Ian Wallace 171; Lis Parsons 359; Mike Prior 371; Paul Forrester 258; Peter Pugh-Cook 249, 262; Russell Sadur 261, 316; Ruth Jenkinson 65, 345; Stephen Conroy 361.**Photolibrary**/BlueMoon Images 145; Fancy 155. **Royalty–Free Images** 241, 265; BananaStock 169; Corbis 173, 228; Imagesource 11; Photodisc 13, 19, 21 top left, 375; Photolibrary 125. **Science Photo Library**/Eckhard Slawik 27; John Sanford 301. **Shutterstock** 140, 321; Joe Gough 353; Scott Rothstein 355. **SuperStock** 246, 293. **Werner Forman Archive**/British Library, London 15.

**Executive Editor** Sandra Rigby
**Project Editor** Ruth Wiseall
**Executive Art Editor** Mark Stevens
**Designer** Peter Gerrish
**Illustrator** Rhian Nest James
**Production Controller** Hannah Burke